Maternal Ethics

and Other Slave Moralities

Maternal Ethics

and Other Slave Moralities

Cynthia Willett

ROUTLEDGE
New York and London

Published in 1995 by

Routledge
29 West 35th Street
New York, NY 10001

Published in Great Britain in 1995 by

Routledge
11 New Fetter Lane
London EC4P 4EE

Copyright © 1995 by Routledge

Printed in the United States of America
Design: Jack Donner

Library of Congress Cataloging-in-Publication Data

Willett, Cynthia
        Maternal ethics and other slave moralities / Cynthia Willett.
            p.   cm.
        Includes bibliographical references and index.
        ISBN 0–415–91209–1. — ISBN 0–415–91210–5
        1. Feminist ethics. 2. Feminist theory. Title
BJ1395.W55   1995
170'.82—dc20   95–35111
                                                                         CIP

For Liza, Joe, and Stefan

Here in this place,

we flesh; flesh

that weeps, laughs;

flesh that dances

on bare feet

in grass. Love it.

Love it hard.

—Toni Morrison
Beloved

Contents

Acknowledgments

The project for this book grew out of my teaching experiences at Le Moyne College in New York. This book owes much of its impetus to conversations with Susan Bordo and Mario Sáenz, both of whom transformed for me the possibilities of philosophy. I am also grateful to Julie Olin-Ammentorp and Mary MacDonald, with whom I spent several wonderful semesters bringing together readings for our tandem course in philosophy, religious anthropology, and literature. The idea of the book, as well as its interdisciplinary texture, evolved out of our preparations for this course.

I wrote the book while teaching at the University of Kansas and becoming a mother. I am grateful to many friends, students, and colleagues for the intellectual and emotional sustenance that kept my project alive. Conversations with Janet Lungstrum, Benjamin Sax, and Thomas Tuozzo not only generated crucial insights for many of the chapters but also turned much of the work for the book into a pleasure. The interpretations of the major texts used in the book evolved out of seminar discussions and are as much my students' as my own. I am grateful to Bryan Armstrong, Mina Blue, Kae

Chatman, Al Cinelli, Greg Conrad, Dawn Jakubowksi (thanks Dawn also for those weekends watching after Liza!), Noelle Henrickson, Harvey McCloud, Dan Norwood, Loretta Pyles, David Reidy, Christina Sharp, Keven Schumaker, Ted Vaggalis, and Heidi Wheeler—to name but a few of the many students who made my classes happen. Many of my colleagues also contributed to my project in ways that were essential. I owe special thanks to Sandra Albrecht, Cindi Hodges, Roberta Johnson, William Andrews, Philip Barnard, Richard Cole, Ann Cudd, Janice Doores, Richard De George, Cheryl Lester, Rex Martin, Julie Maybee, Joey Sprague, and Jim Woelfel. Thanks to Tony Genova, the philosophy department generously provided the funds to support my research assistants, Richard Buck and Ted Vaggalis. It is not at all clear to me how I would have found the time, with my new baby here and my husband away on a postdoc, to have completed the book without their perfect assistance.

I also owe gratitude to the University of Kansas for having granted general research allocations for two articles, "Tactile Sociality" and "The Master/Slave Dialectic: Hegel vs. Douglass." These articles form the crucial sections of chapters 2, 5, and 6 of my book.

Robert Bernasconi, Andrew Cutrofello, Nancy Fraser, Lewis Gordon, Elizabeth Grosz, Irene Harvey, Frank Kirkland, Bill Martin, John McCumber, Dianne Rothleder, Eric Sundquist, and Robert Switzer gave me insights or criticisms at various stages of the project that often enough altered my thinking in ways that are fundamental. I am especially grateful to Andrew Cutrofello for extensive comments on early drafts of the book. These comments, fascinating in their own right, proved enormously helpful in the process of revision. Julie Willett and Randy McBee have greatly expanded my understanding of the dynamics of race and gender through discussions of their own work in social history.

My husband, Stefan Böttcher, has given me his warmth and his wisdom, his good humor, and the deepest possible friendship. When we are together my work is a joy. Finally, I am grateful to our daughter, Liza, who at age one already knows the power and pleasure of subversion. It is from Liza that I have found a "maternal ethics" that is not a "slave morality"—or at least not most of the time.

INTRODUCTION
Master Narrative, Postmodernism, Slave Narrative

Today I believe in the possibility of love;
that is why I endeavor to trace its imperfections, its perversions.
Frantz Fanon

This book weaves together accounts of the self drawn from American and European philosophies, psychoanalytic studies of the mother-child relationship, and slave narratives and social histories of race relations in order to interrogate what Hegel, in his *Phenomenology of Spirit*, locates at the core of the self: the desire for recognition. While contemporary studies on race and gender throw into question Hegel's specific rendition of what he understands as the struggle for recognition, these studies confirm what Hegel takes as the premise of dialectical philosophy.[1] The free and full development of the self rests less on the calculation of individual needs than on the synchronization of the self in the social, or what Hegel conceptualizes as the "movement of Spirit." Patricia Williams recasts this point in contemporary terms in order to account for the devastating effects of racist images in American culture. As she writes, "a fundamental part of ourselves and of our dignity depends on the uncontrollable, powerful, external observers who make up a society. Surely a part of socialization ought to include a sense of caring responsibility for the images of others that are reposited within us."[2] The transmission of cultural images that fail to protect equally the dignity of each one of us commits what Patricia Williams identifies as the gravest of crimes, the crime of "spirit murder" (*ARR*, 73).[3]

While this book does not in any way claim to be universal in its scope, but instead follows through only a few strands of what might be a more inclusive account of struggles for recognition, it does risk a return to what postmodern critic Jean-François Lyotard has identified as the tradition of the master narrative. According to Lyotard, Enlightenment, dialectical, and utilitarian philosophies assert claims regarding the universality of their rather curiously diverse conceptions of freedom and reason. The question is whether these various claims to universality could be anything more than exercises in power. Lyotard "define[s] *postmodernism* as incredulity toward metanarratives." "The narrative function," he observes, "is losing its functors, its great hero, its great dangers, its great voyages, its great goal."[4]

Perhaps the most convincing critiques of the oppressive and exclusionary effects of universalizing reason arise from post-Holocaust postmodernism, and, in particular, from the Jewish philosophies of Jacques Derrida and Emmanuel Levinas. Levinas and Derrida have both exposed the narcissistic forces at work not only in narrative or systematic philosophy but already in dialogic communication. According to Levinas and Derrida, the usual attempts to know the Other aim to assimilate the different into a reflection of the self-same subject.[5] The ethical praxis of mutual respect would entail a willingness to begin the social venture by admitting to a fundamental and, for Derrida and Levinas, irretrievable ignorance of the Other.

The postmodern unmasking of the narcissistic implications of universalizing projects and, even more, the witnessing of the violence of expansionist powers, forbids any easy return to the traditional enterprises of philosophy. At the same time, perhaps not unexpectedly, the very critique of traditional philosophy that defines postmodern theory can be turned against postmodernism itself. Some of the most powerful postmodern writings exhibit symptoms of the very narcissism that is under attack.

There are two respects in which postmodernist writings threaten to submerge difference within the same. First, postmodernism proves unable to produce any principle of change other than that of the iteration of the same.[6] According to this principle, the repetition of social practices or any signifying structure is subject to random displacements ("reiteration," "metonymic slippage," "deformations," or even "the changing same") that account for social change. The problem with this principle of change is that it provides no standard by which to distinguish changes that fundamentally alter the oppressive structures of the past from changes that simply displace traditional with new forms of oppression.[7] Postmodernists can establish no way of making this kind of judgment without resorting to a transcendent or biological basis for the measure of value, and therefore to what is condemned as "essentialism." Without a means for theorizing progressive change, postmodernism reduces difference to permutations of the same.

Secondly, while postmodern theorists expose intersubjective models of communication (e.g., dialogue as well as narrative and argument) as little more than narcissistic projections of the self on the Other, postmodernism does not itself yield any plausible way out of narcissistic conceptions of the self. The problem stems in part from the fact that postmodernism borrows so heavily from the psychoanalytic theory that it deconstructs. Psychoanalytic theory traces the origin of the ego to narcissistic fantasies of wholeness. The deconstruction of narcissistic fantasies unmasks alien dimensions of the self. The problem with postmodern theories is that these theories use the otherness (or "alterity") of the self in order to gain access to the alterity that characterizes the Other. In fact, some postmodern strategies go so far as to equate the alterity of the self with the alterity that defines the other person.[8] Again postmodernism suffers from the very narcissism that it sets out to critique.

Postmodernism has nonetheless thoroughly unmasked the exclusionary politics that underlie the tradition of the master narrative and its various contemporary representatives. There seems to be no way out of the impasse between postmodernism and traditional philosophy—unless, that is, a narrative of freedom were to arise not from the voices of the "masters" but from the voices of the "slaves" of history. Laurence Thomas argues that "some people are owed deference—moral deference, that is." He explains: "Moral deference is meant to stand in opposition to the idea that there is a vantage point from which any and every person can rationally grasp whatever morally significant experiences a person might have."[9] Thomas recommends that those who are socially empowered refrain from pretending to understand the experience of the socially vulnerable. He urges instead that the privileged classes commit to bearing witness. To bear witness is not to dialogue or narrate but to listen to the stories of the Other. Thomas explains, "There can be no bearing witness ... to the moral pain of another without having heard his story and having heard it well."[10]

The task of this book is to transform the master narrative of the philosophical tradition by retelling the story of freedom from the point of view of those who have been systematically marginalized, i.e., the "slaves" of history.[11] The authenticity of this transformation is measured by a single existential test. The assumption is that there are no unbiased rules or neutral procedures, no sympathetical care, and no criterion of reason that could guarantee that an ethical stance is not simply a reassertion of power. Therefore the only possible test for the authenticity of an ethical demand that would claim the force of universality, narrative exemplarity, or otherwise some binding force over another is the statement of that demand from the language and perspective of the disempowered Other.

There is, however, no single vantage point from which a retelling of the master narrative could be told. History reveals a shifting pattern of socially underprivileged groups, which often enough find themselves not aligned but in violent opposition with one another. The strategy of the book is not to impose a metanarrative on divergent voices but rather to weave together several strands of the kind of "large historical narrative" that Nancy Fraser and Linda Nicholson argue to be necessary for comprehending "broad-based relations of dominance ... along lines like gender, race and class."[12]

The several strands come specifically from European feminism and African American movements against sexism and racism. My hope is that this book develops some ways in which these diverse movements can be shown to have—not the same—but corresponding conceptions of selfhood and freedom. Hegel, more than other Enlightenment or dialectical philosophers, develops a concept of freedom from a broad study of different cultures and historical epochs. This understanding led Hegel to transform the meaning of freedom from the modern liberal focus on individual choice to the social process of recognition. The perversions of recognition are well understood by those who have to counter the forces of racism and sexism. As Howard McGary has argued, neither materialist Marxist theories of alienation based in economics nor liberal theories of justice based on rational debate can remedy the "particular estrangement that blacks experience because of the attitude of disrespect generated by the dominant society" (AA, 290). If McGary is right, then, I would argue, only a "dialectic of spirit," that is, a dialectic that focuses on transforming the psychological and cultural sources of oppression, or what post-Lacanians understand as the images, metaphors, and fantasies that compose the "social imaginary," can overcome the alienation that tears apart oppressor and oppressed.[13] The locus of racism as well as sexism resides less in the discursive content of thought than in the colors and shapes of the cultural fictions that constitute the realities of our lives.

But while Hegel locates the source of the self and its oppression in largely cultural processes of recognition, he hardly gives an adequate account of the oppression of the slave. Not only does Hegel develop an allegory of slavery in terms that are abstract and universalist, and therefore without clear historical reference, but, no doubt in part because of the inadequate deference (to use Laurence Thomas's term) given to the lived experience of the slave, Hegel portrays the slave from the point of view of the master. As a consequence, Hegel simply repeats the prejudice of the oppressor when he asserts that the slaves of history are those who lack the spirit for freedom. Hegel justifies slavery, defining the slave as ruled by sensuous desires, not autonomous will, and therefore as too "soft" for freedom. This account of slavery serves the interests and concepts of justice of the slaveholders and not the slaves. Even more, behind these interests and these concepts lies an erotic of domination that is censored in modernist discourses and rationalized as the enlightenment of those who are weak of will. Clearly, it would make a difference if we were to recommence the history of freedom from the narratives written by the "slaves" themselves.

Does there exist for the slave a counternarrative of freedom? Laurence Thomas locates the cause for what he sees as the slow recovery of African Americans from American slavery compared to that of the Jews from the Holocaust in the failure on the part of African American culture to develop a sense of its own identity. "An essential requirement in this regard," Thomas argues, "is a narrative (most often a set of narratives) that defines values and positive goals and fixes points of historical significance and ennobling rituals."[14] If Thomas is right, then there has been no narrative of freedom for the African American, at least none that would preserve an African American identity through centuries of American slavery and oppression.

There are, however, two reasons for rejecting Thomas's argument. First, as Henry Louis Gates argues, "in the long history of human bondage, it was only the black slaves in the United States who ... created a *genre* of literature that at once testified against their captors and bore witness to the urge of every black slave to be free. . . ."[15]

Secondly, Thomas structures his argument not on historical knowledge but on a modernist opposition between form and content, an opposition that may in fact prove alien to some currents in African American cultures. Thomas draws upon this opposition in order to critique the work of various historians who trace African American identity to "a rich oral tradition (story telling) and a rich tradition of rhythm in both dance and song" (VE, 156). Thomas argues that however much African rhythms may contribute to a distinctly African American style, the signifying content of African American culture is not African but Christian (VE, 158). Moreover, Thomas argues, Christian otherworldliness constrains the African American to accept suffering in stoic resignation (VE, 159).

Much of this book demonstrates not only that the content of ideas cannot be separated from the medium in which they are expressed but that, in particular, the cadences of African American cultures break through Christian stoicism and, in the process, transform the very meaning of Western freedom and reason. Hegel repeats the mainline of the Western philosophical tradition when he argues that freedom requires the purging or restraining of erotic and embodied dimensions of the self in favor of a fundamentally stoic conception of reason. While this conception of the free self provokes attacks from such post-Hegelians as Friedrich Nietzsche, Michel Foucault once again foregrounds the ascetic practices that run through various Western conceptions of self.[16] For Foucault, an acquired insensitivity to the desires and sufferings of the body reappears as a constant area of "problematization" in Western constructions of the masculinized self.[17] These practices vary from classical and imperial times through Christianity inasmuch as they demand either a rigid struggle against desire or the restraint of desire. Nonetheless, Foucault, who in some ways follows Nietzsche in order to count himself as an archenemy of Hegel, surprises his reader by emphasizing the larger constants in Western culture. And like Hegel, these forces prove less to intensify or enhance desire than to purge or restrain desire and therefore fall under a reading of freedom and selfhood that can be interpreted as cathartic.

As a more extensive reading of Hegel's concept of slavery will demonstrate, those constructions of freedom that sever a hardened and well-controlled body from the vulnerability of the flesh prove complicit with the subordination or exclusion of women and animals—as well as those "sensuous" men who have not sufficiently distinguished themselves from women or animals. The step from a cathartic concept of the free self to the politics of purgation is not far. That is, the repression of sensuous dimensions of the self is not unrelated to the oppression of others who are perceived through the veil of the disciplined self. Similarly, a dialectic of truth that aims toward an abstract mode of reason, or, more broadly, what Derrida locates as the logocentrism of Western culture, does not transform but participates in the politics of oppression. This analysis is not lost on African Americans who have noted that the European imperialists cited their alphabetic script to distinguish literate from oral cultures and, in turn, to justify the enslavement or subordination (i.e., the "enlightenment") of "primitive peoples."

However, we will discover in some African American texts, and in particular in the slave narratives of Frederick Douglass, practices of the self that are not ascetic exercises of self-mastery or stoic rituals of self-withdrawal, but practices of the self that rekindle in the numbed flesh of the beaten slave a feverous desire for freedom.[18] If the European concept of the self subordinates desire to system, African American slaves found that they might cultivate their desires in order to subvert the systems of oppression. As Audre Lorde explains, in her essay "Uses of the Erotic: The Erotic as Power," European American culture has produced a male model of power that separates the erotic from the spiritual and the political and consequently suppresses the deepest source of power and knowledge within our lives. She writes, "The principal horror of such a system is that it robs our work of its erotic value.... Such a system reduces work to a ... duty by which we earn bread or oblivion for ourselves and those we love."[19] In contrast to the cathartic dialectic that underlies much of Western history, and that finds its way into the Hegelian conception of recognition, the dialectic of the African American slave toward the freedom of spirit is ecstatic.

But, by hypothesis, if practices of the self do not privilege logos over eros, and thereby detach or subordinate the body to abstract forms and artificial constructs of reason, so too these practices of the self would not participate in a schema that associates women or animals (and other so-called primitives) with the weaknesses of the flesh or the irrationality of the biological. A closer examination of the autobiographies of Frederick Douglass reveals that in fact Douglass's affirmation of what might first appear to be a (post)modern reiteration of phallic manhood in fact trans-forms the hard oppositions between man and his Other. Not only does Douglass celebrate what he expresses as the "animal spirits" of the women as well as the men who resisted slavery; Douglass also intimates that he finds critical resources for selfhood in the recognition accorded to him by the spirited hands of the grandmother who raised him. Therefore, I shall argue that the Douglass narratives suggest an alternative origin to what Hegel discerns as the struggle for selfhood through recognition. The self originates not in ritualized struggles for manhood nor in the supposed nar-cissism of early childhood but in what I shall develop, after Luce Irigaray, as the tactile sociality that attunes "bloodmother" or "othermothers" and child.[20] Beyond the logocentrism of Western culture, a new model of self-hood and freedom emerges from the rhythms and tones that articulate infancy and that reverberate through the more abstract dimensions of what we identify as the systems of reason.

Overview

Each of the three parts of the book breaks from mainstream European or Euro-American conceptions of the self and turns instead to the experiences of marginalized subjects in order to reconceptualize the dialectic of Self and Other. Eurocentric conceptions of ethical subjectivity project a dualist model of the self with consequences that are damaging both to the individ-ual and to the social sphere. The detachment of reason from the body pro-duces a pathological rigidity in the individual. This detachment also contributes to the antisocial pathologies of racism and sexism in the dom-inant European cultures. My project draws upon postmodern and multi-cultural critiques of modernist ideologies but only in order to reconstruct a postcolonial, profeminist narrative of ethical subjectivity. From this point of view, the alienation of the self in stoic conceptions of duty or prudential calculation defines not an ethics but a cultural pathology. This pathology results from the denial of the social dimensions of the self and manifests itself in an obsessive focus on control of the mind over the body and its material extensions. It is a culture of solipsism. I argue that ethics needs to be reoriented from the vertical axis of mind over body to the horizontal sphere of social exchange. Ethics develops not from the discipline of desire but from cultivating the social eroticism that can find its roots in the rela-tionship between nurturers and child.

Part 1 reexamines what traditional philosophers and psychoanalysts posit as the first childhood stage in the development of the self. A standard traditional view portrays this earliest stage in terms of a presubjective fusion between the mother and the child (or fetus). As feminists have argued, this view reduces the mother to a biological function. Drawing upon my own experience as well as various feminist writings, I argue that even if the infant is not yet a person, this early relation is already social. Some feminists have made use of the dialogue model in order to account for the first social bonds between nurturers and children. I argue, however, that the synchronization of music and dance provides a better model for the earliest stages of this relation. I conclude that the social eroticism of the nurturer-child relationship establishes the basis for an ethics that goes beyond the altruism-egoism dichotomy as well as the gender stereotypes that this dichotomy sustains in European cultures.

Part 2 reexamines what theorists posit as a second major stage of development, namely, the separation of the child from the mother. Theorists measure this second stage in terms of the ability of the infant to recognize his face in the mirror. Meanwhile, the mother serves as a faceless prop in the drama of the developing infant ego. These theories conclude that the ego is narcissistic. I argue that the mirror in fact serves as little more than a substitute for the face-to-face play with the mother or other nurturer; that self-recognition is not originally egoistic but intersubjective; and, finally, that the dialectic of intersubjectivity should not be understood through the trope of the mirror. The playful eroticism between nurturers and children not only supersedes the altruism-egoism dichotomy of traditional ethics; it also brings out nondiscursive dimensions of intersubjective response and therefore throws into question the rationalism that underlies modernist philosophies from Cartesianism to discourse ethics.

Part 3 reexamines what dialectical and psychoanalytic theories posit as a third stage in the development of the self. The traditional view presumes that only at this third stage does the subject enter into the social order, and that this passage constitutes manhood. Hegel interprets this third stage in terms of a struggle for recognition. According to Hegel, this battle of the wills yields the social hierarchies of "master" and "slave." The slave proves of weaker will and therefore owes deference to the master.

A limitation of Hegel's portrayal of the struggle for recognition is that it reflects the point of view of the master. Part 3 draws upon slave narratives

PART ONE

The Sensuality of the Good

All of Western Culture
rests on the murder of the mother.
Luce Irigaray

A peculiar absence marks the three classic narratives that enframe and validate mainstream Western cultures. The following quotations are interpretations of human origins from the Judaic-Christian religion, the liberal atomism prominent in Anglo-American culture, and European dialectic:

> The Lord God planted a garden in Eden . . . ; and there he put the man whom he had formed. And out of the ground the Lord God made to grow every tree that is pleasant to the sight and good for food. (Genesis 2.2.8–9)

> For the savage people in many places of America, except the government of small families, the concord whereof dependeth on natural lust, have no government at all; and live to this day in that brutish manner [i.e., in a state of war], as I said before. (Hobbes)[1]

> In the beginning, there is the existing shape; as being *for itself* . . . , it comes forward in opposition to the *universal* substance, disowns this fluidity [*Fluessigkeit*] and asserts that it is not dissolved in this universal element, but on the contrary preserves itself by separating from inorganic nature, and by consuming [*Aufzehren*] it. (Hegel)[2]

In each case the narrator draws upon a mythic account of human origins in order to envision the aims and measure the development of humanity. These quotations show that the classic ethical narratives have all begun in speculations that exceed ordinary methods of evidence. Our question then becomes: What images, passions, or experiences could sustain these speculations? What possible sources are there for a philosophical speculation on origins?

If we look again at the three quotations above, we find that they return to a place more familiar than we might first have thought. The first statement tells of innocent pleasures protected by an all-powerful father. The second statement portrays the original human being as the incorrigible child, or as the children's tale relates, "the wild thing," whose world extends only as far as the passions attached to the family. The third statement traces the emerging self from the fluid egolessness of the intrauterine state to the oral stage of primitive appetite. That is, each of the statements projects a familiar fantasy of earliest childhood onto the archaic beginnings of humanity. If, however, archaic origins are to be read by way of adult fantasies of childhood, there is in each of the foregoing accounts an uncanny absence. Genesis begins its story of creation with the father; Hobbes constructs the state of nature around the self-seeking child; the infant Hegelian ego emerges from the nourishing fluids of a vaguely maternal substance.[3] Nowhere to be found in these infantile fantasies, in the mythogenetic beginnings of history, is the first person in the life of the child, the mother. The three classic statements on the origins of the person betray the abstractions—if not sheer fabrications—of a father who in point of fact has all too often been absent from the family scene.

Theorists are beginning to redress the gross injustice and moral ignorance that efface the work of the mother or present caregiver in the formation of the person.[4] In part 1 of this study, I examine revisionary theories of early childhood proposed by three contemporary psychoanalytic thinkers: Julia Kristeva, Daniel Stern, and Luce Irigaray. Each of these theorists contributes to an understanding of the role of the mother or other caregiver in the social development of the self.

Chapter 1 focuses on the work of Kristeva and Stern. Kristeva gains access to the relation between the mother and child by way of the regressive fantasies of adults and the artistic practices of the avant-garde. These psychotic or artistic fantasies reveal nondiscursive dimensions of our language, which Kristeva traces back to presocial drives of the infant. I argue that nondiscursive expressions that are formalized in the artistic practices of music and dance do play an important role in the bond between nurturer and child. Kristeva, however, mistakenly projects onto this bond the misogynist fantasies and self-destructive impulses that define more properly the pathologies of the avant-garde than the prosocial relation between nurturer and child. Acccording to Kristeva, these alien impulses disturb an originary narcissism. My argument, however, is that the original relation between infant or fetus and father, mother, or other caregiver occurs not as a narcissism but as a social eroticism between two distinct beings—beings who differ radically with respect to the experiences that constitute subjectivity but who nonetheless communicate. In this respect, my aim is to demonstrate how the earliest and most primordial experiences of the person break out of the separated self versus shared self dichotomy that drives debates over liberalism versus communitarianism in social theory and over autonomous reason versus altruistic care in Anglo-American ethics.[5]

In order to better understand the "social attunement" between nurturer and infant, I turn to the empirical investigations of the Anglo-American psychoanalyst Daniel Stern. Stern transforms traditional psychoanalytic theory by introducing a model of the self that is fundamentally intersubjective rather than egoistic. Stern, however, does not fully accentuate the rhythmic, tonal, and tactile dimensions of the early social bond. There is in his theory no less than in Kristeva's the tendency to project dimensions of an adult self onto the infant. In the case of Stern, these projections reflect the scientistic fantasies of the masculine self that underlie Anglo-American epistemologies and that find their way into some of Stern's observations of the mother-child relation.

Chapter 2 aims to flesh out Stern's locus of early intersubjectivity in what he terms "affect attunement" with some of the more poetic speculations of Luce Irigaray. Irigaray's musings on the sensuality of touch provide a way of understanding the erotic attraction between mother, father, and other caregiver and the infant or fetus. In contrast with Irigaray, however, I argue that this first social attachment must be sharply distinguished from models of sexuality. The pleasures of sociality cannot be explained in terms of libido.

The sensuality of the originary social bond calls for a reinterpretation of what, after Hegel, we understand as the dialectic of recognition, and so too for a new model of ethical subjectivity. The infant is not to be seen as either fused with the mother or as egocentric, or as originally fused and subsequently egocentric. The infant is neither identified with the Other in an anonymous or collective existence nor alienated from the Other in the abstract constructions of a private subjectivity but is always oriented toward the Other through the kinesthetics (touches, scents, sounds) of an originary social bond.

This reconception of the social dance of early childhood also transforms our understanding of the subjectivity of the mother, father, or other caregiver whose sense of self in part grows out of the intimacy of his or her relation with a young child. This person is not a subject in the same way as is the economic agent in a rational system of exchange. He or she would not define him- or herself primarily in terms of autonomy or rational self-interest. So too caregiving cannot be simply defined as either a form of work or a mode of play. Thus the social work of nurturing marks a blindspot in the modernist systems of exchange. The liminal status of the mother, father, or other caregiver not only locates a constant source of tension in modernist economies; the ethical subjectivity of the nurturer also exemplifies a progressive model for social change.

Part 1 elaborates upon the social attunement that binds nurturer and child before the infant manifests a sense of self-awareness, i.e., at the level that psychoanalytic theories reduce to a function of "need" or "drive."[6] Part 2 focuses on a second stage of childhood, which traditional models measure in terms of the infant's awareness of its objectification in the specular image. I argue that self-awareness should be located not in the recognition of the face in the mirror but, more originally, in the face-to-face play between caregiver and child, and that the expressive dimensions of this play set up an alternative to either rationalistic (e.g., egoistic) or sacrificial (including altruistic and sentimental) models of ethical society.

The revisionary readings of childhood undertaken in parts 1 and 2 prepare for a third major stage in the dialectic of Self and Other. Part 3 reinterprets rites of passage into manhood (locus of the Lacanian notion of desire and so too of Hegel's dialectic of master and slave) through the transformative medium of black expressive culture.

· 1 ·

The Origin of Ethics in Music and Dance

Contemporary Psychoanalytic Theory

According to traditional psychoanalytic theory, the emerging self unfolds in an Oedipal drama that exiles the infant from the primitive libidinal economy (what Freud originally understood as the pleasure principle but later modified to include a death drive) to the demands and prohibitions of social structure (the reality principle and superego). The self-conscious child now finds the world constructed in terms of propositional language, the linearization of time, and the censorship of psychosexual drives. The contribution of Julia Kristeva to traditional psychoanalytic theory consists of her careful exploration of "pre-Oedipal space" (what she also terms "maternal space," or the "*chora*"). According to her hypothesis, the pre-Oedipal experience of the infant takes the pattern of explosive rhythms of libidinal discharge. Eventually, the child emerges from maternal space and only then develops a sense of Self and Other.

It is significant that Kristeva probes the dimensions of maternal space not by way of experiences between mothers and children but through regressive adult fantasies and avant-garde art. These two sources, I shall argue, betray the antisocial politics of her project. Kristeva's heavy reliance on pathological fantasies and avant-garde art in order to understand the mother-child relationship leads her to appropriate two problematic theses from traditional psychoanalysis. The first thesis is that the social structures, which constitutes the constraints that enable all viable forms of *self-expression*, necessarily *silence* the core experiences of the self. The second thesis posits that the *life-giving* maternal space—source of all "*poiesis*" (including the creation of new meaning structures)—is propelled by a drive toward *death.*

Contemporary Anglo-American psychoanalytic research on the observed infant poses an alternative conception of the early relationship between infant and caregiver. According to Anglo-American theories of the last twenty-five years, the infant is neither naturally asocial nor bent on death and destruction. Daniel Stern, in particular, has carefully documented the rhythms of a "social attunement" that punctuate the lifeworld of the infant.[1] In fact, according to feminist theorist Jessica Benjamin, Stern represents especially well the new direction in recent Anglo-American research. This research, Benjamin explains, gives "the mother-child dyad an importance in psychic development rivaling the Oedipal triangle. . . . Where formerly the psyche was conceived as a field of drives and defenses, now it became an inner drama of ego . . . [and Other]."[2]

In this chapter, I shall focus on the contributions of Kristeva and Stern to our understanding of the "mother-child dyad." Each of the two approaches, I argue, reflects only an aspect of infant life. Stern's work strongly indicates that the infant is not a site for savage, warring drives requiring social stricture. On the contrary, even the very young infant expresses a "natural desire" for "social interaction."[3]

On the other hand, there is a tendency for Anglo-American theorists such as Stern to see the neonate as an "ego" in a nonverbal "dialogue" with the parent. Kristeva argues, correctly I believe, that the nondiscursive rhythms of the mother-infant relationship do not resemble anything like the organizing structures (e.g., grammar and syntax) that arise after the development of language and the recognition of the face of the Other.

I conclude that while the early infant-parent relation does not exhibit the abstract features of intersubjective discourse, the articulations of the "maternal space" do exceed biological needs. Already in the womb, the fetus participates in the rhythms and tones of subjectless sociality.[4] After birth, the infant seeks not only nourishment but also the sounds, touches, and rhythmic movements of the parents. From these observations, I think we can argue that ethical engagement with the Other begins not in protodiscursive communication but in the correspondences that compose our most elementary sense of music and dance. So too, the fundamental terms of social exchange would lie not in a logos or a language but in music and dance. Chapter 2 turns to the work of Luce Irigaray for a fuller conception of the sociality that sustains us, as parents and as infants.

Julia Kristeva: From Womb to Tomb

As a theorist of pre-Oedipal space, Kristeva seeks to recover a sphere of lived experience that precedes the point of view of the subject and the objectifying structures of language. Kristeva bases her speculation concerning such a sphere on the "clinical infant," i.e., the infant as it is reconstructed from regressive pathologies in the adult psyche and the antisocial transgressions of avant-garde poetry. In these pathologies and transgressions, Kristeva finds traces of biological drives (*pulsions*) and their displacement or condensation in the primary processes of Freudian analysis.[5] She terms these traces of pre-Oedipal drives the "semiotic" and argues that the semiotic traverses and yet cannot be assimilated into, indeed resists, socially instituted forms of communication, or what she terms the "symbolic."[6] Inasmuch as social systems are not static, they do not completely repress the semiotic. Indeed, language itself cannot be explained solely by reference to the symbolic. On the contrary, Kristeva argues, the dialectic between the semiotic and the symbolic determines the signifying process (R, 91).

The semiotic articulates maternal space. Kristeva figures this maternal site as a womb-like matrix, or *chora* (R, 93). She explains: "We borrow the term *chora* from Plato's *Timaeus* to denote an essentially mobile and extremely provisional articulation constituted by movements and their ephemeral stases" (R, 93). The signifying process, then, depends upon a mythic space of lived experience for which there can be no representation (or likeness) given. "Neither model nor copy," Kristeva writes, "the *chora* precedes and underlies figuration and thus specularization, and is analogous only to vocal or kinetic rhythm" (R, 94). In other words, the *chora* is marked by the more or less irregular variations in tension states that measure the earliest rhythms of infant life.

Does Kristeva in fact succeed in tracing the maternal space inhabited by the infant? There is, as Kristeva well knows, no escape from the paradoxical stance of the theorist of origins. Kristeva specifically carries elements of the Oedipal narrative of European culture into her reconstruction of pre-Oedipal space. The Oedipal motifs of *blindness, incest,* and *mutilation* leave their mark on the reconstructed matrix of pre-Oedipal drive. First, pre-Oedipal rhythms can appear in the signifying process, according to Kristeva, only as ruptures of meaning, *blindspots* that are, by a classical formula of tragedy, the undoing of the subject. Secondly, "radical" poetry and mental pathology are said to betray a ubiquitous but unacknowledged craving to return to maternal space. The so-called illegible space of this fusion portends a narrative of *incest.* Third, pre-Oedipal theory mandates that the "maternal space" be represented not as a subject, i.e., as the mother, but through the fragments of a partial object, breast or even phallus. Maternal space may lack a subject, but as breast and phallus it is originally experienced as replete with being. The child will enter into the paternal space of the symbolic only after the discovery of the absent phallus in the woman. That is, the horror of castration domesticates the child. Finally, then, in order to preempt his own tragic *mutilation,* the young boy must excise from consciousness his (apparently incestuous) attraction to the mother.

What does it mean that Kristeva borrows the elements of her tale of primitive *jouissance* from the Oedipal narrative and its transgression in the "radical" poetry of the avant-garde? Gayatri Spivak, Susan Rubin Suleiman, and others have pointed out the classical pornographic interest of male writers of the avant-garde. The literary perversions of the avant-garde, so-called radicalizations of social norms, invoke elements of a reactionary misogyny.[7] Suleiman poses for her readers the following question: "Did the mutual rejection of the [social norms of the] realist novel put male theorists and practitioners of *écriture* and the female theorists and practitioners of *écriture féminine* in the same camp? Or did the substantive differences between them (for example, the eroticization and aestheticization of violence, including violence against the female body, that one finds in so much avant-garde practice) override the sympathies and similarities?" (*S,* 40).

Kristeva's theoretical appropriation of the avant-garde does not, I believe, sufficiently disassociate the pleasures of the semiotic from willful violence against feminine space. In her theory, Kristeva focuses on the destructive expression of the primitive drives that she finds in avant-garde poetics. According to Kristeva, traditional poetry suspends reference and engenders multiple meanings for its fictive objects. Still, traditional poetry does preserve the signifying structures of experience. On the other hand, avant-garde poetry forcefully breaks apart the syntax (what Nietzsche identifies as "the last god") that structures experience. Subjects and objects fragment. The fluid space that opens up before this aggressive attack on system resists the policed boundaries of signification altogether.

Earlier we noted that, for Kristeva, the symbolic cannot escape the prostitution of meaning that originates in the semiotic. The signifying process, according to Kristeva, depends upon the underlying drift of semiosis. We also noted that, for Kristeva, the semiotic cannot entirely elude capture by the structures of the symbolic. The semiotic appears only in its solicitations of the symbolic. But if we can gain access to the semiotic only by way of its whoring effects on the symbolic, then we are also entitled to inquire about the symbolic overtones of what Kristeva describes as semiotic dispersion. According to Kristeva, primitive semiotic drive erupts in the mature mind through the destruction of social prohibitions. Read through the Oedipal narrative, semiotic destruction signifies socially prohibited intercourse with the semi-depersonalized maternal body. This transgression elicits a *jouissance* at once violent and pleasurable.[8] Of course, near-death experiences, sometimes sexualized, define the element of the sublime in rites of passage into manhood. According to these mythologies of manhood, a scarred and masculinized subject emerges from the passage into darkness intact and even hardened. My question is: *Who suffers* from these peculiar pleasures of manhood ritual? Transgression clearly does not destroy the system of the fathers. Even Kristeva argues that the symbolic sustains itself on transgressions.[9] The irrecoverable effect of the violation is not in the resistance to system but, I believe, in the eroticization of violence against a broken and feminized subject. That subject is the mother.

Nietzsche exposes rather forcefully the dynamics of transgressive eroticism. In *Beyond Good and Evil*, Nietzsche terms erotic discharge "will to power" and proceeds to posit will to power as the original value of nature, locus of all *poiesis*. Supposedly against ego psychology, Nietzsche writes: "Physiologists should think before putting down the instinct of self-preservation as the cardinal instinct of an organic being. A living thing seeks above all to *discharge* its strength [*seine Kraft auslassen*]—life itself is *will to power*."[10] The pleasure of power over that which has no power, Nietzsche explains in his *Genealogy*, is the "pleasure of rape" ["*das Wohlgefuehl, seine*

Macht an einem Machtlosen unbedenklich auslassen zu duerfen, ... der Genuss in der Vergewaltigung"].[11] It is this pleasure of violent discharge that, according to Nietzsche, defines life. Therefore, Nietzsche concludes, "[n]o act of violence [*Verletzen*], rape [*Vergewaltigen*], exploitation, destruction, is intrinsically 'unjust,' since life itself is violent, rapacious, exploitative, and destructive and cannot be *conceived* otherwise" (*GM*, second essay, sec. 11, 208). Nietzsche states in declarative sentences what for Kristeva cannot be made clear and distinct: The seductive force of transgression [*Verletzen*]—the so-called principle of life—draws its unbounded pleasure from the violence of rape. Under conditions of rape, it is clear that he who reaps the pleasure is distinct from she who suffers the violence of the crime. The gift of the warrior binds sex with death, fertility with rape, and perhaps some men with other men, but never men with women.

For Kristeva, the meaning of unconscious fantasies of desire cannot be made clear and distinct because both meaning and image fragment in the explosive charges of semiotic discharge. Primitive drives express themselves, according to Kristeva, only in semiotic discharge. But even if the rhythm of primitive, brute discharge exceeds traditionally figurative or literal meaning, the pattern of this rhythm does not escape the valuations of an economy that is alien to mothers and children. The positivistic language of physics, "explosive charges" and "discharges," signals neutrality but is in fact not neutral.

First of all, the language of quantity is reductive. The infant experience contains not only kinetic variations but also varying qualities of pleasure and pain. Already at birth psychologists identify several distinct cries, each signifying qualities of desire.[12] The cry of pain differs not only from an expression of pleasure but also from the cry of anger.

More significantly, the language of physics schematizes the primitive desire of the infant—a stage allegedly prior to the realization of gender difference—in terms that connote a quite specific myth of male sexuality. According to this myth, the explosive, even savage, charges of male virility cannot be fully domesticated. Meanwhile, the uncathected and liberated explosion of male libido is allowed to suppress the rhythms of female libido. The random discharge of libidinal tension takes its pleasure in the more or less violent prostitution of female subjectivity at a site that is antisocial, anti-ethical, and, I would say, anti-art.

Of course, it is not clear that the transgressions of avant-garde writing can be reduced completely and without remainder to classical misogyny.

Certainly *l'écriture féminine* of French feminism cannot be reduced to the writing of the avant-garde. However, Kristeva's appropriation of the transgressive poetics of the avant-garde incorporates elements of classical misogyny into the very core of maternal space.

Kristeva's various reformulations of maternal space indicate this alien incorporation. In *Revolution in Poetic Language*, Kristeva redescribes the "nourishing and maternal" receptacle that she finds in Plato as a "double helix" of drives simultaneously "assimilating and destructive" and then again as an "ordering principle" that "is on the path of destruction, aggressivity and death" (*R*, 94). The redescriptions end here. The more natural configuration of maternal space as an organic site of nourishment, tactile attachment, and fluid boundaries gives way to the inorganic discharges that signify death. The regulating process of the *chora*, mythic source of life, is said to "effectuate discontinuities by temporarily articulating them and then starting over, again and again" (*R*, 94). Kristeva is clearly alluding to Freud's speculations on a primitive death drive. She explains further: it is "a dominant 'destructive wave' that is drive's most characteristic trait" (*R*, 95). For Kristeva, the repetitions of life imitate the mute reality of death. And so Kristeva transposes the *chora*, or that womb-like place inhabited by the neonate, into the tomb-like space of semiotic dispersion (*sema*, sign, mark, but also tomb), or the principle of life into a brute force of death.[13]

But, a mother might very well ask: Why this transposition?

Suleiman cites a possible motive for transgressive theories of libidinal drive: "According to Deleuze [who is in turn in debt to Melanie Klein on this point], ... the founding desire behind Sadean fantasy [an origin of avant-garde transgression] is *the active negation of the mother*" (*S*, 68).[14] Suleiman suggests that one can interpret the "Sadean hero's aversion toward the womb and the breasts (favorite loci of torture, but not of pleasure), and in general his refusal to accomplish the sexual act in a way that might lead to procreation" as expressions of a hatred of mothers, who are identified as the natural source of life (*S*, 68). Womb and breasts, of course, are women's unique ways of nourishing, and so too of bonding with, the baby. To clarify the irony then, transgressive sexuality may not so much oppose repressive social structures as conspire with paternal law to deny the maternal source of life. But then the transgressive erotics of the avant-garde reveal much less about the early bond between mothers and children than about certain adult male fantasies of self-engenderment (cf. *S*, 69).

Daniel Stern: The Social Dance

I have claimed that the figuration of maternal space through the poetics of transgressive eroticism originates not in the infant but in the absent caregiver who takes his pleasure in projecting antisocial and postpubescent fantasies onto the infant he does not in fact know. A theory of pre-Oedipal space should benefit from the perspectives and experiences of present caregivers. For this reason I turn to the work of Daniel Stern, an Anglo-American psychoanalytic theorist, who bases his theory on empirical observations of the interactions between mothers and their children.

Stern argues against two of the central presuppositions of traditional psychoanalytic theory. These two presuppositions are: (1) that the child is originally in a symbiotic relation with its mother, and (2) that the child then proceeds to develop an autonomous sense of self as it separates from the mother. Stern claims that the infant actively constructs an "emergent self" from birth, and that this emergent self participates in a "subjective social life."

These guiding assumptions of Stern's theory must be based as much in ethical decision as in empirical investigation. Clearly, Stern could have decided to define the person primarily in terms of cognitive and physical agency, e.g., in terms of the power to manipulate or explore objects. In the decision to locate the more significant dimension of the self in its social eros, Stern goes some way toward resisting the asocial atomism of modernist philosophies as well as the repressive sociality postulated by Freud.

This redefinition of the self as social and participatory rather than as private and self-generated is, moreover, critical for a feminist ethics. As Adrienne Rich explains, often enough history has mandated that the "identity, the very personality, of the man depends on power"; the consequence is a society that values technical skills over social skills and that allows the "spectacle of ... bloody struggles for power ... , [with] their implicit sacrifice of human relationships and emotional values in the quest for dominance."[15]

If empirical observation is inseparable from ethical decision, so too ethical decision draws upon experience. For reasons that are at once and inseparably ethical and experiential, I would argue that Stern's claim that the infant can only flourish in a rich social milieu serves as an important correction to the modern *mythos* of the "man from nowhere." I would also argue that, contra Stern, this social life should not be understood through the model of intersubjectivity, a model, i.e., which presupposes subjects.

Let us consider the evidence behind Stern's speculations regarding the subjective social life of the infant. Stern has observed that the infant

> tasks of eating, getting to sleep, and general homeostasis are generally accompanied with social behaviors by the parents: rocking, touching, soothing, talking, singing, and making noises and faces. These occur in response to infant behaviors that are also mainly social, such as crying, fretting, smiling, and gazing. A great deal of social interaction goes on in the service of physiological regulation.... At ... times, parents ... focus on the social interaction and act, from the beginning, *as though* the infant had a sense of self." (*I*, 43; emphasis mine)

While Stern is more careful than the parents who project self-conscious intentionality onto their newborns, his theoretical perspective draws upon more mature structures of social interaction in order to interpret early infancy. This problem is evident from the tension between Stern's own claim to observe emergent selfhood in the infant from birth, if not before, and his more skeptical eye toward the parent who acts "*as though* the infant had a sense of self" (*I*, 43).[16] As a therapist, Stern is of course familiar with the phenomenon of projection. For Stern, however, projection seems to be less a possible source of interpretative error than a necessary element of any theory: "While parents are consummate experts at this alignment with the future states of being of their infants, there is a related phenomenon in therapy.... [The analyst] 'treats the patient as though he were roughly the person he is about to become. The patient will explore being treated that way, and fill in the personal details'" (*I*, 43). My claim is that Stern's endorsement of projection in therapy points to a problem in his interpretative phenomenology of childhood. Because Stern interprets earlier stages in terms of their goal, or telos, in more advanced stages, he produces a more linear account of human development than is supported, I believe, by the evidence. That early social behaviors later take on an intersubjective significance does not imply that the conscious *subject* exists already in early infancy.

Stern supports his interpretative strategies by aligning his theoretical approach with dialectical methodologies. Specifically, Stern takes from a dialectical methodology the assumption that earlier behaviors are preserved and rendered more complex in higher stages of development. Thus, according to Stern, while the meaning of childhood behaviors is altered as these behaviors manifest themselves in the maturational process, our earliest behaviors never leave us. In support of this theoretical perspective, Stern quotes Ernst Cassirer: "The advent of a higher stage 'does not destroy the earlier phase, rather it embraces it in its own perspective'" (quoted in *I*, 29). That is, to make explicit the dialectical language implied in Stern's methodology, the higher stage of human development "sublates" lower stages. However, what I think Stern might have missed in dialectical methodologies is the kind of concern that Hegel articulates in *Phenomenology of Spirit*. Dialectical interpretation must refrain from projecting constructs that emerge only at higher stages of development onto lower stages as though the more advanced constructs were actually given from the beginning.

Stern has the evidence that he needs to establish the sociality of the infant. One clear type of evidence for the sociality of the infant appears in its preference for the more familiar smells of its mother to those of other nursing women (*I*, 39; also cited in Benjamin's *B*, 13). While my argument is that the baby's preference for the smells of the mother does suggest that the baby can only thrive in a hospitable social milieu, this evidence does not establish on the part of the infant either an awareness of the self or an awareness of the mother as a distinct subject.

A second type of evidence for the sociality of the infant centers around infant response to what are called "vitality affects," or, as Stern explains, those "elusive qualities ... captured by dynamic, kinetic terms, such as 'surging,' 'fading away,' 'fleeting,' 'explosive,' 'crescendo,' 'decrescendo,' 'bursting,' 'drawn out,' and so on" (*I*, 54). Stern discovers that these affects appear in such simple acts as how a mother or father picks up a baby (*I*, 54). In general, these affects express rhythms, mood changes, and energy levels that are transferred between infant and caregiver. The appropriate soothing sounds from a caregiver can get the baby to sleep or otherwise alter the way in which the infant finds itself in the world (*I*, 58; here Heidegger's use of the term "*Befindlichkeit*" could be helpful).

Again, however, while these responses do suggest that the infant does not exist in anything like the state of asocial autism postulated by traditional psychoanalysis and modernist philosophies, there is not sufficient evidence to conclude that the social lifeworld of the infant can be understood through the model of intersubjectivity. The early responses of the infant to the sounds and smells of the mother or father do argue for the sociality of the infant. However, it is difficult to see how the transferral of kinetic rhythms implies the recognition of Self and Other that constitutes inter-subjectivity.

The transferral of kinetic rhythms plays a central role in Kristeva's discussion of pre-Oedipal space. Kristeva, however, unlike Stern, is content to treat the kinetic rhythms as an expression of drive states and not of subjectivity. This may in part be due to the fact that so much of neonate behavior is not voluntary but instinctual. Stern himself cites evidence that the "repertoire of facial expressions until about three to four months ... are innate" (*I*, 55). The baby smiles to the caregiver's smile, but the baby smiles also to an inanimate line. These are behaviors that are crucial to social bonding. It is difficult, however, to understand how the first smile could constitute a recognition of the smile of another person when this other person does not yet possess what the child can identify as a distinct face. As Stern himself confesses, "the evidence for recognition of individual faces prior to two months is [not] secure. Many researchers continue to find it, but a larger number do not" (*I*, 64). However subtle and complex the social interactions are between infant and caregiver, these interactions lack what must be fundamental to intersubjectivity: an awareness of the face of the other person.

Stern also notes that observers generally agree that around two to three months something dramatically new emerges in the infant: only then "an infant can smile responsively, gaze into the parent's eyes, and coo, [so that] a different social feel has been created" (*I*, 8). Indeed, Stern adds, a "different person" suddenly appears. A more cautious reading of Stern's observations in relation to his theory would argue that it is not a different person that emerges. On the contrary, this different person is the person. The expression of self-conscious subjectivity appears at two or three months in the face-to-face relation with the Other.

There are ethical reasons for a more cautious definition of the person than Stern allows. In insisting upon the social eros of the developing self, but in resisting the tendencies to project personhood onto the newborn, we can address what at first sight must appear as an utterly bizarre fact: maternal infanticide has been, Adrienne Rich points out, one of the more common crimes in our culture (*OW*, 259). Rich explains that under patriarchy motherhood has often enough meant "penal servitude," i.e., slavery to repressive institutions (*OW*, 14).[17] While infanticide may appear monstrous to the outsider, it may be felt by the mother as the death of a living being that is not yet a person—a being who is, however, already social and who, under conditions of a social nightmare, is already at risk of spiritual death. The self-sacrificing labor required in different ways for different classes and races of women by patriarchal institutions threatens the subjectivity of the caregiver and so too the social interaction that conditions the emergence of the infant self.

If it is the case that the *self* emerges not much earlier than two months, what kind of language or theory could be adequate to a phenomenology of the lived experience of the infant?

The difficulties are immense. Even more immense, in fact, when we see that embedded within Stern's theory is yet another and even more troubling projection of alien images onto infant experience. Despite Stern's emphasis on the sociality of the newborn, Stern falls back upon modernist images in his primary definition of neonatal experience. According to Stern, the lived subjectivity of the infant can be viewed as a "*process* of emerging organization...*, and it is this experience of emerging organization that I call the *emergent sense of self*" (*I*, 45). This claim, supported by much evidence, does successfully oppose the more traditional psychoanalytic view (found, for example, in the work of Kristeva) that the infant experiences "nonorganization." However, in order to alter this psychoanalytic picture of infancy, Stern borrows a conception of the self that takes on a Cartesian cast. This Cartesianism comes out most explicitly in Stern's readiness to claim that "many separate experiences exist with what for the infant may be exquisite clarity and vividness" (*I*, 46). Stern's theory of the infant eschews the anti-rationalism of psychoanalytic theory only in order to revert back to a conception of the self that borrows from analytic rationalism. Paradigmatic of infantile experience is not the mythic space of random libidinal drive in all its polymorphic forms but, Stern argues, a partially organized matrix of impressions that are clear and vivid. Behind Stern's theory of infant subjectivity lies a primitive Cartesian *cogito*.

A Cartesian locus of the self is used to interpret what Stern terms the "global experiences" of the infant. According to Stern, the newborn can "intuitively" grasp holistic phenomena such as the sameness of the visual breast and the suckled breast (*I*, 52). Stern explains this phenomenon as an example of what is sometimes called cross-modal correspondence and at other times amodal perception: "Infants ... appear to have an innate general capacity, which can be called *amodal perception*, to take information received in one sensory modality and somehow translate it into another sensory modality. We do not know how they accomplish this task" (*I*, 51). Constructionist theories rely on "assimilation, accommodation, identifying invariants, and associational learning" in order to explain this mystery of perception. However, Stern points out, the immediate grasp of the similarity between visual and tactile impressions cannot be explained by way of the trial and error processes of construction (*I*, 61, 48). Therefore, Stern resorts to a rather suspicious theory of innate intuition.

Cross-modal correspondence poses a fundamental block to projecting onto infancy a modernist epistemology—Cartesian rationalism or empiricism—that is, any epistemology based on the discrete analysis of the units of experience by a detached observer. If advanced scientists cannot—even for themselves—penetrate the mystery of cross-modal correspondence, the presupposition that an amodal representation exists clearly and distinctly—either as construct or as intuition—in the conscious experience of an infant seems implausible. If neither a "clear and vivid" nor a "well-organized and articulated" network of impressions appears in cross-modal perception, then the language of modern analysis cannot be adequate to the lived experiences of infancy.

Stern's more significant insight remains his decision to define the self not in terms of power over objects (a power that may require a quasi-Cartesian *cogito*) but rather in terms of social-relatedness. We still lack clues, however, as to how the theorist might apprehend the sociality of the infant who is not yet a subject.

The need for a less Cartesian phenomenology of early infancy motivates some theorists to turn to traditional psychoanalytic theory. As the traditionalists rightly insist, from the last trimester through the first few weeks after birth, the infant drifts in and out of sleep. In and out of sleep, the infant begins life in the folds of a dream. Psychoanalytic theorists characterize this early period in terms of the protean drives and fluid boundaries of primary narcissism. The observations of Stern, however, successfully challenge the view that the infant exists in a disorganized symbiosis with the mother. Psychoanalysis imagines the elemental experience of the infant as oceanic.[18] However, after birth intrauterine fluidity is not the primary element of early infancy. Kristeva interprets the rhythmic, tonal, and tactile articulations of infancy in terms of violent and random discharge. However, this distortion of infant musicality fails to question an assumption of patriarchal ideology, viz, that the elements of social structure arise through the categories of propositional discourse. Kristeva buttresses Freudian speculations on a primordial death drive with her work on avant-garde mania. In that mania is manifest a drive to exceed the bounds of productivity and self-preservation, the boundaries that would protect life. The infant, however, instinctively withdraws from dangerous excesses, including intense light, explosive sound, or any source of overstimulation. As a barely conscious, boundless happening of uncertain desire, the infant gropes for nourishment and attachment, not death and antisocial nihilism. Its rhythm is the rhythm of life. In the next chapter, I shall argue that the elementary sociality of the self cannot be known without an epistemology that is also music and dance.

· 2 ·
Tactile Sociality

Irigaray and Child Development Research

Proximity is a Festival.
Enrique Dussel

However forceful the rejections and denials, in fact all the more because of the intensity of the resistance, psychoanalytic theory constitutes for twentieth-century European culture the terms of desire. One of the effects of psychoanalytic theory has been to shake the foundations of Enlightenment philosophies of reason. Utilitarian and Kantian conceptions of reason reappear as ego and superego and thus as mere superstructures of unconscious instinct. However, despite this critique, psychoanalytic theory inherits from the Enlightenment one of its most recalcitrant postulates. According to this postulate, the human being is not *by nature* a social animal.[1] On the contrary, sociality is contrived from predatory instincts that have been "rationalized" in a calculus of self-interest or restrained by the disciplinary practices of pure duty.[2] Psychoanalytic theory, then, does not so much deconstruct as reestablish modern liberalism by providing for it a rich continental genealogy beginning with an elaborate theory of the roots of the self in the animalistic drives of early childhood.

But if the dominant theories of desire postulate that the child is a beast to be domesticated by social convention or subdued by reason, I wonder whose perspectives on childcare these theories represent. I wonder if these theories do not represent the very perspectives of those who in fact have been detached from the childrearing scene. But then what if we were to base a theory of human nature, a philosophical anthropology, not on the experience of absent caregivers but on that of present nurturers? Adrienne Rich observes that patriarchal societies regard women's work to be natural in a way that men's work is not.[3] By "naturalizing" the work of the nurturer, patriarchal institutions of motherhood subject the nurturer to the same subjectless asociality as her infant. Together parent and infant are rendered mute before the forces of a masculinized reason and an oppressive social system.

In fact we now know that much more happens in the "state of nature" than mothers or their infants are given credit for. Already, while the infant is yet in the womb, the mother finds pleasure in her child's movement. In this chapter, I shall argue that the fetal kick should be read not as an act of resistance (a modernist and arguably masculinist measure of the real) but as a step in a dance between mother and child (and thus as an alternative measure of the real). The mother responds to her infant's movement with touch. Between the sensations of the fetal kick and the maternal caress, mother and infant choreograph the boundaries of the real. The infant's first sense of the world—what Heidegger calls "fundamental ontology"— emerges under the direction of the maternal caress.

I am not claiming that the fetus or the newborn already possesses a sense of Self and Other. Until approximately the second month of infancy, when social smiling begins, parents do not find in their child an awareness of self or other persons.[4] Early infancy occurs in a space devoid of *personal* interaction. But even if the experience of early infancy occurs prior to interpersonal awareness, this first infant-nurturer relation need not be innocent of all modalities of ethical exchange. On the contrary, the experience of parenting poses fundamental questions of liberal and psychoanalytic theories of desire. If it is true that the infant possesses as of yet no subjectivity, does it follow that the infant inhabits a space evacuated of all social contact? Does any dimension of infancy already exceed the register of biological need or libidinal drive? A complementary question concerns the parent. How does the mother find herself in relation to the child at her breast? Does the repetitive cycle of infant nourishment, sleep, and excretion efface altogether the presence of the parent, reducing his labor to brute mechanism?

The introduction of the experience of the parent into psychoanalytic theory not only suggests an alternative conception of sociality but also brings the ethical resources needed to challenge the post-Enlightenment critique of the possibility of social progress—especially as this critique draws upon psychoanalytic theory. Psychoanalytic theory centers infancy around cannibalistic pleasures of consuming or refusing maternal fluids.[5] This dynamic of oral pleasure, we are told, prefigures the forthcoming pleasures of the anal and genital stages, as well as the various sublimations and sacrificial repressions that constitute fully socialized desire. If, as the theory suggests, the desires that we articulate in language trace back to biological drives for nutrition and excretion, then there is no manifestation of desire that does not arise from the polarizing mechanics of incorporation and expulsion. Moreover, if it is the case that desire in general borrows its dynamic from the drive to assimilate and/or to expel, any attempt to advance society beyond the social pathologies of domination and sacrifice is doomed from the start. Therefore, social theory lacks a concept of desire that emerges outside of the oppositional pattern of biological drives or asocial discharges in their various manifestations (e.g., drives to consume or expel, include or exclude, control or destroy). That is, social theory lacks a concept of desire that does not fall into the logic of identity or its ever so virile transgression. Without an alternative conception of desire, theory cannot provide for the possibility of a sociality that is not embedded in the sacrificial dynamics of social oppression, the asceticism of disciplinary techniques, or the hyperartificiality of the social construct.

Theories that postulate the inevitability of sacrifice never manage to distribute the social burden of that sacrifice evenly.[6] For example, the psychoanalytic tradition traces the origins of human society to the sacrifice of the pleasures experienced at the *maternal* body and the internalization of the *father's* symbolic power.[7] Consigned to motherhood, women retreat to the background of the social process, where they service the "animal needs" of their infant-machines. Psychoanalysis may be accused of basing the entire structure of the adult personality on early childhood, but in fact it participates in the usual politics of relegating the mother-child relation to a dumb show. If the tradition has its way, there can be no socio-ethical bond between mother and child.

Modern liberalism invokes the same politics of excluding the feminized caregiver from social space. Freed from the material considerations of the caregiver, an abstract and masculinized ego constructs, quite by artifice, a contract for society that binds by unnatural constraint.

So too Lacanian mythology requires that the infant exit from the primitive hedonism of the real and enter into the imaginary, where the infant develops an image of the self through a masculine gaze, and into the symbolic, where the child acquires a position as a subject in the linguistically informed structures of phallic exchange.

It is in particular the texts of Luce Irigaray that demonstrate the complicity of the Western model of sociality with sublimated forms of gender inequality. The imaginary and the symbolic may partially repress but *also* indirectly massage a masculinized id and protect a masculinized ego. For Irigaray, this fact signifies not only that the prevailing *content* of our words and cultural images reflects a masculinized point of view. More importantly, the very *syntax* of experience, in both its imaginary and symbolic forms, excludes a feminist mode of knowing and informs instead an epistemology that has been historically encoded as male.

How could the formal structures that define experience already reflect the interests of a traditionally masculinized subject? Irigaray argues that the masculinist mode of experience rests upon the centrality of visual perception. For modern philosophers such as Descartes, Kant, Hegel, Sartre, and Foucault sensory experience focuses around the objectifying gaze of the autonomous subject. This gaze is not without an economic policy. On the contrary, the excretions of the masculinized subject of European modernity territorialize the world into propertied objects of definition and control, leaving the subject more or less powerful but alone. The gaze prepares for predation, not sociality, or rather, prepares for male bonding in the chase.[8]

But the engrossed absorption of parental eyes need not be the same as the objectifying gaze of the predator. The absorbed eyes of the father or mother do not aim to control an object but seek to gain a feel for the child. As the sleep-deprived parent rubs his or her nose against the child, the scent of the child diffuses the urge to harm. The first social bond occurs not through the dynamics of the gaze but in the mixing of the milky odors of the baby with the milky odors of the mother in skin-to-skin contact.

Therefore, much of Irigaray's work begins with what she takes to be a more elementary and also more feminist[9] mode of sensory awareness, a mode of sensation that only rarely gains the attention of theorists. In effect, Irigaray rewrites the social contract, locating the origin of the social bond in what she takes to be a most basic social gesture. That social gesture is the caress. It is specifically in her response to Levinas in *Éthiqué de la différence sexuelle* that Irigaray reenvisions sociality in the register of tactile experience. There she invokes a return to the presubjective origins of sociality: "On the horizon of a story is found, once again, that which was in the beginning: this naive, or native, sense of a touch, in which the subject does not yet exist."[10] The awareness of tactile sensations precedes and conditions the emerging dialectic of Self and Other, carrying with it the possibility of transformed notions of subjectivity and sociality—notions that, I suspect, are neither modern nor postmodern.

Irigaray's reconception of human origins in the register of touch emerges from a philosophical tradition that traces back from Levinas and Merleau-Ponty to Rousseau.[11] In his "Essay on the Origin of Languages," Rousseau attempts to account for the emergence of social feelings. He argues that the human animal comes to feel for another human being only by way of a transport of the imagination. Perhaps sensing that his various explanations for this transport are not complete, i.e., aware that he lacks an analytic solution to the emergence of social passion, Rousseau finally draws upon an act of god: "He who willed man to be social, by the touch of a finger shifted the globe's axis."[12] It is in particular the pagan god of Michelangelo's *The Creation of Adam* that concocts the primal event by way of a touch. With or without conscious intent, Rousseau nearly puts his finger, so to speak, on what for Irigaray is the origin of the social: the touch itself. The patriarchal tradition strains to grasp what happens in the gap between father and son and cannot. From out of this void, little more appears than the sleight of hand of a creation *ex nihilo*.[13] Never, Irigaray writes, does this void reveal "a God who envelops me, surrounds me, cradles me ... who loves me carnally, erotically."[14] Meanwhile Irigaray takes as the source of social passion—not superterrestrial magic, but the divine and mortal hands of the mother.

Irigaray fastens onto the touch as the most elemental and least self-conscious gesture between two sensuous beings. She develops the social and ethical significance of the touch most fully in her discussion of the renewal, or "rebirth," of the self that occurs in sexual eros. Because, however, the primary concern in her discussion of sexual eros is to salvage an account of heterosexuality that does not sentence women to serving as mother for male self-invigoration and re-creation, she alludes to but does not dwell upon the "amourous exchange" between parent and child. Moreover, as is typical in psychoanalytic theory, her work often approaches the experiences of earliest childhood only by way of projections from an adult psyche. The psychoanalytic mythologizing of infancy flirts with confusing the pleasures between parent and child with those between lovers—if not overlooking the particular eros between parent and child altogether. Elsewhere Irigaray herself warns that the confusion of maternal and sexual eros is typical of Lacanian analysts, who all too readily fantasize infancy as a configuration of sexual desire, or, as she puts it, in terms of what "turns them on."[15] Therefore, I take as an important task the need to sustain Irigaray's discussion of the caress from the position of the parent and child. No doubt the pleasures of the infant-parent caress can be associated with the sexual pleasures of lovers. These primary pleasures, however, also exist independently of sexuality and, therefore, in their own right.[16] If oppressive institutions demand the sublimation and repression of sexuality, so too they demand the sublimation and repression of the eros between parent and child.

The dynamic of parental eros differs from the dynamic of sexuality. One difference is that while sexual love may be initially aroused through the sight of the loved one, parent-infant love is more likely to be initially aroused by touch and smell. Parents often find that the newborn looks misshapen. This is why television commercials do not use images of newborns to sell baby products. But parents who are put off by the elongated head or crinkled face of the newborn are more likely to fall in love with the feel and the scent of the baby. So too newborns do not seem to recognize the faces of their parents. However, these babies respond intently to characteristic smells, touches, and sounds.

Irigaray explains the sensuality of touch by way of an almost Keatsian romance. The caress, she writes, appears as "a gesture, ... which weds without consuming" (F, 232). If, however, personal identity emerges most decidedly with the recognition of the face of the other person, there is no *interpersonal* exchange in early infancy. Therefore, the value of the infant caress—at least until after the first month or so—cannot be the same as that of a gesture. Irigaray is correct, I believe, when she writes: "Before orality comes to be, touch is already in existence. No nourishment can compensate for the grace, or the work, of touching.... The most subtly necessary guardian of my life being the other's flesh." However, I suspect that we should hold back from characterizing this early caress as an "approaching and speaking to me with his hands" (F, 232). The caress of the parent is not yet the gesture of salutation that it becomes after the emergence of face-to-face play. In the early period of infancy, there is as of yet no possibility for either linguistic or prelinguistic signification ("papaese" or "mamaese"). And yet the desire in both infant and nurturer for the sociality of the caress supersedes quasi-biological mechanisms to consume and expel, e.g., the pleasures of oral and anal drives, as well as the ethical dichotomy of maternal sacrifice and infantile narcissism.

Finally, I am taking the liberty of transforming some but not all of the discussion of the "maternal" caress into the tactile pleasures between infant and mother, father, and other male or female nurturers. For against essentialist claims made on behalf of Irigaray (claims that appear unresponsive to Irigaray's efforts to deconstruct the major philosophical sources of inert essentialism in the visual epistemologies of Cartesianism and Platonism), I take as Irigaray's task not the policing of old or new gender lines but the opening of yet unimagined worlds. Rather than speculate on differences between paternal and maternal eros (differences that are as varied as they are real), I anticipate the day when fathers everywhere take a hand in shaping—and giving themselves to being shaped by—the destiny that is the child.

There is in Anglo-American literature "hard" empirical evidence to "support" the so-called "soft" French musings on the caress. Social scientists Golbfarb and Spitz find that if the infant is deprived of the stimulus of the caregiver's caress, it collapses into a state of despondency.[17] Poet-cum-naturalist Diane Ackerman describes the well-known effects of massaging preemies: "Massaged babies ... are more active, alert, and responsive.... [They] had better temperaments, and so were more appealing to their parents, which is important.... Children who are difficult to raise get abused more often. And people who aren't touched much as children don't touch much as adults, so the cycle continues."[18] Ackerman also cites an experiment with monkeys at the University of Wisconsin suggesting that the primary effects of touch will be on the developing social personality: "Those infants who suffered short-term deprivation became adolescents who clung to one another obsessively instead of developing into independent, confident individuals. When they suffered long-term deprivation, they avoided one another and became aggressive when they did come into contact, [proving to be] violent loners who didn't form good relationships" (NH, 76).

I wonder if the extreme personalities of those who have suffered from deprivations of touch, the person who clings to the other and the violent loner, do not map onto a standard dichotomy that informs traditional ethics: the dichotomy between altruism and egoism. It is interesting that this dichotomy also informs an oppressive image of the mother (defined in terms of unconditional giving to the other) and an oppressive image of the father (defined in terms of the instrumental self). The evidence on tactile deprivation in infancy suggests that the detached subject as well as the self-sacrificing caregiver do not condition vital social attachments but instead constitute social pathologies. Thus the rhythms and tonalities of the caress set the stage for an emerging sociality before the appearance of infant subjectivity.

It is significant for Irigaray that the desire for the caress is not reducible to a biological drive to consume or expel; nor can it be modeled in terms of drive mechanisms. That is, the desire to touch and be touched exceeds any conception of drive based on the pleasures of oral assimilation, controlled excretion, or sexual copulation. If these three drives define the Freudian conception of drive as the buildup and discharge of tension, then the pleasures and deprivations of the caress exceed the mechanics of the drive altogether as well as any formalized model of need based on this mechanics. The pleasures of touch exceed the biological. Before the infant self emerges from what is too often reduced to biology, the infant participates in social and cultural life.

The work of the mother must be reinterpreted beyond altruism, or the various sacrifices of self. Because the caress does not aim to incorporate, it resists the fusion dynamics—including oceanic, symbiotic, and organic experiences of oneness—often projected onto the infant-mother relation. Fusion experiences assume that two individual subjects dissolve into a single identity, a sameness that again takes the pattern of an all too fluid assimilation or even final liquidation. But mother no more dissolves into child than child dissolves into mother.

Using ultrasonography, Italian psychoanalyst Alessandra Piontelli has investigated the surprisingly elaborate social activities of the fetus in the womb. In her studies, Piontelli found only a single case of a fetus (named Giulia) that did not exhibit some sense of independent movement within the maternal womb. For the most part, Piontelli writes, this fetus "just floated in the amniotic fluid following the rhythm of her mother's breathing, as if lulled by it, seeming totally in tune and at one with it."[19] After following the stunted social development of the little girl for several years after birth, Piontelli draws the conclusion that "feelings of fusion ... may not be normal conditions to be met in ordinary fetal life, but may represent, even at this very early stage of life, pathological defensive phenomena; perhaps, for example, Giulia in her fusional at-oneness with her intra-uterine environment may have already been resisting or blurring some kind of dim realization of 'me–not me' sensations" (*FC*, 240). It is this dim realization of "me–not me" sensations that brings mother and child side by side, neither identical nor opposed, but, as Irigaray writes, in close proximity.[20]

The work of the father, or the masculinized subject, must also be reinterpreted. The proximity between those that exchange a touch differs from the masculinized economy that is based on a predominantly vision-oriented perception. The gaze of animals that conceive themselves as predators serves to objectify, distance, and target. The hierarchies of the visual register of experience, Irigaray argues, are complicit in the patterns of oppression, including the oppositions between subject and object, that define modernist social structures. The pleasures of the caress, on the other hand, are independent of drives for self-preservation and the predation that ensues. The hand that is not wrapped around the tool, the noninstrumental expression of the hand opened in the caress, resists the logic of predation and traces an alternative dynamic of the social process. As Irigaray writes, "Touch, the substratum of all the senses, acts before any clear-cut positioning of subject and object. Its operation is always almost immediate, the site of a *jouissance* indefinable as such" (*R*, 108). Or, as Enrique Dussel writes, society begins not in exile from the Other but in the jubilation and creation of a festival of touch.[21] The caress between parent and child gives a pleasure that is—unless numbed by the alienating labor of patriarchal motherhood—immediately exchanged. It is, moreover, a pleasure easily overlooked. While Irigaray aims to find in the mother some identity that is not "imprisoned in the reality of need," she too can repress the pleasures of the caress and so reinforce supernatural hierarchies that turn man against animal and woman into nature (*R*, 52). For example, on one occasion Irigaray asks if women might attain a sense of self "in motherhood, relations with children and nurturing functions?" She responds: "But that is not necessarily a human identity. Machines will probably be able to do both in the near future, and animals are not incapable of those functions" (*R*, 192). Much of the labor of the parent addresses biological needs of the child but receives nothing in return. Under patriarchal institutions of mother-hood, maternal labor may indeed be reduced to the alienating rhythms and flat tonalities of mechanistic repetition. However, in a society that values the process of socialization itself, the pleasures and the praxis of the care-giver may be discovered to occur in other animal species without that labor being reduced to the work of Cartesian machines. In cradling, touching, tickling, and nursing, the pleasures between parent and child may often be subtle and barely conscious, only occasionally engrossing. The effect, how-ever, is critical to the social development of both infant and parent. As parental hands bring forth the infant self, so the pleasures of the infant's tactile response can rejuvenate the adult self that has been numbed by the deadening rhythms of economic life.[22] For the parent as for the child, there is dialectical give and take; the feeling between caregiver and child is not identical or even symmetrical. The mother is a person; the fetus or new-born infant is not. But if parent and infant cannot share a "common humanity," they may participate in a feeling that is mutual (cf. *F*, 234).

But then the woman becoming mother attains dimensions of subjectiv-ity in a way that differs from the man or woman becoming subject as an economic agent in civil society. The subject qua economic agent is a ratio-nal and autonomous decision-maker. The subject becoming mother does not construct arguments in her head. She does not rationalize, nor does she emote; she does develop a feel for her child. Discourse theory (Habermas, Benhabib), which models ethical society on the conversation between ratio-nal agents, has nothing to say to the subject as mother. The subject becom-ing mother experiences what Irigaray describes as an "amourous exchange." The attempt to understand all ethical exchanges on the model of rational debate in overdeveloped countries, and the measure of moral maturity in terms of moral reasoning, excludes both parent and child—and the play between them—from the ethical domain. Discourse theory oppresses the playful child in us all.

But it is also the case that the mother ought not superimpose a senti-mental narrative of care upon her infant. Such a narrative would reduce mother to an isolated subject and infant to the topic of a monologue. This suffocating mother-type is herself a projection of patriarchy. Beyond patri-archy, the mother addresses the infant with touch and the infant gropes back. Eventually, after some months of groping, they will encounter one another as persons.

The exchange of feelings between nurturer and child begins not only before the infant is able to recognize the face of another person but already before the infant's own face appears outside of the womb. The mother (and also, if somewhat differently, the father) responds to the kick of the unborn infant with touch. Here in the social space of the caress exists the first reciprocity between parent and child. Before the appearance of the face, in the wondrous flutter of the fetus at play and the jubilant response of the parental caress, there exists a tactile attunement to the Other.

Some male philosophers, including, for example, Nietzsche and Heidegger, have offered their own critiques of the modern liberal construction of the subject as economic machine or machine plus reason (logos). These philosophers also sometimes criticize the romantic conception of the masculinized self as raging warrior in its various oppositional dynamics with the sentimental female self. In order to avoid these traditional conceptions of the masculinized self, both Nietzsche in his *Ecce Homo* and Heidegger in his "What Is Metaphysics?" evoke images of male pregnancy. Man becomes what he is by confronting his death as irretrievable finitude, rather than as the final dare to mastery, and then nurturing what grows within as his destiny. However, when these philosophers speak of their own becoming in terms of pregnancy they do so as men rather than as women. Crucially, with all of their images of male pregnancy, Nietzsche and Heidegger have very little in the way of a positive conception of the social. As men, they would give birth to themselves and not to one another. Women, on the other hand, give birth to the Other, and, I am arguing, beyond patriarchal motherhood, in giving birth to the Other they may rejuvenate themselves. The inner self in the woman becoming mother is ecstatic—out there in social space. While women by their touch re-create Self with Other, men by their visions create themselves alone.

Sociality begins in the caress. Is the caress work or play?[23] Neither, if these opposing terms belong to a modernist hierarchy organized around an instrumental notion of desire, i.e., a notion of desire based on conceiving of the body in terms of hard and pointy organs. Irigaray admonishes: "And does not the fact that you have so much to say about the debt to the father, but very little, if anything, about the debt to the mother, mean that . . . only organs . . . have any value? . . . And it is women who go on providing the material substratum: the body, and blood, and the life which nourish them, whilst you exercise the power of your organs" (*R*, 95). I am arguing that this material substratum is not mechanical labor. Nor is this materiality reducible to random movement, unintelligent flux, or what Irigaray sometimes interprets through Father Plato's notion of the *chora*. The uncalculating *play* of the hand is a necessary and yet unacknowledged *labor* for the emerging sociality between parent and child.

But then again those discourse ethics and ethics of care that exclude the pleasures of play in what is called moral reasoning or a narrative of responsibility for the Other—i.e., those ethics that exclude the child in us—sever themselves from the pleasures that nourish the social. Discourse ethics and care ethics surreptitiously buy into the asceticism of the work ethic.[24] Such an ethic "knows nothing," Irigaray writes, "of communion in pleasure. [It] ... does not ever seem to have experienced the transcendence of the other which becomes immediate ecstasy in me and with him—or her" (*R*, 189; here Irigaray is addressing Levinas on sexual eros and not discourse or care ethics, but the problems are parallel).

The irreducibility of the caress to a biological need for assimilating nutrients intimates a social attachment that is not based on any hierarchical concept of central purpose or disciplinary power. Because theorists will never get a feel for the caress without scientists who are also poets, poet-scientists, I turn once again to Diane Ackerman: "Every other sense has a key organ to study; ... [i.e.] one key center, except touch. Touch is a sensory system, the influence of which is hard to isolate or eliminate" (*NH,* 77). In a closely related passage, Irigaray elaborates: Touch arises from "the desire for the proximate rather than for (the) proper(ty), ... [The pleasures of touch] might ... imply a mode of exchange irreducible to any *centring*" (*R,* 127). In the desire for the proximate, Irigaray traces an origin of social exchange that does not rest on the dualisms of sacrificial generosity and self-centered consumerism, on disciplined asceticism and unregulated egoism, on feminized altruism and the calculus of self-interest. If society is not to consume itself in cycles of predation and sacrifice, ethical theory will have to begin with the tactile sensuality between nurturer and child.

There is in Anglo-American attachment theory a place reserved for touch. Harlow and Zimmerman's well-known study of rhesus monkeys discovered that infant monkeys seek substitutes for absent mothers independent of nutritional needs, or indeed of any biological instinct or libidinal drive.[25] The attachment theorists term the discovered pleasure "contact comfort." They also note that this "comfort" persists in infants violently abused by their caregivers.[26] Whatever the nature of the caregiver's caress, I am suspicious of the flat reduction of the full scale of its sensuality to a single tonality, that is, to the "comfort" of the "holding environment" (see B, 120, and, citing Winnicott, 126–28).[27] Theorists thereby consign the creative work of the parent to a passive backdrop for the drama of the developing child. Mother is uneventful refuge; safe and quiet haven; or, even more poetically, the "seashore of endless worlds [on which] children play" (cited in B, 127). In this account children develop through play; mothers do not.

Such descriptions of the mother bind her arms, restricting their power of expression to the mute cause of settling the child. There is, however, more to the arms of the parent than cradle for the baby. The mechanistic, scientistic model of the mother as "holding environment" no less than the pious poetry of mother as "endless sea" or "elemental flux"[28] conceal the handiwork of interpreting, shaping, and responding to the infant's fluctuating moods. Both scientistic and sentimental discourses reduce the labor of the caregiver to service as what Irigaray terms a "primitive shelter," available for consumption and exploitation and "without any debt, any payment, without any record made of it" (R, 111–12). In fact, the parent is no more passive holding environment than engulfing appetite. The parent finds him- or herself in tactile exchange with another.

The privatization and naturalization of social praxes in a society that models labor on centralized corporate hierarchies renders invisible the elements of reciprocity and decentralized shaping that occur in rearing the child. Rhythms, intensities, and cycles of moods are not imposed by parent on an infinitely malleable child. The infant reciprocates parental overtures with its own score of movements. The ethical bond begins in an attunement that is musicality and dance. Mother and child move one another; through the efforts of both they may learn to move together. Because the infant is not mute and passive material but—from its first kick in the womb—active mover and shaper, the infant threatens to exhaust and alienate but also promises to reshape and reinvigorate the caregiver. The child parents the caregiver as the caregiver parents the child. And if elemental to parenting are the pleasures of decentralized tactile movement, the sources of that pleasure are multiple. The hands involved in caregiving can freely multiply.

Daniel Stern develops his theory of infancy with the observation that already in the first weeks the infant experiences correspondences across modes of perception. For example, the infant knows almost intuitively that the felt nipple is the same as the nipple that is seen (*I*, 48; see chapter 1 above). Correspondence occurs not only across perceptual qualities. The infant also responds to what Stern terms "vitality affects," or those "elusive qualities ... captured by dynamic, kinetic terms, such as 'surging,' 'fading away,' 'fleeting,' 'explosive,' 'crescendo,' 'decrescendo,' 'bursting,' 'drawn out,' and so on" (*I*, 54). "Abstract dance and music are examples par excellence of the expression of vitality affects. Dance reveals ... vitality affects and their variations, without resorting to plot or categorical affect" (*I*, 56). The parent's "there, there, there," properly stressed, together with a rhythmically attuned stroking of the head, soothes the child (*I*, 58).

It is interesting though that relative to the work of Irigaray, Stern does not more fully develop the significance of the caress. This is especially surprising given that Mary Cassatt's painting *Baby's First Caress* decorates the cover of his major work, *The Interpersonal World of the Infant*. Why does the maternal caress remain so much on the outside of his work? I suspect that the underemphasis on the sensuality of touch stems in part from constraints introduced by the "observational approach" of what Stern defines as the "phenomenological" method of his social science. The observational approach construes the empirical method of the social sciences primarily in the visual register. The social distance between observed object (the infant, or the infant-caregiver interaction) and the observer sustains problematic assumptions concerning neutrality in the human sciences. These claims are especially suspect given Stern's remark that already in infancy, "affective and cognitive processes cannot be readily separated.... Learning itself is motivated and affect-laden" (*I*, 42). Rather than bringing this remark fully to bear on his own research, Stern argues for the possibility of neutrality—at least within any given prevailing paradigm of science.

As partial justification for his claim to scientific neutrality, Stern cites Paul Ricoeur, "who suggests that there are some general hypotheses about how the mind works and how it develops that exist independently of the many narratives that could be constructed—for example, the developing sequence of psychosexual stages" (*I*, 16). What could be more uncertain, however, than the "true" nature of human sexuality? The work of Irigaray alone casts substantial doubt on any traditional division of "normal" and "abnormal" sexuality.

Instead of the visually informed knowledge of a patriarchal science,

Irigaray develops the more tactile awareness of self-generation in poetic prose. The work of Stern very much supports Irigaray's project inasmuch as he locates the emerging self not in the physicality of observed space nor in the geometricized space of Cartesian philosophy but only in the fragile web of social space. Social space sublates the physical and metaphysical and exists only through what Stern describes as responsive attunement, and what Irigaray further elaborates in terms of the risk of an encounter (F, 247). An affect-laden interpretation would be necessary if, as Stern explains, the "social feel" of the child is "more than the sum of the many newly acquired behaviors and capacities" (I, 8). Stern does not address the question of how a model of knowledge based on objectifying observation could relate to this "social feel." The neutral and artificial tonality of the definition of the infant self as the "the experience of . . . networks becoming integrated" betrays projections of a censored and alienated science out of touch with the "lived experience" sought by psychoanalytic theory (F, 24). Behind the scientistic demand to objectify, distance, and target lies a modernist pathology, a deprivation of touch. The sterile representational language of social science is doomed to repeat narcissistic projections of a machine-made man.

An epistemology that acknowledges the active participation of the expert in the process of socialization begins by taking responsibility for the shaping of social praxis that occurs in scientific intervention. At the most minimal level, social study risks a stance toward what counts as a person. As long as this task assumes a status that is a priori, it remains materially detached from the praxis that births the social self (cf. I, 6). Beyond patriarchy, the work of social science begins—not by gazing upon the defined Other but in response to an encounter. Only then does social science become (part of) what it studies: social exchange.

From the choreography of parental hand to fetal kick and the fine-tuning of biological rhythms to the shaping that occurs as the baby's yet malleable head advances down the birth canal, in our history it has been women who have single-handedly given material definition to the human. The parental hand plays best when it is not phallic, if by "phallic" we mean the peculiar pleasure found in the urge to reduce the Other to an object of control or observation. Irigaray explains: "The caress does not try to dominate a hostile freedom"; it is not the "voluptuousness nourished by this transgression" (F, 233). Nor can the mother's place be dissolved in the chaotic turbulence of fluids.[29] Parental hands give modest boundaries for the self to come (cf. F, 248).

Irigaray overlooks the molding power of maternal hands when she writes of woman as an unknown quantity, declaring that "woman does not obey the principle of self-identity, or of identity with any particular x. She identifies with every x, without identifying with it in any particular way.... Woman is always already in a state of anamorphosis in which all figures blur" (*R*, 56). But then much of the intent of Irigaray's practice has been to heal those who have been told that their speech does not measure up. The practice of healing would have to begin by opening an uncensored space for the suffering to speak. It is to the silenced and suffering that Irigaray writes: "If you/I hesitate to speak, isn't it because we are afraid of not speaking well? But ... with what are we conforming if we speak 'well.' ... Don't worry about the 'right' word. There isn't any.... There is room enough for everything to exist" (*NO*, 213).

If Irigaray's discourse of fluidity can be read primarily as opening a space for those whose expressive styles run dissonant to the powers that be, then it need not be read as fixing an a priori definition of the feminine. Nor does the discourse of fluidity pose a real alternative to the conception of caregiving as disciplinary action. Irigaray does not simply replace an anal schedule of sociality with an oral one. On the contrary, she is relocating both anality and orality within a larger sociality of touch.

The temptation to dissolve the element of the mother's love into the metonymic discourse of fluids "in which all figures blur" may in part stem from the fantasy of unconditional love. Mother as person is effaced in the image of mother as overflowing breast or engulfing womb. The image of the mother as ever-flowing fluidity destroys the tactile boundaries that condition the social connection between mother, father, or Other and infant already in the womb.

This image also conceals the complexity of the biological connection between mother and fetus. Irigaray asks biologist Helene Rouch to explain "the *mediating* role the placenta plays during interuterine life." Rouch responds: "On the one hand, it's the mediating space between mother and fetus, which means that there's never a fusion of maternal and embryonic tissues. On the other hand, it constitutes a system regulating exchanges between the two ... for both her own and the fetus' benefit."[30] Irigaray concludes: "The placental economy is therefore an organized economy, one not in a state of fusion, which respects the one and the other. Unfortunately, our cultures, split off from the natural order—and the scientific methods used to get back to it more often than not accentuate that distance—neglect or fail to recognize the almost ethical character of the fetal relation" (*J*, 41). I am arguing that this "almost ethical character" emerges fully in the mediations of touch.

Fluids take the identity of their containers. The containers of female identity have been patriarchal institutions of motherhood. As mothers, women will remain unknown quantities until they push back against alien institutions. The discourse of fluidity may erode or destabilize alien institutions, but it cannot choreograph an orienting praxis of psychic generation and social renewal. It is not from the element of water that the "almost ethical character" of early life emerges but from the rhythms and tones of kinesthetic exchange. Ethical life begins in the diffuse intentionalities of dance.

The ethical comportment of the dance brings power to resist the forces of oppression, or that which destroys the social. In the interview with Jacques Derrida, "Choreographies," Christie McDonald recalls the words of Emma Goldman: "If I can't dance I don't want to be part of your revolution."[31] The rhythms of resistance of the mother differ from the rhythms of resistance of the warrior.[32] Resistance that begins by celebrating fertility, and not by worshipping at the shrine of death, demands the guiding praxis of a multiplicity of hands, not ever again the random spill of vital fluids. Beyond patriarchal institutions and their warrior's logic, mother and child perform—to reengage a Heideggerian motif—an originary *poiesis*.

The task of social *poiesis* lies outside of the murderous repetition that measures Cartesian mastery as well as the chaotic turbulence of spilt fluids. While Irigaray insists upon avoiding both Cartesian and postmodern equations of death, her quest for the origins of the fully embodied self is often not heard. Thus she protests against those who find in her lyrical musings only the fluidity of bodies minus organs: "Will you object that we would be straying into the realm of anything goes. Then you are admitting that you have forgotten that any living body . . . brings its *order* to analysis. All you have to do is listen" (*R*, 83–84; emphasis mine).

Listening with Irigaray, we discover in the living body that is not yet a person a desire that exceeds the drives of self-preservation and yet avers death and destruction, a desire that someday—if the right hands are there—finds its self in proximity to the Other. These hands bring forth the first ethical bond, a bond that has disappeared from the dominant narratives of our culture. In the beginning is not the word; it is the touch.[33]

PART TWO

Correspondences: The Attunement of Self and Other

> *My child loves my face....*
> *We are together, my child and I. Mother and child, yes,*
> *but sisters really, against whatever denies us all that we are.*
> **Alice Walker, "One Child of One's Own"**

As Seyla Benhabib has argued, the European tradition interprets the concept of justice through the metaphor of fraternity.[1] This particular use of metaphor points to what I take to be the two central blindspots in modernist philosophy. First, the modernist tradition purges metaphor from philosophical thinking, all the while deriving from metaphor, or cultural images in general, its fundamental intuitions. Secondly, the very modernist philosophies that borrow images from the family for conceptions of justice sever the family as a maternalized sphere from the focal domain of normative inquiry.

For Benhabib, whose own project is to complement a communicative ethics with a moral epistemology of care, this blindness takes the form of a hyper-rationalist deliberation that abstracts from the particular circumstances and narrative history of "the concrete other." As Benhabib argues, the liberal ethics of justice and rights abstracts from precisely those features of experience that play an important role in the moral judgments of primary caregivers. She explains the consequences: "[The] relationship [between] brother[s] is viewed as the humanizing experience that teaches us to become social, responsible adults. As a result of the hold of this metaphor upon our imagination, we have also come to inherit a number of philosophical prejudices. . . . [Most critically, that the] autonomous self is disembedded and disembodied; [and that] moral impartiality is learning to recognize the claims of the other who is *just like* oneself" (*FC*, 85; emphasis mine).

While it is relatively clear that the modernist tradition interprets the autonomous individual in terms of a socially disconnected, masculinized ego, the dialectical and postdialectical traditions would seem to anchor the self in both local and larger social contexts. However, while dialectical philosophies aim to redefine the individual in terms of membership in a family, and that family in terms of its connection to larger ethical communities, Benhabib argues that the point of origin for community in Hegelian thought remains the isolated self-consciousness, which, according to Benhabib, is also where Hegelian-style notions of ethical sociality return. As Benhabib writes, for Hegel the self-conscious individual is the "narcissist who sees the world in his own image; who has no awareness of the limits of his own desires and passions; and who cannot see himself through the eyes of another" (*FC*, 84). If this narcissism is threatened by the encounter with the Other in struggles for social recognition, it returns in sublimated form in civil society. A well-regulated civil society "civilizes sibling rivalry by turning . . . attention from war to property" (*FC*, 85).

While Benhabib, writing as an American feminist in the era of Reagan liberalism, finds that dialectic errs on the side of narcissistic individualism, Levinas, a Jewish survivor of Nazi prison camps, sees dialectic erring on the side of a narcissistic community or nation-state. The totalizing drive of dialectic, Levinas argues, threatens to swallow up individuals whole, leaving in its wake anonymous bodies without faces.[2] Levinas's argument does not turn upon the scale of the totalizing drive. Contra Lyotard, one does not avoid the drive to totalize simply by invoking local rather than grand forms of power. The dynamic of assimilation rises up as readily in local politics and two-person dialogue as in the state. Indeed, as feminists have made known, the most savage violations can occur in the intimacy of the family. Accordingly, Levinas argues that ethical society must be anchored not in duty to abstraction but in an immediate notion of "responsibility to the Other." For Levinas, however, unlike Benhabib, acquiring an immediate sense of responsibility to the concrete Other cannot rest upon the use of narrative elements in ethical deliberation. His argument is that the narrative form (no less than any dialectic) assimilates the unknown into familiar (including ethnocentric, racist, etc.) contexts, failing therefore to respect difference. Thus, unlike Benhabib, Levinas avoids both rational and narrative, or abstract and familial, bases for ethics and recenters ethics around responsibility to the Other-as-stranger.

Levinas provides good grounds for questioning the kind of project that Benhabib is attempting. Benhabib's conjunction of concrete narrative and abstract reason does not adequately address problems of cultural difference. On the other hand, Benhabib's critique of the fraternal metaphor carries over to the ethical philosophy of Levinas. The paradigmatic stranger that Levinasian ethics addresses bears a striking kinship to a lost brother from the modernist tradition of justice. Thus, neither Levinas nor Benhabib by themselves can provide the resources for adequately escaping the ethical vacuity of narcissism.

Benhabib and Levinas share our concern for locating a notion of community that might protect the individual in his or her difference from others.[3] Together they leave us with questions. What kind of account(s) of self and sociality could get beyond the smothering assimilation of, if you like, a domestic comedy, featuring the sentimental, familial scenes of empathetic identification, as well as the abstract tragedy of a global assimilation reflected in the ideological imperialism of Western Reason? If the person is not originally asocial, and if the dialectic of Self and Other begins already in the ethical praxis of the family, then how does the person first emerge in his or her individuality and yet in accord with others?

In order to respond to these questions, chapter 3 returns to the tradition of existential anthropology that grew out of Alexandre Kojève's readings of Hegel and was transformed in the psychoanalytic theory of Lacan. According to this tradition, before the struggles for recognition that structure the public sphere, the self appears in what Lacan terms "the mirror stage" of early childhood. This Lacanian transformation of dialectical philosophy is critical for our project. From the standpoint of the mother-child relation, we can address the major concern of contemporary ethics, namely, the possibilities of a prosocial desire. If the point of returning to an existential tradition of Hegelian philosophy is to yield a dialectic that tunes individual to society without reducing one to the other, such a project requires a concept of the self that is not fundamentally either narcissistic or antagonistic. Hegel himself overlooks the possibility of a harmonious attunement of Self to the Other at the threshold of self-consciousness. In chapter 4, I develop the ways in which Lacan repeats Hegelian themes of struggle in his understanding of early childhood. Lacan's relocation of the scene of recognition in childhood only accentuates the narcissistic and antagonistic elements of the self.

In order to generate an alternative dialectic of Self and Other, chapter 4 appropriates for a reinterpretation of the ethical dynamics of infancy what Levinas locates at the source of ethic comportment, namely, the face-to-face encounter of the Self with the Other. My rereading of the dialectic of recognition through the Levinasian face-to-face turns on Gadamer's aborted attempt to explain Hegel's concept of recognition in terms of the greeting. With this attempt, Gadamer provides a link between Hegel and Levinas. For Levinas draws explicitly upon the everyday occurrence of the greeting in order to understand what is basic to the face-to-face encounter.

By bringing Levinas's phenomenological study of the face-to-face encounter into Hegel's dialectic of self-consciousness, we can avoid some of the worst pitfalls in the dialectical tradition of narrative (*grand* or, as I am arguing, *petit récit*) as well as in the Jewish existential (Adorno, Benjamin, Levinas, Derrida) concern for the nonassimilable Other. Our use of Levinas frees dialectic from the narcissistic conception of the self or social whole, i.e., the conception that requires that human beings in some very abstract (and hyper-rationalist) *or* very concrete (and empathetic) ways must share the same ideas, images, or feelings in order to get along with one another. On the other hand, our use of dialectically based notions of social reciprocity avoids the pious self-sacrifice, if not self-righteous paternalism, that results from what Levinas conceives to be the antidialectical asymmetry of ethical responsibility. The self emerges not in what Levinas (like Hegel and other modernists) portrays as a violence-packed encounter with the absolute stranger but in the ethos of reciprocal exchange.

The event of the Jewish Holocaust has left European thinkers such as Levinas with the suspicion that ethics cannot be unless it is possible to recognize the Other outside of shared contexts of discursive or cultural meaning. The task of Levinas is to show that the face of the Other appears prior to the acquisition of language and culture, or already in something like what Lacanian psychoanalysts term "the imaginary." However, while attempting to account for the appearance, or "epiphany," of the face outside of any specific cultural context, Levinas draws upon the images and language of his own religious tradition. In order to avoid reducing the significance of the face to a single religious tradition, chapter 4 attempts to reinterpret Levinas's ethics of the face by way of the more "empirical" (still, as we shall see, a questionable category) research of Daniel Stern. I suggest that the facial expressions of the flesh-and-blood Other include not only the vulnerability of the eyes, which for Levinas defines the sole basis for ethical comportment, but a multiplicity of psychic-social desires with their non-discursive meanings.

Once we have brought into the foundations of ethics the full scale of responses to the face of the Other, the imperatives of ethics can be expanded beyond the sole principle that Levinas discerns in the eyes of the stranger, namely, the commandment "thou shall not kill." According to Levinas, "The face is exposed, menaced, as if inviting us to an act of violence. At the same time, the face is what forbids us to kill."[4] That is, for Levinas, the Other first engages the Self through "difference," a term whose etymology includes a reference to the violence of warfare. The ethics of Levinas is one-sidedly restricted to the masculinized metaphoric of the warrior.

While Levinas misconceives ethics through the metaphorics of war, he is correct, I believe, to reorient the primary impetus for philosophical thinking away from epistemologies of reason or ontologies of Being to the inter-subjective dynamic of the face-to-face encounter. An ethics that could break down what American multiculturalists term the "us versus them" dichotomy must break out of the logic of identity and difference that supports dichotomy in general. First philosophy should enlist not a logic of identity and difference but an "attunement" to the face of the Other.

As Levinas argues, the acknowledgment of the Other occurs prior to the development of a language, which may or may not be shared. Acknowledgment occurs primarily through the expressive capacities of the face. I argue that this face could be the face of the three-month-old infant who does not yet speak. It could also be the face of an animal who does not belong to the human species. The acknowledgment of the face that is not abstract but made of flesh and blood generates an ethics that crosses over not only differences of culture but also animal species. By reattaching what for Levinas is the transcendent face to the desires and passions of the flesh, the ethics of the face prepares the way for a subjectivity that is not based on animal sacrifice, the politics of warfare, or other ascetic rites of passage that sever the masculinized European subject from his own flesh and blood.

Furthermore, against Levinas, I argue in chapter 4 that the face-to-face encounter with the Other does not derive its most original formulation in the encounter with a fraternal stranger but in the nonverbal interaction between nurturer and child. This liminal mode of social interaction brings the child into being as a person. Chapter 3 examines attempts by patriarchal philosophers to get at the social significance of nonlinguistic communication. The use of the greeting as a way into understanding an elementary form of recognition stems in part from its central place in the philosophy of Levinas and in part from my observation that adults frequently and repeatedly address newborn and young infants with a greeting (a "hi," "hello," etc., accompanied with a smile), sensing that this greeting will eventually bring that infant into subjective and intersubjective awareness. At about two months, and with the beginning of social smiling, the child begins to respond. I argue that what Levinas terms "the face-to-face encounter" should replace what Lacanians term "the mirror stage," Freudians, "anal self-control," and Anglo-American theories, "normal childhood egocentrism" as a second stage of ethical development in infancy.

This social interaction with the parent not only transforms the infant; it also transforms the subjectivity of the one who takes care of the child. For men, this transformation can occur only if manhood is redefined to include not only fathering but also parenting the child. Caring for the child under the appropriate social conditions can foster in the parent ludic and expressive dimensions of ethical subjectivity that are repressed in Western cultures. For example, these ethical dimensions of the self are absent from the modernist loci of the moral person in reason, autonomy, or self-control. Part 3 reexamines various rites of passage in order to yield a concept of masculinity that is rooted in the social eroticism of early childhood.

·3·

The Greeting

Historical Background

Kojève: Self-Creation

Major twentieth-century dialectical, existential, and psychoanalytic interpretations of the self find their source in Hegel, and in particular, in the epoch-making reading of Hegel introduced by Alexandre Kojève in the 1930s in France. According to Kojève, there was no philosophical conception of the self until Hegel. This failure on the part of pre-Hegelian philosophy, Kojève argues, lies in its blindness to the active and transformative dimensions of the self.[1] If a more reactive reading of Hegel would maintain that the *Phenomenology* renders the self relatively passive before the machinations of what Hegel calls "Spirit," Kojève's reinterpretation itself actively transforms the Hegelian corpus. In this transformation, Hegel's superhuman Spirit rematerializes in the shape of an existential anthropology and a human-centered history.[2]

According to this reinterpretation, the active dimension of the self emerges not in an intellectual function, which would constitute for Kojève little more than a passive reflection of the world, but in "human desire" (in

French, "*désir*," closer to the "*eros*" of Plato's *Symposium* than the German "*Begierde*" or the English "desire" with their more animalistic or naturalistic connotations). For Kojève, human desire distinguishes itself from animal desire by actively struggling to reshape nature according to its own freely self-chosen projects. The final goal of the self is to see its reflection in the projects of Others and therefore to attain the kind of mutual recognition that is possible only in a society that is homogeneous.

Kojève's anthropogenetic reading of Hegelian Spirit offers a promising starting point for theorizing individual agency within a social and historical matrix. Two kinds of problems, however, limit the usefulness of Kojève's account of the self right from the start and must be addressed before we can pick up where Kojève left off. One problem centers around the fact that there are cultural expressions of the self that do not resemble anything like what Kojève interprets to be human desire and that such concepts are excluded from the dialectical tradition altogether. Some non-European cultures and European philosophies develop concepts of self that do not call for the active transformation of nature in accordance with human purpose. Moreover, these alternative conceptions appear more immediately relevant to a maternal ethics.

For example, Heidegger's meditative essays adumbrate a conception of a self that emerges in a more gracious openness to alterity, and in particular the alterity of nature. This openness solicits what for anthropologists is a vision quest and what for Heidegger is a disclosure of Being. Heidegger avoids conceptualizing self-creation in terms of dialectical negation and, especially in his later work, emphasizes the receptive role that mortals play in happenings of meaning using images that appear to be more friendly both to nature and to a more "feminine" comportment. Already in the 1929 essay "What Is Metaphysics?" Heidegger speaks of "the anxiety of those who are daring ... in secret alliance with the [more feminized] cheerfulness and gentleness of creative longing."[3] It is, for this Heidegger, from an anxiety before the womb-like "Nothing" that "selfhood and freedom" emerge (*BW*, 106). As has been noted, if nonetheless in his earlier works Heidegger casts scenes of origin predominantly in the Promethean dress of war and challenge, such later writings as "The Question Concerning Technology" recast those scenes in a poetics of birth.[4]

In autobiographical statements of *Ecce Homo* Nietzsche also turns away from the transgressive poetics of the self that he celebrates in the heroic nature and portrays himself through images of male pregnancy. Nietzsche writes: "The real answer to the question, how one becomes what one is, can no longer be avoided.... I never even suspected what was growing in me—and one day my capacities, suddenly ripe, leaped forth in their ultimate perfection. I cannot remember that I ever tried hard—no trace of struggle can be demonstrated in my life; I am the opposite of a heroic nature."[5]

At first glance these nondialectical, nontransgressive representations of self-creation seem to reinvent the masculinized self in terms that are more hospitable to women. However, there is a problematic asymmetry between the representation of male "pregnancy" and female pregnancy. Various patriarchal constructions of self-creation hold in common the imperative that men give birth to themselves (they are agents of their own self-creation) while women sacrifice themselves in order to give birth to others. A more dialectical reconstruction of the self, and in particular a philosophy of self that incorporates male and female images of creation, should allow for the possibility that one gives birth to oneself *as* one gives birth to the Other, and vice versa. It is because of the concern for the social dimensions of the self, beginning with the expression of the self as mother, that I am working with a Kojèvean dialectic rather than some of the more obvious alternative pathways for healing the wound between the European subject and its various Others.

A distinct advantage of a Kojèvean anthropology for an affirmative socio-ethical praxis is that this anthropology conceptualizes subjectivity specifically in terms of social agency. There is no parallel notion of agency in such obvious alternative philosophies as those found in Nietzsche or Heidegger.

But if the existential anthropology of Kojève aims to account for the reciprocal transformation of Self and Other, this anthropology still posits the origins of the Self in narcissistic isolation from the Other. Kojève does not question what Hegel takes to be the originary awareness of the self in the asocial register of biological drives and, even more specifically, in the assimilative activity of digestion: "Indeed, when man experiences a desire, when he is hungry, for example, and wants to eat, and when he becomes aware of it, he necessarily becomes aware of *himself.*... Now, what is desire—one need only think of the desire called 'hunger'—but the desire to *transform* the contemplated thing by an action ... to assimilate it to myself to make it *mine?*" (*IH*, pp. 37–38). The first feeling of the self arises as an unreflective narcissism, without any awareness of another person, in fact, as Gadamer adds in his discussion of Hegel, in the "careless profligacy and sacrifice" of the Other.[6]

. It is also true that for Kojève as for Hegel this unreflective use of the Other for one's own self-preservation, or, more generally, for the deadly syntheses that aim to assimilate the external world to what is "mine," fails to satisfy the self. Unreflective narcissism leaves the self feeling empty, even with a sense of not finding oneself fully realized in the world. The self learns that it is more than mere appetite or animal desire as it experiences its dialectical becoming flattened out into what Kojève takes to be the repetitive cycles of the "biological." The repetitive cycles of nature are, Kojève argues, alien, vegetative, and unreflective of the free transformations that produce the self. It is in particular, according to Kojève, the awareness of death that solicits from the human self a revulsion for the timeless cycles of nature. Therefore, the self aims to distance itself from nature, and in particular nature seen as the *meaningless* slaughter of the individual in undialectical becoming. The self must seek to find itself in something that transcends the natural cycles of birth and death. Or, as Kojève writes, "For there to be Self-Consciousness, Desire must ... be directed toward a non-natural object ... [rather] than a static and given real being that stays eternally identical to itself.... This I will not, like the animal 'I,' be 'identity' or equality to itself, but 'negating-negativity'" (*IH*, 5; citations from Hegel). The self is human only inasmuch as it sacrifices its so-called animal nature—i.e., its fleshly desires and fears—to a higher end. This higher aim is understood initially in terms of the freedom of the individual over nature.

However, the self that emerges in solitary freedom finds that it requires some sense of self-verification in the external world. It is the verification from the outside world that grants an intersubjective recognition to what otherwise collapses into subjective delusion. According to Kojève, this verification could only come from another object that transcends nature, and in a godless world, this means another self. One finds oneself reflected in the absolute negativity (the freedom) of another self. This other can reflect the first self only if the second self also demonstrates a readiness to sacrifice ("negate") its own needs, thereby establishing that it is no mere "animal."

Kojève introduces the existential interpretation of human desire (or freedom) as "a revealed nothingness, an unreal emptiness," or what is also termed "existential negativity" (*IH*, 5). As a result of Kojève's existential reading of dialectical desire, the latter is understood as absolute lack, or what Sartre later deciphers through the dynamics of a "useless passion," and what the French post-Nietzschean tradition (Bataille, Deleuze) identifies as the core impetus of Platonic metaphysics. Bataille and Deleuze counter the metaphysics of desire as absence with their own apparently more Nietzschean reading of desire as excess of power, potency without lack.

However, it is exactly in the one-sided readings of eros, the interpretation of eros as either virile potency or feminized lack, that what I take to be a crucial error emerges in twentieth-century post-Hegelian theories of selfhood. In the more dialectical theory of the *Symposium* Plato clearly characterizes *eros* as the child of *resource* and *need*, that is, not in terms of one-sided negativity. As Plato's dialogue reminds us, only because *eros* is part resource as well as part need can it be creative, transformative, and productive. Therefore, while Hegel does pose self-consciousness as an initially narcissistic freedom and freedom as the sacrifice of the "animal" self, Kojève intensifies the barriers between self and nature, or self and other, with his one-sided representation of desire as pure negativity, or absolute lack. As pure lack, human desire stands in stark opposition to the "resources" of the self that are found in both the external world (with its history and culture) and the body.[7]

One problem with the existentialist reading of desire, and thus of human freedom, in terms of sheer negativity, is that such a reading does not attend sufficiently to the *material* resources of individuals seeking to express a self under conditions of cultural, historical, or physical domination. The free self does not emerge *ex nihilo*. On the contrary, an individual is variously affected in the desire for recognition by the uneven distribution of material (economic but also, crucially, cultural) resources, an unevenness that includes factors of race and gender.

Kojève argues that the slavish consciousness of those who are unfree results from a failure of desire. "This slave is the defeated adversary, who has not gone all the way in risking his life, who has not adopted the principle of the Masters: to conquer or to die. He has accepted life granted him by another.... He has preferred slavery to death, and that is why, by remaining alive, he lives as a Slave" (*IH*, 16). In fact, of course, the prudence of the slave may have less to do with a weak spirit than a strong awareness of limited resources. Kojève's conception of the free self is far too transcendent to account for the materiality of human desire.[8]

The problem reoccurs in Kojève's attempt to account for human sociality by relying upon an analogy between what otherwise he would distinguish, i.e., the transcendent desire for recognition and animal desires to consume or otherwise possess the Other. Kojève writes, "Thus, in the relationship between man and woman, for example, Desire is human only if the one desires, not the body, but the Desire of the other; if he wants 'to possess' or 'to assimilate' the Desire taken as Desire—that is to say, if he wants to be 'desired' or 'loved,' or, rather, 'recognized'...." (*IH*, 6).[9] Compare the above description of transcendent desire with Kojève's earlier description of appetite: "The being that eats, for example, creates and preserves its own reality, by the 'transformation' of an alien reality into its own reality, by 'assimilation,' the 'internalization' of a 'foreign,' 'external' reality" (*IH*, 4). Kojève's Hegel follows the metamorphosis of the spirit from its origins in individual narcissism to its end in a community that is based on group narcissism through an unequivocal process of assimilating what is different to the same. It may very well be the case that Kojève aims, more so than Hegel, to project a notion of community that respects individual autonomy. Nonetheless Kojève presumes a dynamic of sociality based on the assimilation of the different into the same. Of course, the Other can be recognized as the same only if she or he is abstracted from the singular materiality of the body and the concrete historical, cultural, and economic circumstances of individual life, factors that include concerns of race, class, gender, and sexuality and that compose the resources of desire.

Thus Kojève's interpretation of desire perpetuates the opposition between two equally problematic conceptions of society. The society that advances beyond the predatory appetites and/or rational calculus of *homo economicus* transforms itself into a social organism with an appetite for swallowing up individuals whole. The only possible positive model of sociality that could come from such stark alternatives of individual and community is the attempt to balance the two extremes. But even if one were to address the dilemma by balancing the extremes of pure individualism and total community, one still invokes the problematic assumption that sociality is not a pleasure but a sacrifice, or repression, as Kojève writes, of the natural self (see *IH*, 24; cf. the French: "il 'sublime' ses instincts en les refoulant," 30). To be a person is to sacrifice all that is animal, including the body and what I am understanding to be the immediate pleasures of sociality. As argued in part 1, the social bond may emerge not in sacrifice but in various pleasures of sensuality. There is no self that does not begin by drawing upon the social resources of the mother or other caregiver. The divorce of the social sphere from animal pleasures and the related problem of equating the ideal form of sociality with the abstract sameness of community pose fundamental problems for Kojève's rendition of the dialectic between Self and Other.[10]

Gadamer: The Role of the Greeting in Recognition

Gadamer opens the possibility for a more promising transformation of the dialectic of self-consciousness through his rather casual reference to the greeting in his reading of the struggle for recognition. The greeting, Gadamer observes, is a "trivial form of recognition" and yet exemplifies the powers of the Other to create and destroy the psyche (*HD*, 64). As Gadamer explains, "Think of the humiliation when a greeting is not returned ... a devastating defeat for your own consciousness of self" (*HD*, 64). However, Gadamer drops this so-called trivial form of recognition and turns to the tradition of the duel in order to "confirm" the significance of recognition (*HD*, 65).[11] The central use of the example of the duel presupposes that the first awareness of the self beyond the empty feelings of "animal" satisfaction ("animal" used again as a trope for the asocial) occurs after early childhood. That is, Gadamer's reading of Hegel reinforces the modernist conception of a self that, rather magically, would appear from out of nowhere—without a history, without a culture, and certainly without the social force of the mother or other caregiver. It is this masculinist mythology of creation *ex nihilo* that prepares the way for the central delusion of Kojève's anthropology, namely, that the relationship between master and slave constitutes "the 'first' human, social, historical contact" (*IH*, 20–21).

Gadamer's aborted reading of dialectic through the example of the greeting suggests a more fruitful locus for the origins of recognition than does the male-centered tradition of dialectic that he adopts. If intersubjectivity emerges earlier than those struggles for domination that divide the world into masters and slaves, might it not emerge already in the relation between mothers or other caregivers and their children?

Lacan and the Mirror Stage

It is Lacan who anchors the speculative theories of recognition in a more empirically grounded psychoanalysis of childhood. Nonetheless, like Hegel, and in fact even more like Freud, Lacan claims that the ego first makes its appearance in the asocial space of "primary narcissism." One of Lacan's contributions is to locate a measure for the development of the ego in what he terms "the mirror stage." According to Lacan, at approximately six months of age, the infant gives signs that he is able to recognize himself in a mirror reflection. Lacan writes: "The fact is that the total form of the body by which the subject anticipates in a mirage the maturation of his power is given to him only as *Gestalt*, that is to say, in an exteriority ... in which it appears to him above all in a contrasting size (*un relief de stature*) that fixes it and in a symmetry that invests it.... Thus, this *Gestalt* ... symbolizes the mental permanence of the *I*, at the same time as it prefigures its alienating destination."[12]

This alienating distance of reflection can occur without the aid of a mirror in self-reflection. However, the example of the mirror makes especially perspicuous what Lacan sees as the fictive, or illusionary, nature of the ego. The ego is not something that could be given as such in inner sense. The infant constructs an ego as an autonomous agent through assuming an external image, i.e., an image that is alien to the random and incoherent feelings of inner experience. The more or less exclusively *visual* construction of the ego in a self-image distances the infant from the full sensory range of its felt-self. In the process, the infant ego emerges as the unified object of its own alienating gaze.

While Lacan, like Hegel, interprets the first ego as the project of a solitary narcissist, Lacan, unlike Hegel, interprets the ego as originally and finally divided against itself in self-alienation. The use of the mirror as the measure for self-recognition accounts for what Lacan sees as the alienation that necessarily defines the self. The distortions of mirror-like reflection introduce, quite systematically, a fictive element into the constitution of the ego. Lacan indicates two kinds of distortions. First, the reversal of perspective that occurs in the virtual image of the mirror suggests that self-reflection yields only the dialectical irony that the self is not whatever it appears to be. Secondly, the contrasting size of the mirror image recalls the perspective on the ego of one who observes the self from a distance. One's own self-image is produced outside of oneself, i.e., always in opposition to the felt-self.

In order to illuminate the significance of this opposition within the self, Lacan draws upon the language of premodern European warfare. As Lacan explains, the ego is fashioned as "armour" and "fortress" around an "inner castle" that holds what traditional psychoanalysis termed the pleasure-seeking id (*E*, 4, 5). Thus Lacan addresses the development of the ego in childhood only in order to define that self once again through the metaphorics of the battleground.

For Lacan, the first battle occurs in solitude. Self-constitution through self-alienation begins at the mirror stage, where the child's self-construction is said to occur prior to the awareness of other persons. Then what role does Lacan envision for the primary caregiver? How does s/he figure in Lacan's staging of the scene of recognition?

By focusing on the trope of the mirror as a precursor to the face of the Other, Lacan eclipses the very early face-to-face interaction between infants and parents. In effect, Lacan thereby "feminizes" the parent, whose social agency is reduced to a one-way reflection for the "masculinized" infant ego. This effect is reinforced through Lacan's allusions to the myth of Narcissus and Echo in his discussion of childhood narcissism. The mother, like the mythic Echo, passively reflects the pretensions of a narcissistic ego. What this mythic portrayal of childhood misses, of course, is the social force of the mother in the construction of the infant self. It is not that Lacan fails to see any effect of the mother on the child. But for Lacan this means that the mother does not echo the narcissistic self-love of the infant without distortion. The maternal function leaves its mark in the alienation effect of the mirror stage.

Because Lacan interprets childhood through mythology rather than hands-on experience, he fails to understand how the mother might in fact produce some of the effects of alienation that do often enough haunt the self. If we assume that the mother as person and not prop performs the function of mirroring, then the alienation of early childhood could be explained in terms of the parts of the felt-self that are censored or otherwise discouraged by those around one. It is not surprising, however, that Lacan allows mythology to distort his interpretation of childhood, given that his pivotal essay on infancy fails to cite the experience of mothers or other present caregivers.

By reducing the role of the caregiver in the infant's ego formation to the alienation effect of the mirror, that ever-allusive Lacan recasts the feminized caregiver *from* mother *to* whore. That is, Lacan insinuates that behind the sentimental image of the mother who sacrifices in service to her child lies that other side of patriarchal femininity, the man-destroying whore. The mother does not mirror the ideal self; she sullies the virile ego that would fashion itself as free, in control, and independent of women.

Once we see that Lacan's theory of childhood interprets the nurturing role of the mother through images of the whore, we can understand why Lacan abruptly concludes the essay with a sarcastic reference to altruism. "We place no trust in altruistic feeling, we who lay bare the aggressivity that underlies the activity of the philanthropist, the idealist, the pedagogue, and even the reformer" (*E*, 7). The philanthropist, the idealist, the pedagogue, and the reformer recall the altruistic virtues of the primary ethical agent under modern patriarchy, the self-sacrificing mother. Of course, under patriarchy, the work of the mother goes unmentioned. Nonetheless, the Lacanian unveiling of altruism as a weak form of aggression exposes the whore that, according to the same modern misogyny, lies behind the mother.

The transformation of the mother into the whore defines the classic erotic gesture of pornographic art (see chapter 1).[13] The erotic pleasure that drives the pornographic gaze expresses not only a need to debase women, especially mothers; this attack on mothers also constitutes a traditional locus of male self-constitution.

Lacan uses the image of the whore to signify the most fundamental threat to the male psyche. According to psychoanalytic theory, the symptomatic use of substituted objects for the ever-unknowable real thing signifies the original loss of a love object and portends the inevitability of death. The lost object is traditionally interpreted to be the mother, whose replacement may be sought in a series of women who are or are like whores. The most simple narrative of this loss argues that a masculinized ego matures only as it leaves behind its infant attachment to the body of the mother and finds substitutes for her love. The loss of the mother intimates the single loss that cannot be mastered, namely, one's own death. In other words, the claim is that men are afraid not of women but of death and that women signify nothing more than the mortality of men.

It is curious that this old tale of alienation and mortality is fraught with double binds that seem less to weaken than to sustain it. For example, a masculinized ego strips woman of subjectivity and yet also attributes to her responsibility for the original alienation of man from nature. Or again, woman is consigned to motherhood and yet nonetheless rendered accidental to the processes of human creation. Or, woman as womb is also woman as tomb and thus responsible for the accident of death. Lacan perpetuates the same old myths. Woman, dark tain, witch's caldron, concocts the infant ego in the serpentine logic of the unconscious. The result: It is because the selfless mother of procreation and life somehow nonetheless chooses to prostitute herself in the service of death that virile self-construction entails its opposite, self-alienation.

By interpreting the mother-child relation in terms of the effects of the mirror, Lacan precludes understanding the face-to-face play between infant and parent as, most originally, a greeting to be addressed. By confining the first experience of the ego to the visual register, the ego is defined as an object to be seen and not touched.[14] The ego, for both Freud and Lacan, emerges in alienation from both the fully sensuous and the social dimensions of the self. Psychoanalytic theory interprets the interactive caresses and glances of the mother or father through the distancing mechanism of the mirror rather than vice versa. The mirror stage does not require the active participation of the parent as subject. Does the parent, then, have any vital role to play in the formation of the infant ego? The dominant evidence in Lacan's text is against her.

And yet there is a recessive but recurrent theme that emerges in the examples drawn upon by Lacan, a theme that does not cohere with his own speculation. Lacan claims that the alienation effect of the gaze from the mirror *distances* the ego from pleasure-seeking drives and, at the same time, *threatens* the ego with its own impending loss. And yet in Lacan's actual description of the response of an infant before the mirror we find not the anxious defense of an alienated self but, as Lacan writes, "signs of triumphant jubilation and playful discovery ... [that] characterize, from the sixth month, the child's encounter with his image in the mirror" (*E*, 1). According to this description, it is the joyful inventiveness of play and not the illusion of self-mastery that defines the first self: "This act [of self-recognition], far from exhausting itself, as in the case of the monkey, once the image has been *mastered* and found empty, immediately rebounds ... in *play*" (*E*, 1; emphases mine).

This playful exchange in the mirror is, I am arguing, originally derivative from, and not precursor to, the social encounter between parent and infant. That is, under normal conditions, the mother serves not as a mirror but as a face for the child to find itself in. This more playful role of the mother is further hinted at in another of Lacan's examples, this time of the function of mirroring among locusts: "In the case of the migratory locust, the transition within a generation from the *solitary to the gregarious* form can be obtained by exposing the individual ... to the exclusively visual action of a similar image, *provided it is animated*" (*E*, 3). It is significant that the image of another locust effects the sociality of the first locust only if that image is animated. It is a similar story with the human infant. While the infant of six months can be fascinated with its image in the mirror, it shows relatively little interest in the photograph. If the mirror stage cannot find a substitute in a "photo stage," this tells us something about the significance of the mirror stage. The mirror holds the attention of the infant not because it provides a static image of wholeness but because it recalls the interactive qualities of intersubjectivity.

Some Lacan scholars interpret the mirror stage as originally a metaphor for the face of the mother and argue that the ego is social.[15] Lacan himself fails to mention the mother in his crucial 1949 essay. He does, however, mention that the mirror serves as a metaphor for the cortex, which, he writes "psycho-surgical operations lead us to regard as the intra-organic mirror" (*E*, 4). The mirror stage does involve a relation between the "*Innenwelt*" and the "*Umwelt*," but the reflections between inside and outside are said to occur "before the social dialectic" (*E*, 4).

More importantly, the metaphor of the mirror obscures the interactive complexity of face-to-face play.[16] The metaphor implies that the parent primarily functions to duplicate the expressions of the infant.

By restricting ego construction to an interest in a visual form, or *Gestalt*, it seems that Lacan, strong critic of mimetic epistemologies, misreads the playful, sometimes discordant, attunement between parent and child, reducing the fully sensuous encounter to the abstractions of a mere visual representation. In short, Lacan gives a literalistic misreading of his own trope of the mirror. The mirror with its whole image, or virtual object, is not of primary interest to the child. The child attends less to the *literal* image than to the *anima*, the spirit, of the mirror. So too the mother is more than faceless mirror, altruistic servant, or otherwise slave to the child. Perhaps then it is fear before this alien subject, and not fear before death, that motivates the defacement of the mother in pornographic theory as in pornographic art.

Jonathan Bennett and the Face in the Mirror

The literalization of the trope of the mirror in accounts of recognition recurs throughout Anglo-American speculations of the self, including, for example, those found in Jonathan Bennett's essay "Thoughtful Brutes."[17] As a consequence of what I am arguing to be a literalistic misreading of the mirror stage, Bennett turns a skeptical eye toward those who would define self-awareness in terms of mirror recognition. These theorists, according to Bennett, blur differences between human and nonhuman animals. The problem, he argues, is that recognition theorists fail to distinguish the ability to use a mirror in order to observe that body whose image appears in the mirror and the ability to conceptualize that bodily image as *mine*. What we need to know, he writes, is that "the chimpanzee attends to the mark on her brow because 'it is on *me*' and not merely because 'it is on *this*,' where 'this' is the old, familiar, specially interesting body, the one that can be moved directly and that *it hurts* to get damaged" (*TB*, 209; final emphasis mine). Bennett's argument is that quite literally we see not only human infants but also chimpanzees alter their behavior in relation to what they observe of their body in the mirror, but no concept of the self makes an appearance in either the mirror or in behavior before the mirror. The onlooking scientist observes no self in the behavior of the nonhuman animal or the human infant who does not yet speak.

My argument focuses on the depersonalized mode of reflection that is invoked by the detached observer (what I earlier termed the "absent caregiver"). It is the depersonalization of the observer, I believe, that is projected onto the apparently mute Other. In this particular case, the depersonalization of the nonspeaking animal results from the impersonal grammatical construction "it hurts," which characterizes less the animal's behavior in front of the mirror than a grammatical possibility of human speech. A more careful and a more engaged reading of the behavior of the nonspeaking animal in front of the mirror than that offered by Bennett would reveal the expressions of a self.

Bennett's argument repeats a premise of modernism. According to this premise, self-awareness cannot be manifested in any kind of expressions other than those that take the form of propositional speech. The disembodied speech of Cartesian modernism, however, is a speech stripped of the rhythms and tones that compose the moral force of social discourse. On Bennett's account, self-awareness appears specifically in the iterative use of a language that strings together words in sentences: "The so-called vocabulary in nonhuman signaling systems consists of whole utterances (analogous to our sentences) rather than of separately meaningful parts of sentences (analogous to our words). Nothing in those signaling systems resembles the syntactic devices through which our languages assemble meaningful elements in many ways, creating a practically limitless range of possible utterances" (*TB*, 201). He refers to several experiments that demonstrate that nonhuman animals do not use and cannot learn to use words in sentences. He concludes that the range of expressions possible in human language exhibits a relatively high degree of flexibility in response to circumstances and that this flexibility is in turn the sign of intentionality. Bennett does admit that nonhuman animals demonstrate intentionality in nonvocal behaviors. However, only propositional speech—of the kind that modernists use in their philosophical discourse—is allowed to count as an expression of the self. The expressive tones that make up dolphin communication would be excluded. Bennett concludes that humans possess self-awareness; other animals do not.

I am claiming, however, that the fault lies not with the nonhuman animal but in the literalistic mode of thinking that Bennett employs in his argumentation, a mode of thinking that is surprising given that the most convincing example that Bennett offers of the flexibility of human language comes from dramatic poetry, indeed poetry that dramatizes the significance of the fully embodied qualities of such social rituals as the greeting. Here I quote from Bennett: "When Ferdinand said to Miranda 'Here's my hand,' it was not the mastery of a routine that enabled her to reply 'And mine, with my heart in it'" (*TB*, 203). Miranda does not simply and passively echo back Ferdinand's remarks as would a looking glass. She responds in a way that is creative and in a way that expresses an individual style. Through the dramatic interpretation of speech in tone and gesture, the poetized self expresses more than it intends. For example, no doubt her words as his are accompanied by a play of hands, which makes for a kind of gestural dance between them. Thus her self-expressions are embodied in gestures that are not reducible to conceptualization. The self is not some thing that appears originally in the visual register of image or even the visualizable variations of the propositional form.[18] Many species of animals, including human infants, communicate awareness of Self and Other. Self-awareness appears not in an image or a concept but in various gestures that express the self to another person. The distancing gaze of the objective observer destroys the social space in which that self appears. The self can only be read. It cannot be seen.

Bennett's criterion for self-awareness would reduce the self to a linguistic function, no doubt—and here I am reiterating—a specially interesting one that can be affected directly and, as the silenced know, that it hurts to get damaged. However, a linguistic function, no more and no less than a bodily image, is not the self. Body and language, visual object and sentences, can express the self but only if they are animated. Moreover, they are not the sole means of expressing the self. Self-expression occurs not only in novel sentences but also across novel media: property, action, dance, music, art, pantomime, and work are others. The fertility of the self to create novel forms of expression, indeed in media as diverse as music and dance, media that are incommensurate with propositional speech as well as with one another, suggests that dimensions of the self are not reducible to any single register of expression, not even to language. Not everyone expresses herself primarily in permutations of words, as does the academic philosopher, iterations that may be relatively unsurprising products of the disciplinary matrices that constitute academic institutions. On the contrary, styles individualize across different media of expression.

The self is not the power to produce novel linguistic patterns, nor is it the power to express just anything. The self is the power of expression in response not originally to impersonal circumstances but to the equally surprising Other. There is evidence that this happens already in the infant well before the acquisition of speech. Winnicott, Stern, and others have discovered that the play of the face-to-face encounter between infant and caregiver occurs sometime just after the first couple of months. Before the infant speaks, before it can even support its own weight, self-awareness crystallizes in the demand for the attentive look of another person. The self begins not as a demand for autonomy but as a request for acknowledgment. From around two months, the infant is no longer satisfied with being fed, held, and otherwise cared for; like many other animals, the human infant begins to make active demands for attention. The full creative powers of expression, beginning with the social smile, are then engaged in order to gain that attention. An essential dimension of the self lives and dies in that response. All else is mere substitution.

Lacan aims to demonstrate that the self cannot be mapped out in the interior dimensions of Cartesian space. From the beginning, one gains self-knowledge via the alienating difference between self-representation and actual feelings. Moreover, Lacan observes, the self never fully develops apart from the social network that it inhabits. If Lacan is right, the modernist "emancipation" from social rituals such as the greeting yields not a progressive sociality but, as Lacan claims, the "social hell" of the "irresponsible outlaw."[19] That is, the modernist conception of the detached self finds its only real instantiation in the outlaw, what classical philosophers mythologize as the beast. Ironically, then, in the very effort to distinguish man and animal, modernists (including Bennett) reduce man to "beast." As a psychoanalyst, Lacan observes that symptoms of the detached self—the disembodied self of modern philosophy—include the derealization of the world that I inhabit with others (E, 28).

But if the arguments that the modernists employ are so weak, why do they continue to defend them? What would motivate a modernist conception of the self? Bennett argues that the essential dimension of the human person can be modeled after the digital computer. The philosopher's effort to model the self after the computer is not all that different from popular cultural images (in films such as *The Terminator, Star Trek, Rambo, Robocop,* etc.) of the self as machine. The motives for these images of the self are not entirely mysterious. Man as machine is—at least in fantasy—hard, detached, in control, and certainly not dependent upon the mother or her sphere.

Lacan's psychoanalytic theory locates the fully developed self in a world with others. But Lacan also holds that the self begins in the solitary confinement of the self-alienated mind. Lacan thereby reduces the agency of the caregiver to the tain of internal or external mirrors. I am arguing that to deprive the caregiver of social agency and erotic power has repercussions on the infant self. The infant of the "feminized," or selfless, caregiver as slave may find an illusion of mastery in self-reflection, but it finds no real self. Gone entirely are the expressive and playful dimensions of self-creation. The research of Stern and others supports a more interesting perspective on childhood. The significance of the mirror resides not in the instrumental value of locating objects in geometric space but in its substitution for the personal other. The early importance of the face-to-face encounter suggests that the infant self first appears not in the linear space of visual representation but in the figurative space of sociality. As long as theorists define the self as narcissistic, they grasp at images—not the self.

In many contexts, the definition of the person in terms of linguistic skills conspires with what Lacan calls "the Law of the Father." But if language, or rather that papaese that we call language, is under the rule of what for Lacan is the master signifier, the symbolic "phallus," so too, Irigaray has shown, is the gaze that distances. If Bennett has his way, that still mythic category "animals," our infant children, even our silenced selves are not yet persons. This is not a hypothesis that could be borne by a present caregiver. The caregiver who is not muted into service as a nursing machine, who is himself acknowledged as a social agent, encounters the infant self in the face that greets him. In this greeting the infant responds to the *figure* (in French, *"face,"* also figure of speech) before her and solicits a response in turn. But to understand the face not as an image or a logic but as a response to the Other is central to the ethical philosophy of Levinas.

.4.

The Figure of the Face

Levinas and Child Development Research

Before the world, then, there was already proximity,
the face-to-face that welcomed us with a cordial smile
or harmed us with the rigidness, harshness,
or violence of traditional rules.
Enrique Dussel

The Face Stripped Bare

The human being is not born with the ability to recognize the face of another person. Only after several weeks of development outside of the womb does the child show signs of awareness of other persons. The satisfaction of the infant's biological and tactile needs are no longer the primary source of agitation. Now the child demands direct eye-to-eye contact. At about the same time that the infant begins to recognize the face of the parent, but before s/he can articulate or understand words, the infant begins to coo and then babble in what is sometimes called mamaese. What is this language before language? What is it to recognize the face of the Other?

No philosopher has contributed as much to our understanding of the significance of the face in ethical comportment as Levinas. Levinas's ethical philosophy, however, is not without problems. While in this chapter I aim to recuperate the central questions of Levinasian philosophy for a maternal ethics, I criticize those aspects of Levinas's approach that are masculinist and Eurocentric. Levinas's approach is masculinist inasmuch as he passes over the face-to-face interaction between infant and caregiver, including what he denigrates as mere infant babbling, in order to locate the origins of sociality in the encounter with the fraternal stranger.[1] His account is Eurocentric not because he discovers this fraternal Other through images that are borrowed from his own cultural tradition. There is, as I am arguing, no ethical stance that is not laden with culture and history. The problem appears in Levinas's effort to grant to those images a transcendent status. For example, Levinas is clearly drawing more upon the patriarchal tradition of European religion when he describes the appearance of the face as an "epiphany" (O, 149/190). By prescribing the face of the Other as appearing from a "height," Levinas places the face in the vertical dimension of a masculinized space and therefore beyond the reach of the mother (O, 183/231).

Moreover, by casting the face in the aura of the strange, Levinas envisions the Other in the same mythic proportions that are found in the essays of fellow French writer Jean-Jacques Rousseau.[2] In "Essay on the Origin of Languages," Rousseau speculates on the development of human sociality. This development, Rousseau postulates, first occurs between nomadic wanderers. As Rousseau imagines this encounter, the stranger takes on the heightened proportions of the "giant."[3] Like Levinas, Rousseau does not consider that sociality may already develop within the family. As caregivers, we might imagine that indeed the Other does first appear to the child as a giant whose face appears from above. However, Rousseau and Levinas envision the first encounter with the Other as occurring more or less in adolescence, or at least after separation from the mother, and, as Levinas writes, as though one were "an orphan by birth" (O, 105/133).[4]

Levinas deemphasizes the sociality that exists prior to the "fraternity" between strangers because of his concern to address the possibility of an ethical responsibility that would cross over differences of language, culture, and biology. His efforts are supported by the patriarchal tradition, which sees the family as a unified substance and therefore not a source of difference.[5] In fact, however, Levinas constructs the encounter with the stranger from prejudices of his gender and his Eurocentric culture. In this way, Levinas proves himself to be Rousseau's brother. And this brother is no stranger.

There are more cultural affinities between Rousseau and Levinas. These affinities deepen the problems of Eurocentricism as well as masculinism. Like Rousseau, Levinas projects a mythic state of nature (what Levinas terms in his more metaphysical language "*il y a*") from which human consciousness emerges as a figure against a shadowy (or, as he writes, "nocturnal") background. And like Rousseau, Levinas claims that it is the ethical engagement with the stranger that transforms the nomadic animal into social man. Unlike Rousseau, Levinas gives a singular account of this metamorphosis.[6] In its singularity, this account poses as abstractly universal and thereby conceals all the more its own limited cultural resources. In his most striking account of the metamorphosis, Levinas argues that the brute background from which the human existence emerges admits of a single tonality: "Let us imagine all things, beings and persons, returning to nothingness. What remains after this imaginary destruction of everything is not something, but the fact that there is [*il y a*]. The absence of everything returns as ... an atmospheric density, a plenitude of the void, or the murmur of silence ... impersonal like 'it is raining' or 'it is hot.'"[7] The horizon of human existence is not first constructed from the common project of a world. Prior to human time (*temps*) and its imperial projects is the impersonal time of the elements, or, more concretely, the conditions of the weather (*temps*). Whatever the atmospheric variations of humidity and warmth, the overwhelming sense of existence is its brute impersonality. Animal becomes man against a gray and mute background in a mood of panic and lonely isolation. Man overcomes the burden of having been abandoned to the elements (throughout Levinas's early and later work, the mother is mute) only in his desire for the fraternal Other.

While Levinas treats the variations between rain and heat with indifference, Rousseau polarizes the elements around northern and southern versions of human origins. As Rousseau explains, "The great shortcoming of Europeans is always to philosophize on the origins of things exclusively in terms of what happens within their own milieu" (*OL*, 30). Rousseau claims that the development of sociality varies according to the climate in which the human being first encounters another person. In the warm and fertile south, the first encounter is said to spring from the joys of romantic love, i.e., an erotic attraction to a stranger. "The heart is moved by these novel objects; an unknown attraction renders it less savage; it feels pleasure at not being alone" (*OL*, 44). Or, as adolescents sometimes say, it is love that first makes one a human being.

In the harsh and barren north, Rousseau supposes, it is the threat of perishing that instills the need to form social bonds. These bonds do not express passion but rather repress it and thus evolve less around ecstatic celebrations of fertility than the cold labor of forestalling death:

> In those wretched climates where everything is dead for nine months of the year [note that this is also the length of a pregnancy, and that the womb is therefore once again reinterpreted as a tomb] ... society would be formed only through industry ... ; the first words among them were not *love me* [*aimez-moi*] but *help me* [*aidez-moi*].... These two expressions, although similar enough, are pronounced in a very different tone. The whole point [in the mythic north] was not to make someone feel something, but to make him understand.... [The tones] of the south are bound to be sonorous, accented, eloquent, and frequently obscure because of their power. Those of the north are bound to be dull, harsh, articulated, shrill, monotonous, and to have a clarity. (*OL*, 47–48)

Both Levinas and Rousseau explore the airy elemental above for clues to origins. This impersonal elemental—in the vertical dimension—sets the tone for the sociality to come. But why this focus on the atmosphere in the account of human origins? Whatever the variations between their accounts, Levinas and Rousseau agree that human life begins without the mother as a subject or person in her own right. The genealogy of the self in the family disappears into thin air. Levinas hypothesizes, "The great force of the idea of creation such as it was contributed by monotheism is that this creation is *ex nihilo* ... because the separated and created being is thereby not simply issued forth from the father, but is absolutely separate from him."[8] Of course, the present caregiver is aware that the infant is "issued forth"—and that this issuing forth is not directly from the father. The missing "element" in the creation story is the mother. Moreover, the infant is hardly absolutely separate from the caregiver. The infant that is abandoned to the elements does not survive.

On the other hand, already in the uterus, the fetus experiences rhythmic changes in energy levels that come over the mother. The horizon of existing, the pure *il y a* that precedes the categorization of the world, the elemental climate, is not the airy nothing of patriarchal mythology but the temperament of the mother. Nor is the *il y a* of existence, as Levinas assumes, neutral in its genealogy. It varies with the diffuse moods and directed attitudes of the mother.

While Levinas and Rousseau seem to be mystified, in fact a bit in the fog, as to the maternal contribution to creation, they do not render the individual forever or even most originally alone. The human personality, they argue, is fundamentally (at least by adolescence, or, as Levinas always insists, after infant babbling and after the separation from the mother) social. For both, the self develops only in response to the Other. The response to the Other, they both agree, must precede or exceed the development of a common language. The nature of this nondiscursive encounter between two persons is tricky, for both also agree that the encounter with the Other occurs in a kind of language before language. That is, the face-to-face encounter produces signification prior to language, or at least what patriarchal theorists have construed as language and what we might reinterpret as papaese, i.e., the discursive language of conceptual thought.

Rousseau and Levinas diverge in how they construe the nature of preconceptual signification. According to Rousseau, communication begins as "a sonorous and harmonious language, spoken as much according to sounds as according to words" (OL, 24). That is, nondiscursive signification consists of expressions of intonation, rhythm, and intensity addressed to another person. These expressions can communicate love or fear; in fact, a range of social passions. The gradual demand for a clear speech and a common language drains language of its vitality; exchanges exactitude for expressiveness; and thus, according to Rousseau, deprives it of power to energize social passion: "[F]or moving a young heart ... nature dictates accents, cries, lamentations. There we have the invention of the most ancient words.... As man's first motives for speaking were of the passions, his first expressions were tropes. Figurative language was the first to be born. Proper meaning was discovered last" (OL, 12).

In contrast, Levinas, and more problematically I shall argue, insists that the face-to-face encounter occurs in the "nudity" of a bare and inevitably solemn exposure. The Other is said to stand "wholly in relation to himself, ... beyond every attribute, which would ... reduce him to what is common—a being, consequently, completely naked" (TI, 74/71). The face-to-face finds the stranger unclothed in the textuality of figurative speech, i.e., unmasked by the configurations of imagination, which are, for Levinas, nothing more than narcissistic projections. If Levinas finds that he can only evoke the ethics of the face by way of the masks of metaphors, he labors to unweave these very same metaphors by paradox: "The face is at the same time its absence from this world into which it enters, the exiling of a being, his condition of being stranger, destitute, or proletarian ... *and* the master"

(*TI*, 75/73). The projections of metaphor, at play in vertical space, *either* elevate *or* lower the estimation of its object, but in any case the metaphor would not do both at the same time; whether it elevates or lowers its object, metaphorization obstructs the view of the Other through false and familiar images, and this is why Levinas intends to avoid or at least to deconstruct metaphor in paradox. Paradox solicits humility before an alterity that one cannot begin to comprehend. From the violent rupture of a sovereign freedom emerges a self that serves the transcendent and yet, paradoxically, wholly human Other. This stranger is, again paradoxically, named as a brother. Thus, the emergent self appears as a creation *ex nihilo*, a creation that owes not to the flesh and blood of the mother but to the magical appearance of the masculinized Other.

On the other hand, Rousseau does not understand tropic speech (and the otherwise nondiscursive elements of communication) to be a mere figment of the narcissistic imagination. Rousseau argues that only the imagination can bring us to the perspective of the Other and thus engender social passion. If Rousseau is right, the imagination would not simply reduce the strange to some familiar image or category. On the contrary, the metaphoric naming of the Other as "giant" *both* attracts *and* preserves some distance. The Other as he or she is first encountered is sublimely like ourselves. The cry or laughter of the stranger solicits assistance or compels love but in any case brings one out of oneself before a nontranscendent unknown.

While Levinas distinguishes the manipulative use of rhetoric from tropic language, he understands the latter as an equal threat upon human freedom. Like the religious drama of Christianity, poetry would amount to an "involuntary participation in mysterious designs" (*TI*, 79/78). Therefore, poetry is irresponsible. Mystery resides always in exteriority, never to obscure one's own self-understanding or the underlying significance of one's own actions. One's own actions originate in absolute separation from the Other, in oneself as freedom, *ex nihilo*.

But Rousseau is right to claim that an ethical relationship with others requires the poetic dimension of communication, and with it the imagination. First of all, I question the motives behind Levinas's distrust of poetry. The notion of the fully free and self-conscious subject participates in the patriarchal politics of Cartesian modernism. Of course, Levinas's notion of freedom is not Cartesian in any simple way. According to Levinas, one's own sense of freedom is solicited not from interior space but in the exteriority of a response to another person. It is the Other—not myself—who first calls me to my freedom. Nonetheless, Levinas's rejection of poetry is intertwined with the mythology of creation *ex nihilo.* According to that myth, men give birth to themselves, they are fully self-responsible, and they certainly are dependent upon nothing that they do not understand (mothers, a feminized language, poetry). In fact, these self-created men participate in an ideology of freedom that mystifies their interdependencies upon feminized dimensions of the self.

Secondly, it is not clear how one would know to respond to the Other if those responses were not from the start mediated by an imaginative interpretation of diverse facial expressions. By denuding the face of the variables of figurative expression, one responds to nothing in particular in the face of the Other. One's responsibilities with respect to the Other would lack the boundaries that orient ethical comportment. Levinas therefore will have to claim that one's ethical responsibilities to the Other overflow infinitely. Levinas writes of the gaze of the Other: "This gaze that supplicates and demands, that can supplicate only because it demands, deprived of everything because entitled to everything, and which recognizes in giving ... this gaze is precisely the epiphany of the face as a face" (*TI*, 75/73). But I wonder if this open infinity—deeply paradoxical as it is—dissolves before the blank stare of the Other into a silent nothing. Without the possibility of individual self-expression, the Other is denuded of its specificity. Denuded of her "accents, cries, [and] lamentations," the Other is, *precisely in her concrete difference, i.e., in her embodied specificity,* effaced. The transcendent Other serves the piety of the ethical self and not the sufferings and joys of the flesh-and-blood Other.

Levinas does not leave the face entirely blank. According to Levinas, "This infinity ... is the primordial expression, is the first word: 'you shall not commit murder.' The infinite paralyses power by its infinite resistance to murder, which firm and insurmountable, gleams in the face of the Other, in the total nudity of his defenseless eyes" (*TI*, 199/217). But how is it that the multiplicity of expressive features of the human face, often in combination with the hand, posture, etc., could be focused around a sole feature, the eyes? Why would the variable expressions of the face be fixed in a single originary statement: "thou shall not kill"?

Levinas freezes the face-to-face encounter in a single and inflexible tonality, that of the austere and the grave, the element of Rousseau's mythic north. In the Other stripped bare of flesh and blood, I understand one thing and one thing alone: the resistance to the violation of murder.[9] Therefore, nothing in the transcendent face would resist the specific kinds of violations experienced especially by women. As in the Bible, there is no specific commandment against rape.

In his later work, Levinas locates the significance of the face in what he refers to as "the saying" and in distinction to "the said." "The saying," according to Levinas, "is a way of greeting the Other, but to greet the Other is already to answer for him."[10] As a greeting, the saying does not contemplate the Other but makes an approach. However, by reading a priori into every face a single point of origin for ethical deliberation, the saying of the face is congealed into a single didactic said, indeed, the said of a single book: "thou shall not kill." So baldly stated, the commandment is rigid and inflexible. For example, it says nothing to those who would ask to die. A feminized transformation of Levinasian ethics would begin by reattaching the transcendent face to the specific Other. The flesh-and-blood face expresses itself not in abstract nudity but in the coloring of particular circumstances.

Levinas understands ethics as an unmeasured generosity. In order to avoid reducing gift-giving to a calculus of interest, however, he deprives the gift-giving spirit of (an admittedly not entirely conceptualizable) sense. But the gift given without regard to the particular context of the Other, the gift given *ex nihilo*, may be received as an insult or violation, a willful form of misrecognition or misattunement.[11]

The reason that Levinas strips the face of its full range of expressive power is that he cannot conceive of how the face could be read except through an appropriative act of language. This claim rests on the iterative function of langauge. The iterative function of language idealizes and therefore violates the imperative to respect the singularity of the individual, to not reduce the individual to an example of a general concept, mere instance of a repeating function, or the tool of a (linguistic) system. Inasmuch as language abstracts from the idiosyncratic and the individual, the encounter with the Other must exceed language. Levinasian ethics would not follow the Kantian imperative to "respect" another but would instead invoke the Other: "The invoked is not what I comprehend: he is not under a category" (*TI*, 69/65). So too, Levinas claims, the interpretative and hermeneutic dimension of language "approaches the 'this' qua 'that,'" a move that refers the individual to the horizon of a common world (*TI*, 65; 60).

However, Levinas presupposes a theory of language which by now is antiquated. Derrida has demonstrated that language requires a process of idealization that occurs through a context that cannot be mastered, i.e., in "textuality," and which introduces aspects of alterity into every instance of linguistic expression. Meanwhile textuality deprives linguistic expressions of authorship. That is, deconstruction saves the idiom but not the singular self. It resists the violence of system in the name of the idiosyncratic but cannot engender an ethics that affirms the individual. Levinas, on the other hand, gives a locus to ethical response in the naked face. Somewhat paradoxically, however, this face stripped bare of flesh and blood is circumscribed by the teachings of books; worse yet, books from the patriarchal past of a European tradition. In order to secure the face in a more convincing account of ethics, we turn not to a supposedly transcendent speculation on the origin of sociality in the encounter with the stranger but to the more ordinary experience of the face-to-face relation as it occurs between infant and mother.

Face-to-Face with the Mother

Levinas writes: "Filiality itself can not appear as essential to the destiny of the I unless man retains [the] … memory of the creation *ex nihilo*" (*TI*, 63/58). No doubt this is correct. For, as feminists as diverse as Luce Irigaray and Seyla Benhabib have argued, the metaphor of filiality that infuses modern concepts of justice preempts a consideration of the role of the mother as a *subject* in the social matrix. That is, the memory of the creation *ex nihilo* functions simultaneously as a forgetting of the mother.

How does the face that Levinas discovers appear from the perspective of the one who has done a disproportionate amount of the social work in modern Western culture? What is the face-to-face relation as witnessed by the mother?

Levinas describes a face that is infinitely vulnerable and in this vulnerability commands infinite service: "This presence dominates him who welcomes it" (*TI*, 66/62). In a tradition that has feminized altruism, the mother is expected to serve with infinite patience an absolutely helpless infant whose demands know no limit. This myth is called unconditional love. It is not a myth that has proved to be salutary for either infant or mother. On the contrary, from its beginning the elementary dyad of parent and child requires the reciprocal imposition of limits.

Levinas does on occasion allow the metaphor of the maternal to break into a discussion of ethics that for the most part is infused with the metaphor of fraternity. "The evocation of maternity," Levinas argues, "suggests to us the proper sense of the oneself. The oneself cannot form itself; it is already formed with absolute passivity.... This passivity is that of an attachment that has already been made" (*O*, 104/132–33). Moreover, as "a materiality such that ... exposedness to wounds and outrage characterizes its passivity," maternity is "the complete being 'for the other'" (*O*, 108/137). As maternity, ethics is "martyrdom" experienced as "violation," or as the "one-penetrated-by-the-other" (*O*, 49ff./64ff.). But women have not in fact experienced the duty to care for "an attachment that has already been made," attachments, for example, born of a pregnancy against one's own will, as ethical. In order to locate a basis for ethical martyrdom, Levinas weds the metaphor of motherhood to the dynamics of violation.

The desire to serve, Levinas contends, elevates the one who gives: "In [ethical] Desire the being of the I appears still higher [than animal existence], since it can sacrifice to its Desire its very happiness" (*TI*, 63/58). In fact, from the point of view of the mother, the asymmetry of service may or may not be ennobling. And yet however much ethical sacrifice brings honor to the mother, this sacrifice is also suffered as an effacement of the female self.[12]

Levinas writes: "Justice consists in recognizing in the Other my master. Equality among persons means nothing of itself" (*TI*, 72/68–69). Poet Adrienne Rich, however, proves to be the keener observer.[13] If maternity, as Levinas sometimes suggests, reveals something about the origin of ethics, from the start caregiving thrives on mutual recognition. Or, as Rich writes, "mutual recognition, overlaid by social and traditional circumstance, was always there, *from the first gaze* between the mother and the infant at the breast" (*OW*, 32). In effect, by denying the possibility of mutual recognition in elementary sociality, Levinas stalls the master/slave dialectic in the unhappy vertical hierarchy of feminized submission before the infinitely commanding and masculinized other. Or, as Levinas mixes his metaphors, ethics begins in the maternal submission to a fraternal other. But then what equivocation, what cruel irony, allows unethical self-effacement to be called sacred sacrifice—unless it is the feminization of ethical work in a society that profits from the rhetoric of the sacred?

Levinas characterizes the face-to-face encounter with the Other as "direct." He condemns both rhetoric and poetry as oblique forms of address and as therefore useless for ethics. Nonetheless he also insists that a masculinized Other make his approach not along the horizontal plane of mutuality but from a height. The verticality of the approach of the Other obliquely renders mother supine before her infant's every demand. That is, Levinas defines ethics in a rhetoric that is blind to what it borrows from its own familiar patriarchal past, a past that effaces women in the name of a mythology of the unconditional good, or, as we might say, a good created *ex nihilo*.

In his retreat from dialectical sociality, Levinas encounters the enigmatic voice of the Other echoing *within* himself but not outside of himself. Levinas experiences the Other as a violation of the narcissistic ego and not in the diverse pleasures of interpersonal exchange.[14] Levinas thereby excludes what for the mother must be a more viable conception of self, a self that is discovered in the joys of fertility. Adrienne Rich writes that the bond between infant and parent engenders the passions of a "love-affair" (*OW*, 36). However, as Irigaray points out, Levinas cannot conceive of how a "love-affair" could engender ethics. In his discussion of heterosexuality, Levinas finds not an ethics but the threat of castration and lost mastery. This threat of sexuality presents the thrill of a near-death experience, from which the male ego is challenged to emerge with its verticality intact.[15]

No doubt, just as Levinas's ethics is limited by a masculinist cosmology, so too Rich's personal account of the maternal bond recalls what we might call, after Rousseau, a mythology of "southern" passion. That is, her account of motherhood is not unconditional but inescapably limited by cultural allegiances.

The cultural allegiances of Rich, and in particular the locus of elementary sociality in the mutual pleasures of sociality, do not, however, participate in what must be one of the gravest injustices of the West: the effacement of maternal agency in the construction of sociality. As Rich observes, "The child gains her first sense of her own existence from the mother's responsive gestures and expressions. It's as if, in the mother's eyes, her smile, her stroking touch, the child first reads the message: *You are there!*" (*OW*, 36).[16] The notion of a separate ego is a mythic abstraction without reality. But if the hypothesis of a disconnected ego belongs to the mystifications of a hypermasculinist mythology, then the concern for the Other need not be experienced as violent intrusion.

If Levinas must understand the concern for the Other as violation, perhaps it is because he holds on too rigidly to the masculinized ego of patriarchal myth. This ego cannot acknowledge ever having been a little lost in the poetry that revitalizes adult speech, tunes one self to another, and recalls the primal bond to the mother or caregiving father. That poetry, or what Levinas dismisses as mere infant babbling, is also sometimes called mamaese.

The Saying before the Said, or Mamaese

Levinas puts forth the claim that the "primordial manifestation of the Other" occurs as the "total transparence of the gaze directed upon the gaze, the absolute frankness of the face-to-face proffered at the bottom of all speech" (*TI*, 182/199). In other words, Levinas claims that however we might attempt to communicate with one another through various verbal and nonverbal signs, these signs, or what Levinas calls "the said," never present the alterity of the Other. The person manifests herself over and above whatever she might say or do. This pristine manifestation of the person occurs through what Levinas discerns as the gaze and develops further through "the saying." By developing the manifestation in the register of the saying, Levinas aims to locate the encounter with the Other in the address that precedes any speech, rather than in the content of that speech.

Behind Levinas's efforts to distinguish the pristine manifestation of the gaze from various adulterated modes of expression in signs lies a concern to secure the claims of the singular individual against the assimilating drive of any kind of system. Levinas argues that if it is the case that signifying events can only be interpreted within a shared sign system, and if the individual is understood solely in terms of his signifying acts, he disappears as an individual and acquires a status solely in relation to the system. This shared sign system may be politically necessary for the complete development of sociality, but it could not, according to Levinas, provide the ethical origin of sociality.

For similar reasons, for Levinas, any dialectical conception of the self constitutes a politics and not an ethics. Because dialectical conceptions of the self locate what is real solely in that dimension of the self that finds a reflection in the other person, Levinas argues, these conceptions efface the individuality of the person and are blind to deeper concerns for justice. If Levinas is right, ethics cannot be based on reciprocity. Levinas writes: "In political life ... humanity is understood from its works—a humanity of interchangeable men, of reciprocal relations. The substitution of men for one another, the primal disrespect, makes possible exploitation itself.... Justice consists in again making possible expression, in which in non-reciprocity the person presents himself as unique" (*TI*, 298/332).

Therefore, when Levinas writes that the response to the Other can only occur via "the straightforwardness of the face-to-face" and adds that the face-to-face encounter "is not a play of mirrors" (*TI*, 183/199), his first intention is to avoid reducing the individual to a mirror reflection of the same. However, in the attempt to secure the ethical nature of the encounter with another, Levinas portrays the face of the Other in a single and sober light. The responsibility to the Other is portrayed as deadly serious. Occluded from the fixity of the gaze are the animated exchanges of play.

And yet contemporary psychoanalytic research into the origin of the face-to-face relationship in the parent and child suggests that this encounter takes place originally not as a fixed gaze into the eyes of another but in the varying expressions of play. In *The First Relationship*, Daniel Stern reports that "we are, it turns out, extremely playful animals.... We ... play with our voices and faces and movements in the sense of experiencing pleasure in the creation of new variations, elaborations, and combinations of simple behaviors. Song, mime, and dance are most probably the cultural ritualizations of this process."[17] The ludic reciprocity of the face-to-face encounter brings about mutual recognition between parent and infant.

But if the face-to-face play between parent and infant introduces a conception of mutual recognition that throws into question Levinas's mythic portrayal of the encounter, it also poses a major challenge to the identity logic of dialectical philosophy. Dialectical philosophy aims to subordinate differences within a larger identity. In the *Phenomenology*, Hegel gives a reading of mutual recognition as the process in which the individual comes to recognize the Other as similar to oneself. Stern finds, however, that the complex features of face-to-face play cannot be explained in terms of mirroring resemblances. Thus, I would argue, the face-to-face play invokes a process of recognition that is outside of traditional models of the dialectic of recognition.

In particular, face-to-face play is primarily the effect of what Stern explains as "affect attunement." Stern's work on affect attunement is especially exciting because it offers a way of understanding social reciprocity that is not based on a logic of identity, or, in general, on the presumption that individuals aim to be the same. On the contrary, Stern construes communication primarily in terms of correspondences between individual styles of self-expression.

Stern's speculations begin with the observation that infants yet unable to speak (i.e., unable to speak what traditionally is understood in terms of the language of the father, or even language proper), and only nine to fifteen months of age, indicate, at least to their parents, that they understand some of the feelings of those around them and in turn signal when they have themselves been understood. The question for Stern is how parents know that infants understand what in alienated philosophical jargon is termed "other minds." Even as a neonate, the infant expresses a smile of recognition in response to the smiling face of the caregiver. However, Stern argues, strict imitation, or mirroring, of behaviors, however expressive they might appear to be, cannot indicate the infant actually understands the meaning of the other person's behavior nor that the infant intends anything through her response. The infant signals that she understands the meaning of the parent's smile, Stern argues, only when she is able to respond with some behavior that does not literally copy but instead "corresponds" (Stern borrows the notion of correspondence from the French poet Baudelaire) to that of the parent. According to Stern, investigators have been able to describe "in detail how caregivers and infants mutually create the chains and sequences of reciprocal behaviors that make up *social dialogues* during the infant's first nine months."[18] These "dialogues without words" vary a theme in a manner that is most aptly characterized as "musical" (*I*, 139).

Stern's research suggests that Kristeva (see chapter 1) misunderstands the musical dimension of self-expression in what she terms the "semiotic." Through the notion of the semiotic, Kristeva rather narrowly interprets the rhythmic, tonal, and gestural dimensions of communication as violent disruptions or transgressions of meaningful propositional ("thetic") discourse. While Kristeva aims to use the notion of the semiotic in order to account for the sources for new systems of meaning, she can only understand the semiotic itself as a disruption of sense and structure. She fails to see that the semiotic might constitute a source of nondiscursive meaning. In effect, Kristeva conceives of the violence of semiotic nonsense from the perspective of patriarchy with its fear of the creative power of the mother, rather than as part of the sociality between mother and infant. Stern's analysis of the musicality of infant–parent communication suggests that emphasis, tone, and rhythm are not airy nothings but constitute expressions of affect in a fully embodied speech act. If the semiotic were reinterpreted as mamaese, then philosophy of language would no longer be centered around the language of the father, a center left intact throughout the various deconstructions of postmodern theory.

Language begins in the coos that rebound between infant and parent. These nondiscursive dialogues emerge fully not when they are reduced to thetic discourse (propositions or concepts) but, as Stern's research suggests, when these nonthetic dialogues take on the power of figurative transformation. That is, at around nine months, the dialogues between infant and parent draw upon the process of cross-modal correspondence, or what Stern is calling affect attunement.

Stern only really defines affect attunement by way of various examples of exchanges, vocal and nonvocal, between parent and infant. In one example, the infant sounds out an enthusiastic "aaaah!" at a new toy and the mother responds with a little dance, "a shimmy," that is "equally excited, joyful, and intense" (*I*, 140).[19]

What kind of theory accounts for the correspondence between the musicality of an infant's expression and the mother's dance? Stern claims that only metaphor can fully account for the correspondence between sensuous expressions of affect in different modalities, e.g., the correspondence between a roll of the torso and a vocalization.

The movement of the torso or vocalization expresses an affect that itself does not literally exist but, Stern explains, appears in "virtual time" through a process of imaginative interpretation. Stern clarifies the distinction between what literally exists and what exists in virtual time through the example of music. "Music as an actual physical temporal event is one dimensional and homogeneous in time, yet it presents virtual time—that is time as lived or experienced, rushing, tripping, drawn out, or suspenseful" (*I*, 158). Only after one responds to the sound by giving it a certain reading does it become music. This process of reading the sound as music and then in turn the process of responding to the music with dance invoke nonverbal uses of metaphor.

However, while Stern at one point describes attunement as metaphoric and mysterious, he later claims that cross-modal expression can be given a literal explanation. This is an important point. If he is right, then the use of metaphor in the explanation of affect attunement would be superfluous. Metaphoric description would be superfluous, for example, if the mother's gesture and the infant's sound could be referred to a single referent, itself existing independently of either particular mode of expression and thus entirely severed from its expression in the body. Stern concludes his discussion by making such a claim. He writes:

> An attunement is a recasting, a restatement of a subjective state. It treats the subjective state as the referent and the overt behavior as one of several possible manifestations . . . of the referent. For example, a level and quality of exuberance can be expressed as a unique vocalization, as a unique gesture, or as a unique facial display. Each manifestation has some degree of substitutability as a recognizable signifier of the same inner state. (*I*, 161)

Here Stern implies that there exists a literal mental referent apart from its expression that serves to guarantee correct translation from one medium to another.

And yet Stern's examples of affect attunement often involve expressions that lack any discernible common referent. One of Stern's first examples comes from a metaphor that he finds in Defoe's novel *Moll Flanders*. Stern claims that he can clarify with exactitude how the metaphor works: "When the heroine is finally caught and imprisoned after a life of crime, she says, 'I had . . . no thought of heaven or hell, or at least that went any farther than a bare flying touch.' . . . The activation contour of her ideation reminds her of the activation contour of a particular physical sensation, a fleeting touch. And they evoke the same vitality affect" (*I*, 58).

In fact, however, Stern cannot demonstrate—by measurement—that a bare flying touch and a thought of heaven or hell have the same—i.e., literally identical—energy levels. First of all, a touch that is bare and flies suggests an immaterial touch, which is literally nothing at all. Metaphorically, the nature of its impact remains open to interpretation. But if it is not even clear how one would measure the vitality affect of a bare flying touch, it is even less clear how one might decide upon a common standard of comparison between this peculiar touch and a thought of heaven and hell. The comparison is fitting, but this fit is not due to some common measure.

Stern also claims that the vitality affect of the mother's roll of the torso is identical to that of her child's exuberant "aaaah!" And yet the only literal resemblance that Stern does in fact locate is the length of time that each response takes (actually only approximately the same). Of course, any indefinite number of responses would meet this minimal criterion. Apparently a lot more is going on. One might try additional dimensions of vitality affect in order to account for the relatively limited number of appropriate responses to any given stimulus. Stern's full list includes not only duration but also absolute intensity, intensity contour, temporal beat, rhythm, and shape. For example, one could certainly claim that the loudness of the infant's vocalization at least in some sense equals the intensity of the mother's roll. But it is not clear how the observer would decide to define the units of intensity of the mother's movement so that we might then compare this kind of intensity to the intensity of the vocalization.

Secondly, it is not clear that the basis for this decision is ever available to the discursive consciousness of the infant or parent. As long as the definition of the unit of the dance remains open to interpretation, it is difficult for Stern to claim that the measure of affect intensity can be, as he puts it, "absolute." The evidence for affect attunement (i.e., cross-modal communication between affects) argues that parent and child communicate more than they could ever conceptualize. Therefore, our most fundamental level of communication is, like artistic expression, beyond intentionality, causal explanation, or any literalistic verbal account. We cannot explain how our elementary communication happens, but we sense when it goes wrong. We express much more than we could ever say.

Communicative responses between infant and parent may exhibit in some sense or another identical levels of vitality affect. Still the choice of an appropriate response requires an element of imaginative interpretation. As Stern himself points out, without an act of imagination, music remains a series of sounds that express nothing. But musical interpretation is in part a matter of individual style. The communication of style is not a matter that can be brought fully into discursive analysis or into conscious awareness. Therefore, the very musicality of our speech acts calls into question the fantasy of self-presence that founds traditional conceptions of autonomy and reason. This fantasy represses not—as the early Kristeva would have it—an antisocial and symbiotic fusion of infant and mother but the primary bonds of sociality. These bonds provide a source of significance that exceeds individual consciousness but not individuality. Therefore, the notion of affect attunement allows us to understand the face-to-face encounter as playful and yet responsive, in fact, responsive inasmuch as it is playful. Attunements occur through cross-modal correspondences that cannot be subsumed under a logic of identity, conceptual explanation, or intentionality. These correspondences provide a mode of mutual recognition that would not reflect the Other as the same but respond with imagination to difference. There is no element of consciousness that is not fraught with the oblique enigmas of material expression. The mind severed from the flesh is nothing.

A Correspondence Theory of Ethical Exchange

Observations of the parent-infant relationship support what Levinas speculates to be an origin of intersubjectivity in the face-to-face encounter. These same observations fail to support Levinas's particular interpretation of that encounter. According to Levinas, the protective stance of the maternal emerges from the asymmetry of the somber gaze and expresses itself as infinite duty. The observations of Stern and others suggest that sociality emerges from the reciprocity of play.

While the reciprocity of play locates an origin of ethics in the face rather than in discourse, it is tempting to explain this reciprocity as a kind of dialogue, and thus by way of discourse ethics.[20] The evidence from social theory supports the claim that the source of ethical judgment lies not in systems of reason but in participatory communication. Discourse ethics, however, cannot account for nondiscursive dimensions of communication, specifically for the ways in which the unreal abstraction of what philosophers analyze as propositional content connects with the tonal, gestural and cultural dimensions of a fully embodied act of expression.

The embodied dimension of communicative acts poses problems for what Seyla Benhabib argues to be the fundamental principle of communicative ethics, namely, "the capacity to reverse perspectives" (SS, 8). In effect, Benhabib's interpretation of dialogue as an exchange of perspectives relies upon the Cartesian mapping of the subject in a geometricized space. Space (originally the body of the mother) would be a big empty nothing, and exchanging perspectives would be a matter of changing places. Benhabib develops the principle of reversed perspectives by citing Hannah Arendt: "This enlarged way of thinking, which as judgement knows how to transcend its individual limitations, cannot function in strict isolation or solitude; it needs the presence of others 'in whose place' it must think, whose perspective it must take into consideration" (SS, 9). One must respond to the *expressions* of the Other. However, if, as Benhabib well argues, the self is not disembodied, one cannot simply change places (e.g., bodies with racialized skin and sexed flesh, histories of slavery or conquest, cultures that repress or enhance desire) with another self.

A correspondence theory of ethics, unlike the rationalist theory of dialogue that Benhabib takes from Habermas, would begin by acknowledging the unique modalities of expression that define individuals in their attunement to others. These responses testify not only to a fully embodied person but to some body with a history that cannot be transferred from one to another. Communication cannot provide a basis for ethical judgment unless ethical theory acknowledges the nonreversible status of these bodies and these histories. I would agree therefore with Laurence Thomas, who argues that "we cannot simply imaginatively put ourselves in the shoes of another ... [for] if we had a complete description of the person's experiences, we would nonetheless not be the subject of those experiences."[21] So too the task of ethics requires moral deference—not to the sovereign masters of Hegelian lore but, as Thomas argues, to those who have suffered. Sounding a Levinasian note, Thomas defines moral deference as "bearing witness to the moral pain of other" (*MD*, 246). Like Levinas, Thomas breaks with the inclination to defer to the masters of history and aims instead to defer to the slaves.

The arguments of Thomas, however, would return us to the asymmetry of ethical response and therefore, I assume, to the kind of ethical stance developed by Levinas. In part 2, I have attempted to address the concerns of philosophers such as Thomas and Levinas. A correspondence theory of ethics begins with the irreversible differences between individuals; therefore the central task of ethics is to respond to the voices of the disempowered Other. At the same time, however, in this chapter I have suggested that there are problems with reducing the Other to the alien victim of injustice stripped of the resources of culture. If the Other is not to be reduced to the unknown object of an alienating gaze, then we must find paths of communication that do not presuppose sameness. A theory of correspondence provides one such way.

Benhabib is not insensitive to the fact that individuals vary in their histories and concrete circumstances. She attempts to address the problem of individual difference and yet save the Habermasian project of a reason-based ethics by ordering relationships "along a continuum, extending from universal respect for all as moral persons at one end to the care, solidarity and solicitation demanded of us and shown to us by those to whom we stand in the closest relationship at the other" (*SS*, 10). However, this solution simply compounds the problem. Both the masculinized reason of the Enlightenment *and* its complement, the sentimental narrative of care, presuppose that each of us is capable of changing places with the Other. Both respect and empathy conceal the erotic possibilities for responding to, corresponding with, a person whose lived experiences are fundamentally different from our own.

Benhabib further argues that effective ethical dialogue demands mature persons who have agreed upon a universal standard of moral reason. The requirement that individuals exhibit the kind of rationality that determines maturity excludes children from the moral conversation. However, as parents we know (as Benhabib so well argues) that dialogue does not originate in fraternal rivalry. Communication happens already in the face-to-face play with our infant children. In fact, because face-to-face play does not require abstract skills in reason, it also provides a basis for communication across animal species.[22] Other mammals besides humans have developed highly mobile facial skin in order to communicate. In fact, only less social mammals do not need facial expressions; as a consequence, their facial expressions are relatively hard and stiff.[23] For social animals generally, communication trades less on concepts constructed *ex nihilo* than on the flesh-and-blood mysteries of attunement across differences of style.

PART THREE

Dissonance
and Social Struggle

structed the concept of the subject. These theories demonstrate the various ways in which the subject is an effect of the technologies of power/knowledge ("discursive formation," "text," etc.), and therefore not a possible agent of social change.

The task of what follows is to locate at least one exemplary model of an "adult self" (traditionally demarcated in terms of the readiness of the individual to leave the family of origin and enter into the social sphere) that lies outside of dominant European or Euro-American philosophies of freedom. While postmodernism forbids us to posit any particular conception of the self or freedom as the final telos of history, it must not preempt the contextual valorization of some groups of outsiders as agents of progressive change at any particular juncture of history. A postcolonial narrative of freedom would differ from the universalizing narratives that are attacked by postmodernists on exactly this point. Postcolonial philosophies emerge not from the perspective of an empowered group but from the lived experience of a social outcast or liminal Other. The refusal to valorize a specific perspective as definitive of the social goals of an epoch risks falling back into an impasse between the aimless violence of postmodern transgression and the cathartic violence of universalizing reason, i.e. between the adolescent violence of "bad boys" and the power of the "good old boys."

Foucault exemplifies the impasse that cripples postmodern theories of social change. On the one hand, Foucault has, as he claims, "tried to show how we have indirectly constituted ourselves [as rational and responsible social agents] through the [arbitrary] exclusion of others: criminals, mad people, and so on."[1] But while Foucault's research demonstrates the arbitrary and exclusionary nature of what Enlightenment and nineteenth-century thinkers idealize as the march of reason through history, Foucault also disengages himself from commitment to a theory of social change: "For a rather long period, people have asked me to tell them what will happen and to give them a program for the future" (*TS*, 10). Why the refusal? "We know very well that, even with the best intentions, those programs become a tool, an instrument of oppression. Rousseau, a lover of freedom, was used in the French Revolution to build up a model of social oppression. Marx would be horrified by Stalinism and Leninism." What is left for the postmodern theorist? "My role—and that is too emphatic a word—is to show people that they are much freer than they feel" (*TS*, 10). And so Foucault's final work begins with the premise that one is forever enslaved to powers beyond control. Foucault's response to such a fate seems to be indicated in his final turn to Greek and Roman programs for "the care of the self," and, in particular, his interest in stoicism.

It is not surprising that Foucault's final work turns to the philosophy of stoicism in order to locate the freedom that is possible for the unfree. The Hegelian system, whose discursive power Foucault feared might prove inescapable, posits stoicism as the philosophy of the enslaved. While Foucault refuses to prescribe revolutionary theories of change, his retrieval of the stoic program for the care of the self orients his reader toward individual self-mastery, not in order to effect social change but as a project of numbing the self in order to endure the lacerations of what is taken to be one's fate. Foucault uses the example of the stoic to demonstrate a constant (if nonuniversal) theme of manhood from classical to modern times. The production of a masculinized subject typically requires tests of self-mastery that are designed to harden the body against the impact of the external world.[2] In particular, the stoic hardens himself before a fate that might include such extremes as economic, political, or social enslavement. In the face of domination, the stoic does not resist but retreats into quietism. Thus, Foucault's final writings on the practices of the self fail to locate an agent for progressive historical change.

Can we locate a model of a slave who becomes subject through resistance rather than retreat? One of the most significant places in which this question comes up is in connection with the development of African American identities during American slavery. As many new studies have shown, African Americans found various ways to reconstruct their social, psychological, and cultural meanings in the midst of the alienating and demoralizing circumstances of slavery.[3] One of the most striking ways in which African Americans constituted an identity for themselves under conditions of slavery takes the form of the "slave narratives."[4] Indeed, at the same time that Hegel was constructing a master narrative of freedom in Europe, African Americans were constructing the most substantial accounts ever left by slaves of their own struggle for freedom (*CSN*, ix). These *slave narratives* provide a supreme test of the power and scope of the *master narratives* of European theory.

In particular, my interest here concerns to what extent the African American slave narratives challenge European or Euro-American conceptions of selfhood and freedom.[5] Even more narrowly, I will focus on specific narratives of Frederick Douglass. In his 1845 *Narrative of the Life of Frederick Douglass* as well as in its 1855 revision, *My Bondage and My Freedom*, Douglass tells how he regained a sense of agency, or "manhood," that led to his resolve to escape to the North and freedom.[6] At first reading, it appears as though Douglass is able to tell his 1845 narrative if not also his 1855 revision only by way of the dominant discourse of nineteenth-century Eurocentric culture. In fact, however, even in his early writings, Douglass does not appropriate elements from the dominant discourses except to transform them.

William Andrews offers one of the most thorough attempts to locate assimilative and transformative elements in the Douglass narratives. Andrews argues that while the 1845 *Narrative* accommodates the Garrisonian abolitionists' pacifistic stand against violence and in favor of the moral purity of the self, as well as accommodating the late-eighteenth- and early-nineteenth-century celebration of self-reliance and assimilation into white America,[7] the 1855 revision relocates the search for self within a quest for a "truly communal Afro-American home" (*BF*, xix). *My Bondage*, according to Andrews, should be read as "an evolving dialectic between these two sides of the man: the side that sought plenitude within, through some sort of ideal of the free self, and the side that sought plenitude outside, through an ideal of communal attachment" (*BF*, 220).

It is specifically the thematic issues raised by Andrews that I address in the chapters that follow. My larger question concerns the extent to which Douglass creates a uniquely African American dialectic of freedom. In response to this question, I attempt to show that Douglass's narratives project a concept of freedom that appropriates and transforms a nineteenth-century dialectic of freedom and therefore, only less directly, an eighteenth-century liberal concept of freedom. The dialectical philosophy of the nineteenth century yields a positive conception of freedom in contrast to the negative concept of freedom that is anchored in Enlightenment Europe and that continues to inform Anglo-American culture. Enlightenment and post-Enlightenment Anglo-American culture locates freedom primarily in terms of the absence of external constraints and thus in the protection of a sphere of private rights that one exercises on the basis of individual choice. This detachment from external constraints can be elaborated in terms of the eighteenth-century notion of natural rights or in terms of a Romantic notion of self-reliance that is associated with such

European American writers as Emerson and Thoreau. The consequence for twentieth-century America is a very weak sense of the participation of the individual in such apparently external realities as the social and cultural sphere. Dialectical European philosophy, on the other hand, does not reject the liberal concept of freedom as choice but redefines as *the primary dimension* of the free individual his or her place within a community, nation-state, or other yet-to-be-defined social and cultural context.

In the introduction to *The Philosophy of History*, Hegel lays out the distinction between the two notions of freedom. Hegel writes:

> Morality is Duty—substantial Right—a "*second* nature" as it has been justly called; for the *first* nature of man is his primarily merely animal existence.... The error which first meets us is the direct contradictory of our principle that the state presents the realization of Freedom; the opinion, viz., that man is free by *nature*, but that in *society*, in the State—to which nevertheless he is irresistibly impelled—he must limit this natural freedom.... Limitation is certainly produced by Society and the State, but it is a limitation of the mere brute emotions and rude instincts.... We should ... look upon such limitation as the indispensable proviso of emancipation.[8]

The Douglass narratives appropriate Euro-American conceptions of freedom, conceptions that include the image of the self-made man and the atomistic individualism of Enlightenment philosophy, within a dialectical conception of freedom as recognition. In this respect, Douglass's social philosophy is unique, not in the full European context but in America.[9]

But at the same time, Douglass's narratives fundamentally alter some of the repressive, and specifically antifeminist, tendencies in the European project. In chapter 5, I demonstrate how the dominant European concepts of freedom, concepts that Hegel reinterprets as various moments of the ultimate goal of universal recognition, "preserve" (in the sense of "*aufheben*") the Western opposition between nature and sociality. Behind this opposition lies the presupposition that human nature is originally (where "originally" refers both to so-called primitive tribes and childhood) ruled by narcissistic impulses (e.g., self-centered inclinations). The individual acquires moral, social, and political status, and in this sense "comes of age," only when he (maybe she) is able to control natural impulses and act in accordance with what Western culture reads in terms of abstract principles of reason. This opposition between the natural and the social self supports variations of the altruism/egoism dichotomy which recur from modernism through contemporary Eurocentric cultures. As I have argued in parts 1 and 2, this dichotomy not only sustains unhealthy gender oppositions (oppositions that pose mothers as altruistic and therefore selfless servants, infants as egocentric and asocial animals, and men as egoistic by nature and to varying degrees capable of rational control over their impulses); it also preempts what I am arguing to be a much more favorable conception of ethical life, one that accentuates the pleasures of sociality.

Chapter 6 argues that such an alternative conception of ethical life emerges out of the Douglass narratives. In these narratives, Douglass rewrites the dynamic of recognition, or what Hegel allegorizes in the dialectic of master and slave and what I am analyzing in terms of rites of passage into manhood, through the eyes of the defiant slave. My argument is that Douglass retells the encounter of the slave with the master not in order to portray how he as slave was able to "master the master," and thus reverse the terms of power, but in order to transform the meaning of social and personal empowerment. Marginalized images of the autobiographies suggest that already in his 1845 *Narrative*, Douglass appropriates the dialectical concept of self as social only in order to alter the very terms of this sociality. These efforts on behalf of an alternative conception of the self are strengthened in his 1852 fictional narrative, "The Heroic Slave," and in *My Bondage and My Freedom*. The mere reversal of the terms of power, of course, would leave the hierarchies of power, a dichotomy between those who are recognized as persons and those who are not, intact.[10] The dominant dialectical and liberal discourses of the nineteenth century rationalize oppression by representing the Other in terms of the alien self, specifically, in terms of the child or beast, whose narcissistic impulses or egocentric desires are not under rational control.[11] Not only in *The Philosophy of History* but already in the earlier and more romantic *Phenomenology*, Hegel makes clear that the free (and, according to the patriarchal tradition, the masculinized) subject must finally overcome the animal within. Similarly, the white Christian abolitionists in America require that the black slave demonstrate worthiness for freedom through ascetic tests of moral purity at the same time that these abolitionists represent the slaveholder in terms of abject bestiality.

A marginalized pattern of images in the Douglass narratives challenges the European Christian dichotomy between "animal" and "man" and projects not the abstract freedom and moral purity of liberal and dialectical philosophies of freedom but a fully embodied and social self. Even while the fully embodied self is physical and passionate, to the point of being combative under conditions of oppression, Douglass's narratives deconstruct the socially regressive dynamic that severs the rational or morally pure self from a mythical animality. Douglass's narratives in effect develop what is deeply lacking in both European and Euro-American culture, a self that is by nature (and here I mean "first nature" and not what Hegel calls "second nature") a social animal. For Douglass, selfhood does not require rituals that would harden the already scarred body against further infliction of pain but, on the contrary, practices that reawaken the body to the pleasures and desires of recognized sociality that originate in early childhood. In this way, Douglass's narratives alter and even strengthen the dialectical conception of our social nature—a conception that is left far too underdeveloped, even what we might call primitive, within the Enlightenment philosophy of Anglo-America.

Dialectical conceptions of the self argue that the individual is embedded within a sociality whose origin in the material and cultural forces of history is incommensurate with powers of the individual to conceptualize or to control. At the same time, no doubt in part because of its bourgeois origin, dialectical philosophy aims to preserve individual freedom as a moment of irreducible difference in what would otherwise degenerate into total system.[12] It is not clear, however, how successfully Hegel preserves individual agency within the larger spirit of the community and historical change. Most problematic is Hegel's heavy reliance on stoicism in order to locate the place of the individual in the system that is his or her fate. On the other hand, Douglass quite clearly rejects European stoicism in order to define the self as an agonistic agent of social change, or, in other words, as a "freedom fighter." It is only because Douglass is able to overcome that numbing of the flesh that deadens the passions and breaks the spirit of the slave that he is able to rekindle a sense of freedom and self. But if the struggle for a free self requires the reawakening rather than the purgation of sensuality and the agitation of desire, the cathartic dialectic envisioned by Hegel must give way to a dialectic that is ecstatic. Chapter 6 concludes that while the Douglass autobiographies do repeat some of the major themes of the Hegelian narrative, these autobiographies appeal to a notion of recognition that does not sublate but, on the contrary, transforms the mind/body dichotomies that sustain European constructions of the self. According to Douglass, the primary locus of ethical life is not in the vertical dialectic of mind over body but in the horizontal dynamic that mediates the differences between Self and Other.

The final chapter, chapter 7, compares the agonistic self that emerges from the slave narratives of Douglass with a somewhat similar notion of selfhood found in Nietzsche's *Genealogy of Morals*. Like the Douglass narratives, Nietzsche's *Genealogy* offers a critique of the asceticism that defines mainstream Western culture. However, while both Douglass and Nietzsche challenge the asceticism of the European tradition and aim to reattach the self to the body and its drives, they interpret the body and its drives very differently. The warrior self projected by the Nietzschean narratives breaks free from one type of asceticism, the asceticism of rational duty, only to lapse into another asceticism, namely, the asociality of the will to power. On the other hand, the agonistic self projected by the Douglass narratives attune the self as will to power—or will to empowerment—to the goals of a larger social narrative. This larger social narrative reverberates with the resources of self that trace back to the social eroticism of the nurturer-child relation and reinvoke the origin of ethics in music and dance.

Chapter 7 ends by concurring with postmodern and multicultural theorists who argue that European-based concepts of the self sever a rational ego from the body and its desires and sustain a politics of oppression in the name of freedom. The reconstruction of the self in the Douglass narratives provides the basis for a concept of freedom that does not disavow social and expressive dimensions of the self and which therefore offers a future that would be less oppressive than the past.

·5·

Hegel's Master Narrative of Freedom and the African American Experience

In the *Phenomenology of Spirit* (sec. B, "Self-Consciousness"), Hegel interweaves a modernist locus of the self in the will and its freedom with a classical conception of the self as social.[1] But if sociality is our second nature, it is not, according to Hegel, our first nature. For Hegel shares with liberal, Nietzschean, and psychoanalytic theories the claim that human beings are in part animals driven by asocial desires. Nonetheless, Hegel's dialectical method engenders what more reductive modernist theories lack, namely, an elaborate phenomenology of the social dimension of the self and a corresponding notion of freedom. According to the *Phenomenology*, the first climactic turn toward the development of the self takes the form of what has become known as the master/slave dialectic. Those who are able to prove that they are not slaves to their own animalistic desires attain the social status of a person. Those who prove weak of will fall into physical bondage and social shame, and according to Hegel deservingly so.

Despite the arcane language of the *Phenomenology*, Hegel's dialectic of self-consciousness continues to provide the theoretical framework for major historical and sociological studies of American slavery.[2] These studies cite Hegel as an authority on the socio-psychological dynamics of master and slave, as well as of the sado-masochism behind contemporary white racism. Hegel provides an account of socio-psychological aspects of domination that do not lend themselves to a materialist explanation or formal analysis. While these studies suggest the importance of a nonmaterialist and specifically a culturally-informed dialectic in studies of domination, many of these same studies present empirically based accounts of slavery that, I shall argue, pose problems for Hegel's version of the dialectic.[3] According to dialectical logic, as Hegel develops it, the identity of the slave reflects those liminal elements of the self that are overcome (or sublated) by the master. The duplicitous symmetries of Hegelian logic conceal, however, what African American history demonstrates: The slave was not in fact the mirror reversal of the master. The slave did not inevitably see himself or herself in terms of desires disavowed by the master.

Moreover, Hegelian philosophy appropriates and so too validates dualisms of European asceticism that are alien to major currents of African American culture.[4] Major currents of black expressive culture lie outside of the dialectic between pure reason and embodied desire, and thus the central poles of mainstream European cultures. On the contrary, I shall argue, the experience of the African Americans during the period of slavery gives rise to a second dialectic, and thus a social vision that is irreducible to the Hegelian project of subjectivity and freedom. Chapters 6 and 7 follow one strand of this alternative model of self-transformation and social change in the narratives of Frederick Douglass.

Will over Desire

Hegel introduces his discussion of master and slave (or *Herrschaft und Knechtschaft, PS*, secs. 178–96) with an excessively abstract account of the emergence of self-consciousness out of a simple biological existence (*PS*, secs. 166–77).[5] Unfortunately, the abstract language invites the reader to treat this section of the *Phenomenology* as an a priori and quasi-mathematical description of concepts.[6] This is, I believe, a mistake. As Hegel construes it, dialectical phenomenology discovers concepts not from intuition (*Anschauen*), nor from any other source of disembodied and ahistorical knowledge, but from experience (*Erfahrung*).[7] The uprooting of concepts from their historical, anthropological, or other empirical sources reduces dialectical phenomenology to a formal and neo-Kantian phenomenology and therefore transforms the Hegelian project into the kind of alienated speech-act that it was meant to critique. As Hegel writes in his preface, "The formalism which recent philosophy [including his own] denounces and despises, only to see it reappear in its midst, will not vanish from Science, however much its inadequacy may be recognized and felt, till the cognizing of absolute actuality has become entirely clear as to its own nature" (*PS*, sec. 16). It is the nature of this "absolute actuality," or what for Hegel must be historical experience narrated in terms of what he perceives to be the overarching purpose of human existence in freedom, that I aim to make clear. Whatever experience signifies in the *Phenomenology*, it is not reducible to either a neomathematical formalism or to a causal web of events without narrative meaning.

On the other hand, to the extent that Hegel's phenomenology of experience does show symptoms of a Cartesian reification of self-consciousness, I would ask if this reification does not itself have, at least implicitly, a certain history. Would not the most basic experience (feeling, intuition, etc.) of the self vary according to such factors as race, culture, sexuality, and gender?[8]

One of Hegel's primary hypotheses regarding the structure of human experience is that the development of individual consciousness recapitulates the development of historical consciousness, or, as it was commonly expressed in the nineteenth century, ontogenesis mirrors phylogenesis.[9] Of course, this hypothesis, as well as its particular interpretation, hardly stands beyond empirical critique. My strategy is to read the phenomenology of self-consciousness not as an abstract deduction of concepts nor as contingent chronology but as a psychohistory, and in particular as a psychohistory that accounts for both ontogenetic and phylogenetic events that might explain dominant expressions of the masculinized self in Western culture.[10] Through this interpretative strategy, I aim to clarify the empirical, psychological, and historical foundations of Hegel's concept of self-consciousness in order to demystify that concept and discern its implicit ideological allegiances. While these allegiances reflect dominant and recurrent themes in Western Eurocentric culture, they are not universal. On the contrary, I shall argue that Hegel's uncritical appropriation of these themes reinforces asymmetries of power that his dialectic otherwise aims to overcome. For, as it turns out, Hegel portrays the beginnings of self-consciousness in terms that are not as unfamiliar nor as innocent as his abstractly metaphoric language might suggest.

According to the *Phenomenology*, in the beginning of human history, the self is submerged in what Hegel terms "Life." Hegel defines "Life" as a "simple fluid substance of pure movement within itself" (*PS*, sec. 169). He implies that at its origin the not-yet-conscious creature lacks any awareness of its own existence. From the organic flux, the *Phenomenology* continues, a "being for itself ... comes forward in antithesis to the universal substance [i.e., the whole cycle of Life], disowns this fluent continuity with it and asserts that it is not dissolved in this universal element, but on the contrary preserves itself by separating itself from this its inorganic nature, and by consuming [*Aufzehren*] it" (*PS*, sec. 171). This most primitive form of consciousness occurs strictly in terms of the awareness of oneself as an appetite to consume (e.g., as hunger). For Hegel, the self that does nothing more than consume is passive. It lives off of other things but in a manner that is not aggressive.

In order to develop a phylogenetic reading of Hegel's account of primitive consciousness, I borrow from Hegel's discussion of nascent forms of culture in a later section of the *Phenomenology*. In this later section, Hegel distinguishes primitive and female-centered religions, which center their worship around vegetation, from more developed and male-centered religions, which are based on animal worship (*PS*, sec. 689).[11] In the earlier female-centered cultures, the individual survived by the seemingly effortless and unintelligent task of gathering fruits and vegetables. For Hegel, this kind of existence would support the passive and feminine self that defines the first stage of human self-awareness and that comprises the most primitive pre-European culture.

An ontogenetic reading of Hegel's discussion of early consciousness yields an image of the infant as an asocial creature defined entirely by its various biological appetites. These appetites take the single pattern of assimilating fluids that are provided by a vaguely maternal substance.

Under either the phylogenetic or ontogenetic reading, the most primitive experience of a self occurs as an awareness of a passive and therefore feminine and/or infantile appetite to consume for which a selfless, sacrificial, and therefore maternal nature unconditionally provides. Neither account acknowledges the material but also, and more crucially, the social and cultural work that a mother or nonindustrialized and even nonagricultural people performs in the development of the self and sociality. This failure to appreciate the often well-developed social practices of non-Western cultures reflects the underdevelopment of social and expressive dimensions of the self within the economically overdeveloped Western cultures.

In the second stage of separation, the self is experienced no longer in terms of the passive consumption of what is provided by nature but as an aggressive and egocentric drive to appropriate all of nature (what Hegel calls "the genus of Life") for itself. The self is now characterized in terms of "*die Begierde*," which signifies the predatory nature of animal desire. As Hegel writes, "The simple 'I' is ... certain of itself only by superseding [*das Aufheben*] this other that presents itself ... as an independent life" (*PS*, sec. 174). Hegel interprets this superseding of the Other as the need to destroy the independence of the Other ("*vernichtet den selbstaendigen Gegenstand*") (*PS*, sec. 174). The self aims to sacrifice others, not simply to satisfy passive appetites but in order to assert itself as a power at the center of all things.

Desire, understood as a territorial imperative to dominate all of nature, recalls the "destructive being-for-self" of the hunter in the *Phenomenology*'s account of male-centered religions. According to Hegel, the "warring life" of the hunter defines the less passive and therefore more advanced cultures based on animal worship (*PS*, sec. 689). In these societies, man does not yet oppose the Other-qua-man. What he does do is oppose the Other-qua-nature in a continual struggle for power.

Hegel's account of self-consciousness as desire corresponds as well to a second stage of infant development. According to this account, the yet unsocialized infant asserts an absolute and unyielding claim over the objects of its world. The infant who begins life in vegetative passivity becomes, so to speak, a little animal.

The centripetal forces of early selfhood, however, do not suffice to organize a fully human self, or what Hegel terms "the person" (*die Person*) (*PS*, sec. 187). According to Hegel, the primitive self transforms into a fully human person only after experiencing dissatisfaction with an existence defined solely in terms of gratifying biological appetites and animalistic desires (*PS*, sec. 175). This dissatisfaction cannot arise merely from the fact that the self seeks to overcome cycles of dependency upon external objects.[12] For, according to Hegel, self-consciousness will turn its attention from the external object of desire to the equally external other self-consciousness. In both cases, the self aims to control what it experiences as the external world.

There is, however, an important difference between the social dependence of the self upon another person and the natural dependence of the self upon the object of desire. The potentially human self that is defined by a natural existence comes up against the possibility of its own death. It is this awareness of death that prompts the human being, already constituted as masculine, to seek a sense of self that is not embedded in nature. Hegel presumes that animals, now sharply distinguished from man, are not aware of their mortality and so do not feel the urge to overcome it. Thus, apparently in distinction to the animal, man strives to overcome the meaninglessness of death and gradually transforms itself into the only creature capable of defining itself in terms of larger social and historical purposes, or what Hegel calls "Spirit."[13]

In more contemporary terms, the mortal and masculinized human being cannot console itself in the pleasures of hedonistic consumption nor in the acquisitions of the instrumental self. The awareness of the possibility of death opens a space for seeking in the Other something more than an object to be consumed or appropriated, some object of desire that might elevate the self out of what the masculinized subject perceives as the death-bound cycles of nature. It is at this moment of awareness that self-consciousness seeks out other persons.

It is only as the human being leaves the state of nature (defined quite reductively as cycles of appetite and desire) and becomes a social creature that he can achieve any substantial notion of freedom. Hegel explains what he means by freedom in terms of a dialectical notion of negation. It is only in the "person," Hegel points out, that "negation is present as absolute negation" (*PS*, sec. 175). As I understand the distinction, absolute negation signifies not a desire (à la Kojève and Hegel's French interpreters) but a *will* that strives to define itself above life and therefore above itself as a living thing.[14] It is this will to resist the status of an object, and thus a thing to be consumed or otherwise used, that provides the impetus for freedom. That is, in order to prove itself above nature, the self seeks to manifest a will and not simply a desire (and certainly not a mere appetite). This will—or what for Hegel must be a bold indifference to life and death—seeks to establish that it is free from nature.[15]

An assumption of dialectical methodology is that self-consciousness is defined in terms of its objects and vice versa. Or more broadly, we might say that self-consciousness finds itself through its reflection in the Other. If the person seeks to define itself through its alienation from nature, then it must find some other object that reflects this same alienation. That is, the self must prove its freedom not in a world of nature but in a world inhabited by other persons.

The Hegelian dialectic presumes that the self first encounters the Other as a threat. This is because, in a move that is distinctly modernist and arguably masculinist, Hegel measures the reality of the external world in terms of its force of resistance.[16] Or, to use his terms, the alterity of the external world originally appears as the dialectical "negation" of the self (*PS*, sec. 175). The other person as well as the fully human self first appears on the scene in a contest of wills.

A test of man against nature cannot substitute for a test of wills. As Hegel explains, "On account of the independence of the object [now conceived to be an object that likewise possesses a will], ... [self-consciousness] can achieve satisfaction only when the object itself effects the negation within itself; it must carry out this negation of itself in itself, for it is *in itself* the negative, and must be *for* the other what it *is*" (*PS*, sec. 175). Only those objects that possess a will (or "persons") can "negate" themselves. The human being must have in the Other a verification of (or a reflection of) his own freedom from nature and desire. Only then does he gain a sense of self. The direct assertion of the self over nature (including such rites of passage into manhood as killing an elephant, etc.) retards the human being at the level of the animal. And for Hegel this apparently low level of existence characterizes cultures that are socially primitive.[17]

Hegel's concept of freedom is more fully developed in his discussion of master and slave. Two crucial presuppositions with regard to Hegel's concept of freedom, however, emerge already in the preliminary discussion. First of all, freedom requires a radical break from nature (including the body and its desires, women, and African men). According to Hegel, a maternal nature signifies "nothing" in relation to itself and requires a masculinized person to give it a unifying purpose—or, as Hegel writes, that "for which" it is (see *PS*, sec. 173). One of the implications of this concept of freedom is that those entities that are not recognized as persons (and Hegel would claim to hold the universal definition of the person) exist only as sacrificial means to higher and distinctly "human" ends. Human existence provides the meaning and purpose for all other life forms, including those vegetable- and animal-like selves (e.g., primitive and naturally slavish peoples such as women and Africans) who fail to pass through specifically those rites of manhood that define the person and mark what according to the tradition is the entry into the social. Meanwhile, Hegelian genesis repeats the biblical bequest of nature and things natural to human (or rather manly) domination.

The second presupposition of dialectic is that freedom is defined primarily in terms of the mutual recognition among those who count as persons. Reconciling the various independent wills without subordinating one to another constitutes for Hegel the primary goal of historical development. This end, Hegel writes, is nothing less than "the unity of the different independent self-consciousnesses which, in their opposition, enjoy perfect freedom and independence: 'I' that is 'We' and 'We' that is 'I,'" or what Hegel calls "Spirit" (*PS*, sec. 177). The advantage of this conception of freedom as recognition is that it locates the crucial dynamic for self-expression not in the domain of property but in the sphere of the social. The problem with Hegel's analysis of the foundation of recognition is that it allows for only a single concept of the moral person, and this concept defines the person as antiwoman, antinature, and anti-African.

In the Hegelian narrative, the self advances from immersion in a fluid substance, to the passive consumption and then active sacrifice of other living things, and finally to the struggle for mutual recognition. Read as a phylogeny, Hegel's dialectic of self-consciousness narrates an evolutionary tale about human beginnings in elementary fluids, the rise of feminine gatherers and then masculine hunters, and finally an ethical community whose common principles presuppose shared rites of manhood. Read as an ontogeny, Hegel's dialectic presents a tale about the socialization of the individual from its early experience in the womb, to its passive consumption of its mother's milk and then aggressive assertion of its own autonomous power, and finally to the achievement of social status through rites of passage into a community of men.

The phylogenetic reading of self-consciousness renders non-European societies primitive copies of a self-same European culture. This narrative of world history legitimates such predatory or paternal practices as the physical or economic slavery of those who are deemed animals or children because they are not socialized as white male subjects. A more radicalized dialectic, i.e., one that does in fact mediate difference and not assimilate difference to the same, would work to destabilize the predatory and consumptive practices of imperial culture by meeting alternative cultures *in their own terms*. To the degree that the European imperialist reduces other kinds of persons to impersonal objects, the imperialist is himself not a fully free, i.e., fully social person but, in Hegel's terms, underdeveloped. If Hegel's hedonist hides from the realities of death in the pleasures of consumption, the imperial subject retreats from addressing those who are constituted through alternative rituals of selfhood. On the contrary, the Hegelian subject flees from the Other and circumscribes himself within self-reflective circles of narcissism.

Read as a narrative of individual development, Hegel's dialectic of recognition poses similar problems. As I have argued in part 1, the work of contemporary psychoanalysts ranging from French feminist Luce Irigaray to American empiricist Daniel Stern strongly suggests that Hegel's presuppositions concerning childhood conceal the one-sided mythology of a patriarchal culture.[18] This mythology dissolves the distinct personalities of both the mother and the infant into formless fluids. If, contra Hegel, the infant is from the beginning aware of its difference from the mother, the child need not undergo the ritual of severing itself from its mother, and what the mother represents in the Western imaginary, in order to establish a claim to selfhood.

Moreover, while twentieth-century reinterpretations of the Hegelian concept of the self center the polemics of recognition around the objectifying gaze (see my chapter 3), contemporary feminist revisions of psychoanalytic theory suggest that the self begins prior to the visual economy of the gaze and its objects.[19] Before the visual contact that is established some weeks after birth, the infant and the parent already seek one another's recognition in touch (see my chapter 2). Even in the womb, the fetus responds to the parent's caress with the fluttering of a kick. Immediately after birth, the infant seeks the voice, smell, and touch of the mother, and not solely to satisfy an appetite to consume. The mother or other caregiver seeks the sounds, touches, and smells of the child. Hegel's dialectic misses the pleasures of sociality between different kinds of persons and so too the dimensions of the social self that grow out of the dynamics of recognition between nurturer and child.

Freedom as Self-Mastery

My focus in the remaining chapters of this book will be on what Hegel calls "the person" and what I am reinterpreting in terms of practices of manhood. Hegel discusses the crucial elements of the person in the sections of the *Phenomenology* that immediately follow the introduction of self-consciousness, i.e., the discussion of lordship and bondage and the development from slavery of the preindustrial philosophies of stoicism, skepticism, and Christianity, or what Hegel calls "unhappy consciousness." I read these sections not as the empirical application of aforementioned concepts of recognition, concepts that would then have to be taken as somehow a priori valid, but as the beginning of a detailed development of stages of recognition that Hegel sketches out in the introduction (I interpret sec. 178 as making this point). In the remainder of this chapter, I will focus on the dialectic of master and slave.[20] This climactic scene in the phenomenology of self-consciousness tells us something about the development of the person that is mainstream European but, despite the history of European expansion, not universal.

Hegel's primary aim in the *Phenomenology* is to put into practice the Kantian notion that every individual should be treated with respect, and thus not merely as an instrument of another's desire, but as an end in his or her own right. In order to realize the Kantian notion, Hegel must find some way to make the noumenal side of the person as pure freedom phenomenally accessible. According to Hegel, this means that each individual must "accomplish the movement of absolute abstraction, of rooting-out [*vertilgen*] all immediate being, and of being merely the purely negative being of self-identical consciousness; in other words, [the various self-consciousnesses must have] ... exposed themselves to each other as pure being-for-self" (*PS*, sec. 186). Hegel adds that "pure being-for-self" requires "the pure negation of its objective mode, [which means that the person must show] ... that it is not ... attached to life" (*PS*, sec. 187). The German word *vertilgen*, used also in the context of a war of extermination or a war to the death (*Vertilgenskrieg*), emphasizes that freedom finds its origin in total opposition with the natural self, whatever and whoever that may be. The task of self-consciousness is to manifest its freedom in a world where living things seem to be determined by hedonistic appetites and powerful desires, finally the desire for life itself. Therefore the human being proves he is free only if he can undertake some action that is not reducible to appetite or desire, i.e., to any of the interests and satisfactions that define the hedonistic or instrumental self.

But this struggle does not reduce to a contest of man against nature. The supreme test of courage, at least for Hegel, occurs only in the confrontation with one's true equal—another self-consciousness defined in terms of will. Therefore, each self-consciousness must seek to establish its self by engaging in a life-and-death struggle with another self-consciousness (*PS*, sec. 187). Such a struggle need not signify an actual battle (e.g., a duel).[21] The test might require putting at risk the means of one's livelihood, and thus the interests that define the instrumental self. Or the test might require that the initiate demonstrate courage before pain and thus prove himself superior to the soft-willed hedonist. In any case, personhood, or what historically has been read as manhood, requires not just a test of *will* over *desire* or *appetite* but a test of *will* over *will*.[22]

Thirdly, each of the parties must realize that even though he is to risk his life, that risk should be a bluff. The more courageous combatant proves to the other (as in a game of "chicken") that he is the "real man" (and by this very fact, not a woman or child). At the same time, the loser shows himself to be weak not of intelligence or strength, but of the non-natural attribute of will. He who proves weak of will is by this very fact like (but not the same as) woman and/or child a slave of desire, and so too nothing better than a thing to be used, servant to the master.

Hegel's justification, in his *The Philosophy of History*, of the enslavement of the African gives a more concrete picture of what he sees as the contribution of slavery to the advance of the European spirit. The "sensual Negro," Hegel writes, "has not yet attained a consciousness of freedom."[23] For in his or her passion, the African manifests a "want of self-control" (*PH*, 98). Thus, Hegel argues, the enslavement of the African within the boundaries of the rational European state constitutes an "advance from the merely isolated sensual existence—a phase of education" (*PH*, 99).[24] The sensuous slave endures the chains of slavery for his or her own good, i.e., slavery is a necessary condition of freedom, or so Hegel argues.

The relation between master and slave is, for Hegel, the most primitive expression of intersubjectivity. It is also, according to Hegel, intrinsically unstable. For entangled in the very core of the dialectic of master and slave lies a double irony. The first irony is that the master finds himself dependent upon the slave not simply as chattel or some other instrument of desire but for recognition. The subordination of the will (not just the body) of the slave establishes the honor (or selfhood) of the master. The primary contribution of Hegel's account of slavery is his conceptualization of the paradoxes of domination. The slave is not simply viewed as property, and therefore as a means to the desires of the master.[25] On the contrary, the master attains self-respect through rituals of deference and therefore must also see the chattel slave or subhuman servant as a person.

There is a second irony. The master finds himself recognized not by another person who in fact counts as a person but by a mere slave, someone who is dependent and not independent of the will of the master, and therefore someone whose recognition does not count. In truth, the master knows that he is no better than the slave upon whom he depends for recognition. He has yet to find himself recognized by an equal. The recognition that stems from domination is a fraud. This failure is reflected in the actions of the master. Just as the master treats the slave as a brute, so too the master proves to be little better than the brute. The relation of master to slave (or more generally, the expression of the self through domination) hopelessly entangles honor with power, will with desire, human being with "animal."

While the master's existence regresses to that of the brute, the slave performs what Hegel calls the "labor of the negative," the work that advances history toward its end in universal freedom. More specifically, it is self-humiliating service and the self-consuming terror of certain death that define the experience of the slave-worker and account for his or her role in the liberation of the human spirit.[26] Through labor for a cause beyond oneself (initially, for the master) and through the certainty that death is "the absolute Lord," the slave develops the potential for understanding himself as "pure being-for-self," or as the freedom that he apparently lost to the master. As Hegel explains, in the total terror of death, the slave-worker "has been quite unmanned [*es ist darin innerlich aufgeloest worden*], has trembled in every fiber of its being" but has in this slavish fear achieved what the warrior achieves in an act of courage, namely, the detachment of the self from its natural existence (*PS*, sec. 194).

However, the detachment (and therefore the freedom and manhood) attained through fear differs from that attained through courage. The test of courage cultivates the will of the warrior. The sovereign warrior, however, is not able to subordinate his individual will to a higher universal, or at least not according to the Hegelian model. The warrior (not to be confused with the dutiful soldier) proves the strength of his *particular* will over the power of death. On the other hand, the worker negates the biological self not by conquering the fear of death but by knowing through his fear the reality of death. That is, the worker overcomes his animal nature by coming to accept what the animal does not know and what the master believes that he has overcome: the inevitability of death. An awareness of the finitude of his particular existence prompts the worker to acknowledge that the self that is disconnected from what turn out to be the larger purposes of human history signifies, like all things natural, nothing. Personal meaning derives not from the particularity of natural desire, nor even from the particularity of the individual will, but from what endures, namely, the movement of *universal* spirit. For the individual meaning and purpose ultimately lies in working not for his own freedom alone but for the freedom of his brothers in humanity.

In work the slave creates something that survives the transitions of death and the transitory desires of the egocentric individual. By working on the raw materials of nature, the slave realizes the transcendent self that death bares. This actualization of the self occurs first in the worked-on object and finally in the spirituality of history. Thus, alienated labor realizes the higher personality of the worker once that worker has been set free from egocentric desire by the certainty of death.

As a worker, the slave contributes to the actualization of freedom in a way that the idle master cannot. By demonstrating that it is the slave and not the leisure class of slaveholders who creates culture, Hegel undermines the classical concept of the person. Aristotle's leisure class lacks the spirit of contradiction, i.e., the awareness of death and the labor of the alienated self, that moves the larger processes of history toward freedom.

If the intertwined concepts of the person and freedom first emerge in the struggle for recognition, these concepts develop only in the hands of the laboring slave. The master invokes a warrior's concept of freedom and manhood. He is free inasmuch as he proves himself in a battle of wills. The irresolvable paradox in the position of the master is that he can only prove himself before the eyes of the loser. Having been humiliated in battle, the loser's respect for the master does not count. Therefore, the master's notion of freedom through domination of the Other self-destructs.

Hegel's slave, on the other hand, replaces a *warrior's* concept of freedom with a *worker's* concept of freedom. The sacrificial work ethic of the slave is motivated by the fear of death and performed through "the discipline of service and obedience" (*PS*, sec. 196). Without the certainty of death, the worker would not accept the futility of desire and animal existence. And without the selfless and humbling discipline of service and obedience, work would instill only an "empty self-centred attitude" (*PS*, sec. 196). Hegel requires what modernist Enlightenment philosophies preclude: the individual self finds purpose in laboring for larger social and historical processes that are irreducible to the interests and desires of the individual and yet advance humanity toward the freedom of Spirit. It is this higher notion of self as Spirit that supersedes the self-centered freedom of the master and can only be developed by the laboring slave.

Of course, it is not as a slave that the worker proves himself to be fully free. The path of the dialectic of the *Phenomenology*, like that of history, is long and tortuous. However, it is significant that this path begins in obedience and humiliation and proceeds through what Hegel identifies as the philosophy of slavery, namely, stoicism. As Hegel writes of stoicism: "Whether on the throne or in chains, in the utter dependence of its individual existence, its aim is to be free, and to maintain that lifeless indifference which steadfastly withdraws from the bustle of existence, alike from being active as passive, into the simple essentiality of thought" (*PS*, sec. 199). Under conditions of quietistic withdrawal from the body and the social, the slave produces a culture that is based on what the stoics identify as "reason." The asceticism of what according to Hegel defines slave culture provides the basis for the emerging cultures of Christianity, modern rationalism, and the Protestant work ethic.

While there are important differences between Hegelian master and Hegelian slave, both master and slave share a notion of freedom that manifests elements of European asceticism. Both develop a notion of the free self that severs human being from nature and requires the subordination, denial, or dialectical negation of embodied dimensions of human existence. Freedom is defined in terms that include as a necessary element the notion of self-mastery, or what is more often understood in terms of the will.

While the master proves no better than the egocentric brute to which he would reduce the slave, the master nonetheless contributes what for Hegel is the crucial element in the abstract idea of freedom. In the battle for recognition, the master exhibits a will that is stronger than his desire.

The asceticism of the slave begins in the slave's escapist withdrawal from the material world. No longer slave of the master because servant of a higher authority—first the Christian god and finally the Hegelian *Geist*—

the slave performs the labor of the negative, and thus the cathartic movement of history.

For Hegel, freedom cannot be understood apart from self-control, where self-control is interpreted in terms of the sublation of sensuality in what is called reason.

The Slave as the Liminal Self

It is under conditions of extreme oppression that the slave must reconstruct an idea of the free self. According to Hegel, while the body of the slave serves as instrument, even—as we know from African American slave narratives—raped victim, for the pleasure and power of the master, the slave finds his essential self in a realm of pure thought. The progress of humanity toward universal freedom requires an intermediate step in which the slave proves indifferent to his fears and passions. Rather than giving in to his desires, he must dedicate himself to the purposes of work and, finally, to the common purposes of humanity that Hegel interprets as spirit.

It is suspicious, however, that as Hegel understands the slave, he happens to serve the project of the *Phenomenology*, and thus a master narrative of European history. In particular, I wonder whether Hegel comprehends the slave from the perspective of the slave or, on the contrary, reduces the position of the non-European slave to a function in a master European discourse?

From the master's perspective, the slave performs two roles. Inasmuch as the master represents himself through the negation of the passive pleasures of the appetites, the slave must play the role of what in nineteenth-century American slavery is called the "Sambo," i.e., the "child-like" or "castrated" creature who serves the will of another.[27] Inasmuch as the master represents himself through the negation of predatory and sexual drives, the slave represents the violent and overly sexual "brute." In either case, the slave is seen as a body without a face, the passive child, uncontrollable beast, woman, primitive African, etc., without the will to be a man.

By the very fact that the slave serves as an instrument of the master's desires the master gains a sense of self. For through the continual subordination of the slave the master reenacts the mastery of his desires or appetites. Therefore, the master is not only physically dependent upon the slave's labor; the master also depends upon the slave, with whom he struggles for a sense of self. For Hegel, there is no sense of self that is not vulnerable to the processes of intersubjectivity, or the complex dynamics of recognition. The master cannot gain a sense of self without looking into the eyes of the Other with whom, according to Hegel, he must do battle.[28] The master finds verification that he has won the battle of the wills through averted gaze, bowed head, and other signs of deference of the slave. There is no self apart from the dynamics of recognition.

Hegel's concept of self-mastery, as it originates in the master and develops in the slave, projects a dynamic of freedom that in some respects is more useful than that of modern philosophy. For Hegel, freedom is primarily measured not in terms of an economic concern for controlling one's property but in terms of social and psychological needs for overcoming alienation and acquiring respect from others. By locating freedom in intersubjectivity, Hegel rejects the Anglo-American myth of the self-reliant individual who is most free when he is least dependent upon others. If the self is constituted through the social processes of recognition, then the self can only be free through its dependency upon the Other.

Hegel's analysis of the origins of freedom is faulty, however, inasmuch as his phenomenology of self-consciousness does not provide access to the alterity of other persons and non-European cultures. That is, inasmuch as Hegel's understanding of the psychology of the nineteenth-century slave turns out to reflect nothing more than the master's encounter with his own liminal self, the dialectical positioning of the free self in intersubjectivity collapses into reflections on the egocentric self of European modernism.

Hegel demonstrates that the intersubjectivity between master and slave is marred by the asymmetries of power. It is these asymmetries that create distortions in the dynamics of mutual recognition and that drive the slave to alter the conditions of what is called freedom and manhood. While Hegel's concept of freedom as intersubjective rather than atomistic cannot be fully developed in the dialectic of master and slave, the concept of freedom nonetheless originates in that dialectic. Therefore, we must ask whether Hegel adequately understands the relation between master and slave not only from the point of view of the master but also from that of the slave. Did the slave see him- or herself in terms of an infantile passivity or animal primitivism reflected off of the face of the master?

The African American Experience of Slavery

In a historical and cross-cultural study of the patterns of slavery, Orlando

Patterson provides some factual evidence in support of what Hegel argues to be the social and psychological dependency of master on slave. At least under certain conditions, the powerful depend upon the deference accorded by the powerless for what Patterson analyzes in terms of honor and what I am identifying as a dominant and problematic expression of manhood.[29] Patterson explicitly cites Hegel in order to account for the ironies of domination in slavery: "As Georg Hegel realized, total personal power taken to its extreme contradicts itself by its very existence, for total domination can become a form of extreme dependence on the object of one's power, and total powerlessness can become the secret path to control of the subject that attempts to exercise power" (SSD, 2). Patterson also provides a distinction that points to the conditions under which domination would turn into dependency. Patterson contrasts what he calls the "liminal social status" of the slave with the less paradoxical status of the "outcast," who, as a kind of "untouchable," is excluded from the community altogether. If we use this distinction, it is the invisible outcast, and not the slave as liminal other, who would exemplify the pre-Hegelian, or classical, concept of slavery. The classical concept neglects the peculiar social ironies of slavery and consigns the slave to the less problematic status of tool. On the other hand, according to Patterson, the slave, unlike the outcast, "was marginal, neither human nor inhuman, neither man nor beast, neither dead nor alive, the enemy within who was neither member nor true alien" (SSD, 48).

Hegel's interpretation of the contorted intersubjectivity between master and slave accounts for the peculiar status of the slave as a liminal person within a social system. The slave must be a person inasmuch as the master seeks from the slave recognition. Without the deference accorded by the slave, the master's sense of self crumbles. At the same time, the slave is used to satisfy the appetites and desires of the master and reflects the master's animal-like existence. The slave is perceived as lacking a will and therefore depending upon the master for a sense of purpose. As a consequence of his liminal status, the slave loses not only physical freedom but suffers social alienation, or what Patterson terms "social death." Unlike the "outcast" (to use Patterson's terms), whose exclusion from the social system is total, the slave exists as dialectical contradiction and therefore as an instability in the system and an impetus toward social change.

However, while Patterson argues that the master might seek to confirm his sense of self through the subordination of the slave (and everything the slave represents) he, along with Hegel scholar Allen Wood, argues that Hegel fails to allow for the possibility that the master could find recognition from other slaveholders.[30] If this is the case, the master could avoid the implosive paradox of slave as thing-and-person and use the slave (like the outcast) solely as an instrument of power. According to Patterson, the master not only could in theory but did in practice (e.g., in American slavery) preempt the alleged dynamic for change by satisfying the need for recognition through interactions with other free persons. Patterson and Wood argue that by relegating the slave to the nondialectical and thus unproblematic status of thing or animal, slavery and other extreme forms of oppression continue to acquire stability.

Hegel's argument, however, is somewhat stronger. The passages from the *Phenomenology* imply that the kind of recognition that one slaveholder might gain through another slaveholder could only constitute a fraud. At least for the particular kind of self that Hegel conceptualizes, there is a necessary connection between the demand for recognition and a battle of wills. The master wills not the body nor even the desire but the very will of the Other, and to get it he must prove that he can stand up against his desires when the slave cannot. He cannot acquire this recognition from other slaveholders because they have not resisted his will and therefore have not proved to be sources of willful purpose in their own right. The acknowledgment of one slaveholder's honor by another slaveholder—without a contest—*proves* nothing. Like any number of other defaults (e.g., the death of one of the contestants in the battle for recognition), the mere acknowledgment of honor signifies nothing and therefore can at best constitute a dead end, so to speak, in the history of freedom.

The master no doubt shares interests with other slaveholders (e.g., in the institution of slavery), and in this sense there is something like a common purpose or even, loosely speaking, a common will. However, the notion of honor or will, as Hegel conceptualizes it, cannot be based on the self-interest of the instrumental self. On the contrary, one receives recognition only by staking interests and desires in the name of a higher conception of freedom. Therefore, without a contest of wills—a contest that involves the risks of slavery and death for both parties—acknowledgment of honor is hollow. Proof of manly honor requires that one encounter the Other in his Otherness and proceed to challenge ("negate") that alien will.

Freedom, as Hegel understands it, is realized only in the symmetry of mutual recognition, and this symmetry requires a shared sense of purpose. This sense of shared purpose, or common will, is not, however, equivalent to shared interests. Hegel's conception of freedom requires a sense of honor that is distinct from the more practical and utilitarian concerns of the instrumental self, or what Hegel understands as so-called animal satisfactions.

Hegel's strong claim regarding the *social* and *psychological*, and not simply economic, dependency of the master on the slave finds supporting evidence in African American slave narratives. For example, Frederick Douglass often remarks that the gravest of all crimes committed by the slave is neither idleness nor even the destruction of property but sheer impudence.[31] My claim is that impudence would threaten the master only if the master depends upon the oppression of the slave not simply as property but for a sense of self, and that the master cannot obtain this sense of self elsewhere. The socio-psychological dependence of white master on black slave can also serve to explain, at least in part, why the South refused offers from President Lincoln for compensated emancipation and the colonization of blacks.[32]

Because the master depends upon the oppression of the slave not only for labor but also for a sense of self, slavery (or, by analogy, any form of oppression that produces persons of liminal social status) proves to be an inherently self-destructive institution. It is Hegel's understanding of the social pathology of domination, and its inherent dynamic toward change, that constitutes an advance over the classical conception of the slave as akin to the tool or other property.

Nonetheless, Hegel's incomplete familiarity with historical accounts of slavery also blinds him to a fundamental error in dialectical logic. While the slave may serve as mirror for the master, it is not at all clear that the master serves as mirror for the slave. As Patterson observes, masters deceived themselves as to the true cleverness of their slaves, hardly knowing their slaves as well as their slaves knew them (*SSD*, 338). For example, while the African American slave might perform the Sambo role before the master, there is, Patterson argues, historical evidence that slaves played the role as a farce (*SSD*, 96; cf. 337–38). As historian John Blassingame argues, many African American slaves developed a strong sense of identity apart from the roles they played for their masters.[33] These slaves managed not to internalize the projections of the dominant culture and turned to African-based communities for a sense of self.

American slaveholders obtained slaves through kidnapping or various forms of trading and not through conquest of the slave in battle. Nonetheless, the identity of the slaveholder as well as the legitimation of slaveholding would often make use of the mythology (what Hegel calls the phenomenology) of heroic conquest. Slaveholders (e.g., Captain Auld or Colonel Lloyd in the Douglass narratives) would adopt for themselves military titles or otherwise perpetuate the image of the plantation as a battleground where deference was earned.

It is also the case that some American slaves displayed a willingness to risk their own lives before the slaveholders in order to defend their honor or even the honor of other slaves (*SC*, 211–12).[34]

But if the sense of manhood invoked at least on occasion by the African American slave exhibits the warrior's courage, this construct cannot be assimilated into the Hegelian model of the slaveholding master. The ascetic European tradition defines freedom as the "absolute negation" of desire and this negation in terms of a cathartic "rooting-out all immediate existence." Hegel preserves this negation even as he sublates it in his conceptualization of the universal Spirit. For example, the rational will that develops, according to Hegel, out of slavery emerges in opposition to affective and other embodied dimensions of the self. The store will aims to control or otherwise master these desires. On the other hand, the African American brings a culture that does not aim to abstract from but on the contrary may aim to intensify desire and yet have reason on its side. For example, in his complex analysis of the 1831 slave rebellion of Nat Turner, Eric Sundquist argues that the "excessive emotionalism" or even "messianic passion" of its rebel leader expressed a "'rational' political intelligence."[35] It is a variation on an ecstatic model of the self in various African American cultures (in contrast with the cathartic models that predominate in European cultures) that I shall explore in the remaining chapters.

While the standard Hegelian reading of slavery assumes that the slave lacks the courage (and thus the will) to resist oppression in open struggle and would instead redefine freedom through the kind of virtues that are acquired in alienated labor, a different picture emerges from the history of American slavery. As Sundquist documents,

Black antislavery, some time before the advent of [Frederick] Douglass, did not hesitate to invoke violent resistance, and Henry Highland Garnet provided one of the most striking articulations of a countertradition of black American patriotism in his 1843 "Address to the Slaves of the United States of America." Berating slaves for their timidity, challenging their manhood ... , Garnet asked: "Where is the blood of your fathers? Has it all run out of your veins? Awake, awake; millions of voices are calling you!" (*WN*, 66)[36]

While European Christianity attempted to "instill docile passivity" among the slaves, Sundquist notes that "black spirituals were often laden with messages of resistance ... and that Christ appeared in them less as a forgiving, benevolent savior than as a warrior-leader" (*WN*, 57). Hegel's tale of the history of slavery from stoic resignation and Christian alienation to Christian forgiveness appropriates the values of European dualism, or what Nietzsche critiques as European asceticism, and therefore cannot reflect the militant spirituality that defines one significant strand of African American history.

Finally, while European slaves, including the indentured servants who emigrated to America, defined themselves through the discipline of work, blacks, as Paul Gilroy argues, are more likely to equate work with slavery, not freedom, and define themselves through music and other expressive dimensions of black culture.[37] Those slaves who were forced to devote their lives to labor in the fields did not, as did whites, separate their work from emotive forms of self-expression but, according to historian Eugene Genovese, measured their work by the rhythms of their song.[38] Black slaves and ex-slaves resisted demands for regulating their labor in accordance with what social historians term the "industrial morality" of the North. As historian David Roediger demonstrates, white American immigrants internalized ascetic Protestantism in accordance with the demands of the white work ethic.[39] These immigrants, Roediger explains, derived a sense of self by identifying whiteness with worker and in opposition to blackness and slavery. Thus the repressed worker imitated the master-boss by expressing himself through the punitive control over those who did not subject themselves to the ascetic drive of European culture. On the other hand, slave culture in America culminated not in the repression of the enslaved body through the discipline of the worker, and the abstract and technical rationality that ensues, but in the expression of the lived black body in the erotic energy of the spiritual. Therefore, Hegel's phenomenology of slavery as stoic withdrawal from materiality introduces into his conception of freedom an ideology of Euro-Christian asceticism that does not fit African American slave culture.

Black Dialectic/White Dialectic

The symmetries of dialectical logic require that the master serve as the mirror-opposite for the slave just as the slave serves as mirror-opposite for the master. Hegel constructs the position of the slave in terms of the dialectical moment of "negation." According to Hegel, the slave represents what the master would overcome. The master aims to prove he can discipline instinctual drives in the name of a higher sense of self. His attempts to control the slave are in part to prove that he can control himself. The slave represents for the master animalistic desire and/or infantile appetites that the master has under control. However, if, as historians of African American slavery argue, the deference accorded by the slave to the master was a farce, then the slave has not internalized the animal-like or child-like roles performed for the master.

But if master and slave live in two at least partly distinct worlds, then the dialectical history of the slave does not correlate with the dialectical history of the master. The problem for dialectical phenomenology is that it cannot find its way out of a mirror-like logic that subordinates difference to identity.[40] Of course, Hegelian logic is not a simple logic of identity. The alterity of the master as represented in the slave is not excluded from dialectical phenomenology as it would be from a more linear conception of selfhood and freedom. It is this alterity of the master that drives the dialectic forward. The limitation of Hegelian logic is that it lacks a concept of alterity that is strong enough to support a concept of freedom as the mediated difference of intersubjectivity, where this intersubjectivity crosses over Eurocentric and Afrocentric cultures. A genuine concept of freedom as recognition must account for a difference that is not a shadow of the same.

The discoveries of psychoanalytic theory cause us to suspect that the projection (through dialectical negation) of animal- or child-like desires onto the slave betrays the symptoms of an impossible self-mastery on the part of the slaveholder. So too arises the suspicion that the master does not so much transform (or sublate) as frustrate (or repress) his desires. But then the adumbration of the liminal self in the image of the slave must pose a constant threat to the identity of the master. While I have critiqued the specific models of childhood or animality that inform traditional psychoanalytic theories (see parts 1 and 2), my discussion supports one of the major assumptions of psychoanalytic theory: Significant features of our childhood persist in the adult self. The self that would transcend childhood desires or the animal self necessarily depends upon dimensions of itself that it cannot accept. Therefore, the master needs the slave not only for rituals of deference but also to play out the fantasies of his own repressed self. The antinature and hypertranscendent stance taken by the master demands a servant to do his living for him.

Hegel's master does not fully encounter the Other. Instead he projects onto the Other his own unmastered desires. Thus, Hegel's concept of freedom as intersubjectivity complicates but does not advance beyond a modernist concept of freedom as individual self-restraint.[41] Moreover, the concept of freedom as the dialectical negation of biological appetites and animal desire goes hand in hand with Hegel's appropriation of the modernist prejudice against so-called primitive cultures. Religions of flowers and animals, Hegel argues in a later section of the *Phenomenology*, are not religions of freedom (*PS*, sec. 689). But while Hegelian Spirit sublates the worship of flowers and animals among "primitive peoples" in the name of a more European concept of the free self, the bearers of those so-called primitive desires return to reclaim history.

For finally what European dialectic fails to acknowledge is what the master fails to acknowledge: that mastery subsists—not only in its economics but also in its imaginary—upon what a master discourse of European origin cannot control. No wonder the oppressed provokes not only rage and fear but a peculiar attraction for the oppressor. But therefore too, what the oppressor apprehends of that "primitive consciousness" belongs not to the Other but to alien dimensions of the Self. Chapters 6 and 7 take up a model of selfhood and freedom that lies outside of the dialectical oppositions recounted by Hegel. This alternative model develops out of the slave narratives of the mulatto American, Frederick Douglass.[42]

· 6 ·

A Slave Narrative of Freedom

Frederick Douglass and the Force of Manhood

Silent submission ... is bound to sap the manhood of any race.
W. E. B. Du Bois

The white race will only respect those who oppose their usurpation.
Martin R. Delany

For me identity is fundamentally about desire and death: desire for recognition,
quest for visibility.... Persons who construct their identities and desires often do
it in such a way that they're willing to die for it ... or ... kill others....
That's what's frightening ... it's a shaking of the rationalist foundation.
Cornel West

One of the crucial questions concerning the slave narratives of Frederick
Douglass as well as those of other African Americans is to what degree these
narratives are able to express freely an African consciousness as opposed to
reflecting dominant European or Euro-American modes of self-expression.
At the time that Douglass is writing his slave narratives, the "master narratives" projected by Enlightenment and dialectical philosophies of freedom
control the intellectual scene in Europe and European America. As argued
in chapter 5, Hegel's *Phenomenology of Spirit* contributes what may be the
most powerful analysis of slavery and freedom in any classical European
text.[1] Hegel draws upon the tropic resources of dialectic in order to demonstrate the dependency not only of slave on master but also of master on
slave. In fact, according to Hegel, it is this second dependency that is more
revealing. For the great irony of history, Hegel demonstrates, is that the
European slave and not the master constructs the idea of freedom that
drives history forward. The question is, can this master discourse of
European culture narrate a history of freedom for the African American

slave? Or might it be that the master narrative of Europe would depend upon the narratives of non-European slaves for a more inclusive conception of freedom?[2]

Perhaps it is because Hegel attempts to recapture the contribution of the slave (albeit the European slave) as central among the forces of history that he develops a more suggestive trajectory of freedom for the African in America than that which is found in the Enlightenment philosophy of Anglo-America. In particular, Hegel breaks from the atomistic model of the self that grounds Anglo-American conceptions of freedom and proposes instead a vision of the self as fundamentally social. As I shall argue, it is a nineteenth-century dialectic of freedom as recognition rather than a modernist concept of freedom as individual choice that animates the slave narratives of Frederick Douglass.[3]

The Douglass narratives, however, do not simply assimilate a European model of freedom without asserting a difference. On the contrary, these slave narratives transform significant normative and epistemological strands of what Hegel represents as the history of freedom in the West. In particular, these slave narratives reject what Hegel locates as the stoic underpinnings of the Western conceptions of freedom and reason. Hegel claims to have uncovered a historical condition for freedom when he argues that the slave exemplifies that stage in the development of the self that aims to overcome the natural proclivity toward sensuality and to acquire the discipline of the rational will. He traces the origin of the modern concepts of freedom and reason to the stoics, who were able to construct an experience of freedom in slavery by severing an inner self from desire and sensuous existence. The stoics defined their essential self in a realm of reason alone. While Hegel argues that the inward spirit of the stoic must eventually reconnect with the ethical practices of the community, the Western project as Hegel represents it perpetuates a repressive asceticism that recalls (or preserves in the sense of *Aufhebung*) its stoic origins. Hegel exemplifies the asceticism of Western models of rationality when he proclaims that his *Phenomenology* purges or otherwise sublates the sensuous dimensions of cultural experience in order to instate a total concept-based knowledge (*PS*, sec. 787, "Absolute Spirit"). In contemporary terms, Hegel's *Phenomenology* privileges the disciplinary practices of a culture based on literacy over the expressive and social resources of cultures that are oral.

The autobiographies of Frederick Douglass portray an image of selfhood that challenges both liberal and dialectical variants of European asceticism and incorporates the desires, passions, and concrete modes of expression of sensuous human existence and oral African American culture.[4] Douglass thereby parts with mainstream Western traditions of freedom and reason. These traditions perpetuate a series of regressive dichotomies, crucially, the opposition between animal-like desire and the rational will, that are used to justify the domination of people who are deemed irrational, uncontrolled, primitive, etc., but who in fact are simply different. The European dichotomies are regressive not only because they sustain classic sources of domination embedded within such rational categories as race, gender, and culture[5] but because these dichotomies also sustain a nondiscursive pattern of images that associate blackness with irrational violence and whiteness with moral purity. Because the non-European African represents for the dominant white culture the negative of the self rather than a self that is different, in the white mind the black looms large as an ever-present threat to selfhood and sanity.

As I shall argue, the Douglass narratives traverse the abstract categories and concrete images of European culture in order to project a construct of freedom that is rooted in the social eroticism of the self and that challenges the very basis of what is called "reason" in the history of the West.[6] If my argument is correct, then the Western conceptions of freedom (liberal or dialectical) cannot provide a standard for social advance in racist America. On the contrary, the Western conceptions manifest a pathological detachment of the self from social desire and this pathology expresses itself in the dialectic of attraction and repulsion for the black body. Without the construct of freedom that is embedded within the Douglass narratives, we lack a way of theorizing one of the more fundamental sources of oppression for both white and black in America.

I am not arguing that the writings of Frederick Douglass develop the only or even the most advanced conception of freedom or selfhood. In fact, Douglass, who claimed a white father and a black mother, not only refused to identify with a European model of freedom; he also rejected black separatist movements (including the Afrocentric philosophy of Martin Delany) along with the ecstatic religiosity of black expressive culture. Following W. E. B. Du Bois, who argued that Douglass stood for "ultimate assimilation *through* self-assertion, and on no other terms," I shall argue that Douglass embraces a universalizing dialectic (not the abstract universal of modernist philosophies but the mediating and concrete universal of dialectic) that speaks to white and black Americans but reflects the specific mulatto origin of its maker.[7]

The Ecstasy of Struggle

Narrative of the Life of Frederick Douglass: An American Slave, written by Douglass in 1845, is sometimes regarded as heavily under the influence of William Lloyd Garrison and like-minded Christian abolitionists. These abolitionists located the basis for the self and social change in the dictates of moral purity and the resources of moral suasion and consequently renounced the use of violence or indeed any political action. Douglass, however, clearly centers the climax of his 1845 autobiography around a physical struggle between himself and the slavebreaker Mr. Covey. This struggle not only foreshadows his impending break with the Garrisonian abolitionists; the fact that Douglass focuses on the struggle as "the turning-point" in his life as a slave also constitutes in part his response to European expressions of freedom and selfhood. Moreover, while Douglass subordinates a second crucial event within the autobiography, the attainment of literacy, to his struggle with the slavebreaker, the theme of education interweaves an epistemological strand into the story of emancipation.

The twin themes of struggle and literacy define what Douglass identifies as the locus of questions of self-identity at the time of African slavery. Slavery was justified on the basis of the fact that blacks lacked two moral criteria of a person. First, the status of slavery was seen as proof that the slave lacked the will to be free. According to the argument, if the slave truly possessed the manly virtue of courage, then he would rather be dead than a slave.[8] Secondly, because African-based culture did not express itself in the European logos, which in the nineteenth century was primarily interpreted in terms of the skills of abstraction acquired in learning to read an alphabetic script, blacks were thought to lack the rationality that defined the fully developed human being. The Douglass narratives demonstrate not just that the black can measure up to the European standards of the person. More than this, these narratives aim to alter the criteria of a moral person. This transformation of the identity of the self would be, according to Douglass, the basis for a second American Revolution.

The central elements in Douglass's confrontation with the slavebreaker express both a kinship and a difference from those dominant European conceptions of the self that are centered on the will. Of central importance is the fact that the encounter demonstrates that this black slave does indeed possess that relevant virtue of the moral person that was to divide the slave mentality of the inferior creature from the assertive will of the sovereign individual. The details of the struggle, however, suggest that the will exhibited by Douglass in struggle differs from its European variants. Elementary to this model of manhood is not necessarily an ethics of regenerative violence (à la Frantz Fanon) but certainly a force that asserts itself in the world.

The critical struggle occurs after Douglass appeals to his owner against what Douglass perceives to be arbitrary punishment at the hands of the slavebreaker. The slaveowner, who in nineteenth-century slave ideology is posed as a father, fails to intervene. Douglass returns to the slavebreaker. Douglass writes:

> I was called to go and rub, curry, and feed, the horses. I obeyed, and was glad to obey. But whilst thus engaged, ... Mr. Covey entered the stable with a long rope; and just as I was half out of the loft, he caught hold of my legs, and was about tying me.... Mr. Covey seemed now to think he had me, and could do what he pleased; but at this moment—from whence came the spirit I don't know—I resolved to fight.[9]

Covey backs off. Douglass concludes:

> This battle ... was the turning-point in my career as a slave. It rekindled the few expiring embers of freedom, and revived within me a sense of my own manhood.... The gratification afforded by the triumph was a full compensation for whatever else might follow, even death itself.... I resolved that, however long I might remain a slave in form, the day had passed forever when I could be a slave in fact. I did not hesitate to let it be known of me, that the white man who expected to succeed in whipping, must also succeed in killing me. (N, 113)

While the will to struggle evidenced in this passage does prove the manhood (and hence the moral status) of the slave, it does not exactly fit the various models of the self that develop in white culture. Most significantly, as I shall argue in this chapter, the black self forged through the visceral dynamics of struggle with the oppressive Other exceeds eighteenth- and nineteenth-century projects of grounding a moral self either exclusively or dialectically in the rational will. As I have argued in chapter 5, according to the European models, the rational will is defined through abstraction from (or what Hegel terms the "absolute negation" of) desire, affect, or other embodied dimensions of the self. In America the Garrisonians exemplified this conception of the self. According to the view, the rational will (or again, the moral locus of the person) is fully assessed through moral reasoning stripped bare of physical, emotive, or political force. My claim is, if the self is fundamentally embodied, then to strip the self of its force is to destroy it. And this of course is the strategy not only of rationalism but also of slavery and other forms of oppression.

According to the *Phenomenology*, the origin of the doctrine of the rational will lies in stoicism, which, the *Phenomenology* also claims, is not only the authentic philosophy of slavery but also the real beginnings of "thought" (*PS*, sec. 199). Throughout Hegel's philosophy is found the argument that the slavish human animal (the primary example in modern European culture is the African) requires the disciplinary practices of slavery in order to act in accordance with rational thought. Because human nature tends to succumb to the blind impulses of desire, slavery is a historical condition for the development of freedom. Hegel's narrative of freedom does favor the position of the slave over that of the master. But according to Hegel this eventual victory of the self-consciousness of the slave is due to the fact that once the conquering master returns home to enjoy the fruits of slave labor, he becomes soft. The core element of the slaveholder's sense of self is refocused from the death-defying quest for honor to the satisfaction of desires served by the slave. Meanwhile, the slave who is white (unlike the slave who is black) is able to turn inward, sever the mind from the flesh, and devote himself to abstraction. The Western project of freedom develops out of the stoicism of the slave.

The philosophy of freedom in the slave narratives of Douglass is not stoic. Behind his conception of freedom lies a notion of the self that is not based on the rational will. As Hegel has made clear, the rational will emerges in European history from a self-effacing retreat of the slave into quietism. Differences between Douglass and the European-based model of freedom that would be exemplified in the Garrisonians intensify with the publication of the 1855 revision of the autobiography, *My Bondage and My Freedom*.[10] Again the autobiography turns on the encounter between Douglass and the slavebreaker. This time, however, Douglass adds a direct commentary to his description of the critical event. The act of self-assertion implied in the inclusion of commentary is itself already indicative of Douglass's strengthened position vis-à-vis the Garrisonians. The Garrisonians required that colored men serving the cause of the abolitionists restrict themselves to reporting the bare facts of slavery. The interpretation of the facts, and therefore the power to define the goals of the movement, was to remain in the hands of the white abolitionist leaders. Therefore, Douglass's insertion of direct commentary into his story of slavery would already in itself constitute a challenge to white domination, in this case the domination exercised by the white abolitionists over black fugitives from slavery.

"A man, without force," Douglass comments, "is without the essential dignity of humanity. Human nature is so constituted, that it cannot *honor* a helpless man, although it can *pity* him; and even this it cannot do long, if the signs of power do not arise."[11] By envisioning the manhood of the slave in the spirit of struggle, rather than in stoic retreat, Douglass rejects what Hegel recapitulates as the necessary education of the slave to freedom in the West through the alienation of desire and the imagination in the cathartic exercises of duty-bound labor and abstract reason.[12] For Douglass, the freedom of thought for the black slave begins with the intensification of desire and its expression in the will to resist degradation through the moral, physical, or political force of struggle.

At the same time the commentary makes clear that Douglass rejected the ethics of sentimentality (a predecessor of contemporary care ethics) that opposed the modern rationalist philosophies in eighteenth- and nineteenth-century Europe and America.[13] The rhetoric of sentimentality no less than the Enlightenment project of educating the slave up to the standards of European reason could only support nineteenth-century forms of paternalism (among both the slaveholders and white abolitionists), which took its pleasure in stripping the slave of moral authority. According to this paternalism, the child-like adult (or "Sambo") no less than the child lacks the rational will that defines the person, and therefore would depend upon the moral agency of the great white father (replaced in contemporary care ethics by the white middle-class mother). The oppressed who poses himself as victim before the sympathetic gaze of the paternal (or maternal) Other only strengthens the ideology of oppression. Seeking not sympathy but respect from his oppressor, Douglass rejects any normative philosophy that would further the infantilization of the oppressed and embraces instead the spirited conception of the self as agent of resistance—as freedom fighter.[14]

Writing the Self: Douglass versus Foucault on Literacy

Douglass interweaves the acquisition of literacy as a second major theme into the dialectic of freedom. While Hegel argues that the abstract skills developed in the acquisition of the alphabetic script are essential for the development of mind, he does not address the emancipatory function of literacy in his account of stoicism and slave culture. This oversight on the part of Hegel becomes more evident when we compare his analysis of stoicism with that of Michel Foucault. Like Hegel, Foucault discounts any strong thesis with regard to human agency in history and focuses instead on the emancipatory effect of stoic retreat into a program for the "care of the self." However, unlike Hegel, Foucault adds to his analysis of stoicism a discussion of literacy.

According to Foucault, the literacy of the stoic strengthened the resources of the inner self against the insurmountable forces of fate. As Foucault explains, "The stoics say you must attend to the self, 'retire into the self and stay there.' ... Writing was also important in the culture of taking care of oneself.... The self is something to write about, a theme or object (subject) of writing activity. That is not a modern trait born of the Reformation or of romanticism."[15] What Foucault does not say is that the self that is quintessentially the object of writing is acquired through the alienation of the mind from social and expressive modalities of oral cultures.

A crucial element of the culture of the stoic, Foucault notes, is what the Greeks understood as *askesis*, or the particular practices to which education is put. If, "for the stoics, the truth is not in oneself but in the *logoi*, the teaching of the teachers," among the uses of these teachings, according to Foucault, are the "eidetic reductions of future misfortune" (*TS*, 35). For example, one might imagine oneself in situations of various forms of suffering such as torture or poverty "in order to convince oneself that they are not real ills" (*TS*, 36). These practices do not encourage the stoic to challenge the sources of suffering but instead provide techniques for numbing the flesh against one's fate. The stoic forms a sense of self by undergoing ritualized tests of suffering, purification, or even self-mortification.

What is striking about Douglass's account of how he acquires a sense of self in slavery is that it eschews the path of outer obedience and inner retreat and in the process fundamentally reconstrues the role of writing in the education of the slave. While Douglass spends much of his life as an ex-slave reworking his autobiographies and writing for his newspapers, he

adds to the account of his "turning-point" as a slave the following dis-
claimer: "My learning—it was really precious little," for "book learning...
[as the slave Sandy had said] had not kept Covey [the slavebreaker] off of
me" (*BF*, 147). Contrary to the practices of the European stoics, Douglass
does not rely upon a mastery of the European *logoi* or the abstract produc-
tions of the rational mind in order to establish a sphere of freedom and
declare his status as a person. The achievement of literacy is, at least for
Douglass, embedded in the process of self-transformation not in lieu of but
via social and cultural change. This is a process that must enlist the "force"
of "manhood" exercised in struggle. In his autobiographical narratives,
Douglass in effect renounces what Hegel elaborates in terms of the
"inwardizing" of the European spirit and struggles for a kind of recognition that is reminiscent of the self-consciousness of the Hegelian master.
Unlike the stoic, Douglass refuses to await the reconciliations of the supra-
individual spirit of nineteenth-century Christian European and Euro-
American culture. Douglass instead rekindles the "spirit" of "manhood"
within himself and thereby becomes an agent for historical change.[16]

The question is, what is this spirit of freedom that Douglass calls forth?
Does this spirit betray a particular cultural or racial affinity? Does it exclude
women from participating in the rituals that constitute the self and in the
narratives that define social progress?

Liberal and Dialectical Constructions of Manhood

The tendency among the many literary scholars and social theorists who
have made passing reference to the connection between the dialectic of the
master and slave in the writings of Douglass and Hegel is to draw parallels
between Douglass's struggle for recognition and the self-consciousness not
of the slave but of the "master" in the *Phenomenology*. Specifically, the black
slave stakes his biological life and/or economic well-being (what Hegel associates with an animal-like existence) in order to display the self as will. By
subordinating the theme of literacy to the struggle with the slavebreaker, the
narratives anchor Douglass's conception of self in the spirited will of Hegel's
sovereign master rather than in the rational will of Europe's stoic slave.

The significance of this reversal as well as the specifics of its interpretation, however, are not at all clear. Paul Gilroy makes the connection
between Douglass and Hegel and goes on to draw one important implication. As Gilroy argues, Douglass's departure from the pacifism of the white

Christian abolitionists "is directly relevant to his critical understanding of modernity. It underscored the complicity of civilization and brutality while emphasizing that the order of authority on which the slave plantation relied cannot be undone without recourse to the counter-violence of the oppressed" (*BA*, 63). By narrating the resistance of the slave in a discourse of honor, Douglass dares incorporate the will to violence into African American manhood. This identity of the colored man transgresses what must be a moral taboo of specifically that paternalistic element of white society that was strong at the time that Douglass was writing. The black who refused to perform the role of the Sambo risked reviving monstrous images of the dark savage that have alternately haunted and delighted the European imaginary at least since the fifteenth century and in which Douglass traces a deep-rooted pathology of white culture.[17]

While I agree with this implication of Douglass's stance, Gilroy's specific account of the kinship between Douglass's self-portrait and the Hegelian sovereign master mistakenly links the will to resist to the death with the practice of slave suicide and the existential meaning of freedom that this practice might imply (*BA*, 63ff.).[18] For both Douglass and Hegel, the spirited warrior accepts the risk but not the necessity of death. According to Hegel, the certitude of death is experienced only by the slave mentality, which eventually succumbs to total despair. Of course, for Hegel, it is the alienation of the slave mentality that gives rise to Western culture. On the other hand, Douglass clearly aligns himself with the position of the Hegelian master when he indicates his disrespect for suicidal projects and lets it be known that the valiant slave should not rebel when the odds against him are overwhelming. But this similarity only strengthens the comparison between the self-consciousness of the Hegelian master and that sought by Douglass for himself and the other ex-slaves.

This kinship is nonetheless not enough to establish that Douglass was in some definitive sense an Hegelian. The idea that manhood emerges through a struggle of the wills, and thus that the criterial test of the moral person resides in the will, appears not only in the Romantic motifs that are conceptualized in Hegel's *Phenomenology;* the notion of virile struggle occurs already in the modernist culture of Enlightenment America. Throughout his writings and speeches, Douglass appropriates the motto of revolutionary America, the call for liberty or death, in order to prepare for the resistance of the colored man to slavery (e.g., *N*, 124). The black slave, like the white revolutionary, would forge an identity not in alienated service to a greater power but in the struggle for "freedom."

In fact, according to Eric Sundquist, it is the Enlightenment philosophy of the self-made man that controls the Douglass narratives. Sundquist cites as evidence Douglass's desire to overcome his status as "a *'chattel'*—a *'thing'*—a piece of southern *'property'*" and take possession of his body and his life as his own.[19] Sundquist then draws the conclusion that Douglass's attempt to control the meaning of his life through the various revisions of the autobiographies further locates Douglass in "America's revolutionary tradition of liberal individualism and ... [its] principles of autonomy, property, and equal rights" (*WN*, 90).

There is, however, a distinction between the eighteenth-century Enlightenment concept of freedom as autonomy and a nineteenth-century dialectical concept of freedom that leaves its mark in the Douglass narratives. The Enlightenment concept of autonomy not only frees the individual from patriarchal authority and religious superstitions; it would also uproot the individual from social, historical, and intersubjective resources of selfhood. Anglo-American philosophy posits the atomic individual as the natural condition of the self and as the foundation of society. The dignity of the person resides in the capacity to exercise rational self-restraint over anarchic desires. Since the person is defined in terms of ownership over his own life, autonomy is primarily understood as possessive individualism, or in terms of property rights.

The interpretation of freedom in terms of what Douglass calls "honor" and what Hegel terms "recognition" begins with the assumption that the individual constitutes a sense of Self only in dialectic with the Other. Freedom does not signify most originally the rights of self-ownership but intersubjective recognition, or, as Cornel West aptly puts it, a quest for visibility together with a deep, visceral need to belong.[20]

Douglass indicates his allegiance to a notion of freedom as recognition most directly in an 1863 speech, delivered in the Church of the Puritans, entitled "The Present and Future of the Colored Race in America." In this speech, Douglass accuses the Northern people of a "compromising servility" to the slave power of the South and proceeds to attack not only the institution of slavery in the South but also the social prejudice against the colored race in the North. While Douglass sees no satisfactory argument one way or the other regarding the socialist concern for the equal distribution of property, he also does not simply fall back on a liberal conception of freedom as self-ownership and its attendant political rights. On the contrary, Douglass explains, "the depressing power of oppression" means that "as a people we have moved about among you like a dwarf among giants—too small to be seen. We were morally, politically, and socially dead."[21] It is in particular the moral and social death of the slave that the ideal of freedom is to address.

Therefore, it is not only inequality in political or economic spheres but more specifically moral and social alienation in an antiblack culture that demands what Douglass looks for in the Civil War, namely, a second American Revolution. "The one [i.e., the first American Revolution] had respect to the mere political birth of a nation, the last [i.e., the second American Revolution] concerns the national life and character, and is to determine whether that life and character shall be radiantly glorious with all high and noble virtues, or infamously blackened" (*LWFD* 3, 306). In a speech several months later, Douglass calls forth in the people a "martial spirit" that would challenge the slaveholding practices of the South. The final goal of the struggle would be to "reform the national heart, quicken the national conscience, root out wicked prejudices, ... and destroy the great moral evils" (*LWFD* 3, 338). Clearly, the second revolution would not restrict its goal to the establishment of political or economic rights but would aim instead to reconstruct the national spirit. Douglass's use of the language of revolution indicates that he does not think that the problems of racism can be remedied by actualizing a potential for freedom already embedded within American culture. On the contrary, the revolution against racism would have to root out colorphobia—i.e., the moral and social pathology that runs through antiblack cultures, and that includes among its symptoms the American conception of freedom.

Douglass, like Hegel, appropriates aspects of the Enlightenment concept of self-ownership and the American work ethic that this concept supports in his critique of economic and political slavery. For example, Douglass contrasts the use of the whip to drive slave labor and the self-regulated work of free ship workers: "I saw no whipping of men; but all seemed to go smoothly on. Every man appeared to understand his work, and went at it with a sober, yet cheerful earnestness, which betokened the deep interest which he felt in what he was doing, as well as a sense of his own dignity as a man" (*N*, 148). Similarly, Douglass remarks on the injustice of surrendering the wages for his work as a calker over to his master, Hugh Auld (*N*, 135).

However, Douglass does not see the dialectic of freedom as residing primarily in the individual and his or her right to self-ownership but more potently in the recognition gained in struggle. If in his *Narrative* Douglass does commend the sense of self-worth that accrues to one who owns his body and the fruits of his labor, in general Douglass did not, according to biographer Waldo Martin, show much interest in black labor union movements.[22] My argument is that this lack of interest in the cause of workers is due not to what Waldo Martin takes as an overly intellectualized lifestyle but to a revolutionary social vision.

Clearly, in his autobiographies as well as in his fictive narrative, Douglass subordinates his concern for the power of self-ownership to a social struggle for "honor" in an antiblack culture. Throughout these writings, the slave generates self-respect by asserting the counterforce of his will against that of his oppressor. As he writes in *My Bondage*, the slave becomes a man when he acquires not power but "the *signs* of power" (*BF*, 152; emphasis mine). As I understand the distinction, Douglass strives not for power (or empowerment) per se, but for the intersubjective recognition of his power, or honor. Power and property in and of themselves signify nothing. Douglass can acquire "manly independence" only by way of proving himself to his Other—including even the slavebreaker. Without this proof of self before the Other, the slave no less than the slaveholder may acquire the comforts of property and power but lacks the identity of a self.

It has also been noted that the "strength, courage, and masculinity" of a Douglass protagonist "makes him a model classical hero with Old Testament and Greek analogues" (*WN*, 118). No doubt, Hegel's concept of the sovereign master similarly reinvokes a model of manhood as basic in the West as the Homeric heroes. However, the interpretation of manhood as a struggle for honor over self-preservation occurs not only in pre-Christian Western culture.[23] On the contrary, Hegel's analysis of the battle for recognition distills major narrative elements of a large number of historical, literary, and anthropological accounts of masculinity. What Gadamer, in his commentary on Hegel's concept of recognition, interprets in terms of "the institution of the duel—two people fighting it out to restore honor which has been offended"—offers only one variant of a more general phenomenon.[24] Anthropologist David Gilmore finds that near-death experiences and various win-or-lose tests of daring performed on a "public stage" constitute one of the more frequent rites of manhood across a number of cultures (*M*, 14). While not all struggles for recognition require physical combat, these struggles typically involve some threat of force (*M*, 14). Thus, by portraying the slave hero as a warrior, Douglass invokes a rite of manhood that does not so much imitate European practices as repeat what anthropologists identify as constant themes in the construction of a selfgendered male.

However, Douglass, like Hegel but distinctly unlike thinkers of the Enlightenment, does not discount the formative role of social and historical resources (including institutional practices) on the self. Hegel makes it clear that not only the struggle for recognition but the entire discussion of "Self-Consciousness" is an abstract moment of what he calls "Spirit," by which he means a larger social and historical context that supersedes the understanding or control of the individual. In a similar vein, Douglass argues that the institution of slavery is larger than the individuals within it. For example, Douglass explains that "the slaveholder, as well as the slave, is the victim of the slave system. A man's character greatly takes its hue and shape from the form and color of things about him" (*BF*, 54).[25] Similarly, in reflecting upon a slaveholder, Douglass writes, "Had the man no bowels of compassion? Was he dead to all sense of humanity? No. I think I now understand it. This treatment is a part of the system, rather than a part of the man" (*BF*, 56; cf. 77–78). Moreover, like Hegel, Douglass takes the forces of history to be inevitable. Again, in a speech in 1863, Douglass addresses the "Negro question." "The term, Negro, is at this hour the most pregnant word in the English language.... A divine energy, omniscient and omnipotent, acting through the silent, solemn and all pervading laws of the universe, irresistible, unalterable and eternal, has ever more forced this mighty question of the Negro upon the attention of the country and the world" (*LWFD* 3, 348).[26]

But if, like Hegel, Douglass acknowledges forces in history that are incommensurate with self-consciousness, unlike Hegel, Douglass casts off the model of the slave-cum-stoic and thereby challenges as "superstitions" what European cultures term "history." As I have argued, this does not return Douglass to the Enlightenment notion of the self-made man. For Douglass, the second American revolution, unlike the first, must begin with the premise that no individual is immune from the power of a dominant culture to weave a veil of prejudice within one's innermost concept of self.[27] Because there is no inner sanctum from the images projected by dominant cultures, the acquisition of self-respect cannot occur apart from a social struggle. Neither individual fortitude nor separatist communities can shield the oppressed from vulnerability before the gaze of the Other.[28] The psychology of self-respect must be reconceptualized through the social dynamics of recognition.

Black Spirituality

If Douglass's portrayal of manhood presents a variant of what Hegel conceptualizes as the self-consciousness of the master, there are some pivotal differences. Central among these differences is that the 1845 *Narrative* and, more forcefully, "The Heroic Slave" and the 1855 revision of the *Narrative* reject transcendent and antinatural elements that are appropriated in the *Phenomenology*'s recapitulation of the Western project of freedom. As Hegel stages the dialectic of master and slave, the transformation of the animal in the state of nature into a transcendent human consciousness capable of history cleaves apart animal and human, natural and unnatural, matter and spirit.[29] Moreover, while Hegel does not make explicit the role of gender in his discussion of self-consciousness, the assertion of the self in terms of a life-and-death struggle throughout Western and non-Western cultures divides men from women. My argument is that Douglass's narratives invite the reader to reconceptualize the basis for one of the more ubiquitous models of manhood, and in such a way as to complicate the issue of gender difference.

The association of masculinity with artifice and femininity with biology continues to circulate among feminist and nonfeminist theorists alike. Notoriously, Simone de Beauvoir argued that the "woman who gave birth ... did not know the pride of creation; ... giving birth and suckling are not *activities*, they are natural functions.... [In becoming a mother,] she submitted passively to her biological fate.... Maternity imprisoned her in repetition and immanence."[30] But even some contemporary feminist writers claim as a truth of poetry that women experience nature as continuous with their own bodies, while men strive to transcend nature and their bodies.[31] Similarly, anthropologist David Gilmore draws upon a large number of cultures and argues that in contrast with femininity, "masculinity is an artificially induced status ... achievable only through testing and careful instruction" (*M*, 106). Compare Hegel's remark that "the individual who has not risked his life may well be recognized as a *person*, but he has not attained to the truth of this recognition as an independent self-consciousness" (*PS*, sec. 187). Unlike Hegel, however, Gilmore makes explicit the underlying issue of gender:

> This recurrent notion that manhood is problematic, a critical threshold that boys must pass through testing, is found at all levels of sociocultural development.... Rarely is [a woman's] ... right to a gender identity questioned in the same public, dramatic way.... An authentic femininity rarely involves tests or proofs of actions, or confrontations with dangerous foes: win-or-lose contests dramatically played out on the public stage. (*M*, 11–12)[32]

The significant disagreement between theorists who share these views concerns their interpretation of traditionally feminine expressions of subjectivity. As has been argued in parts 1 and 2 of this book, feminists such as Irigaray aim to break the association of female childbearing practices with the ascetic virtues of alienated labor. These feminists claim that women do not or at least should not experience sexuality or motherhood as selfless, ahistorical, or otherwise passive. On the contrary, practices whose genealogy is female provide the basis for conceptions of subjectivity that cannot be schematized through the dichotomies that perpetuate the pathologies of Western culture.

At the same time, rites of passage into manhood through struggle and testing are sufficiently widespread to factor into discussions of black manhood. This does not mean, however, that these practices can be or should be assimilated into white models of manhood. Critically, while Douglass identifies the existential force of black manhood with the courage to undergo a life-and-death struggle, his narratives do not always repeat the sharp dichotomies between nature and transcendent freedom, animal and man, and male and female that structure white—including Enlightenment, dialectical, and postdialectical—concepts of self. Douglass's protagonists—including himself in his 1845 and 1855 autobiographies and the portrayal of Madison Washington in "The Heroic Slave"—do not appear as "brutes," i.e., as the antithesis of the European model of manhood as self-mastery. They do, however, renaturalize the transcendent self of the European *mythos*.

For example, Douglass describes his triumphant encounter with the slavebreaker as having "rekindled ... embers of freedom." The spirit of freedom expressed through the element of fire does not evoke a transcendence of nature but a fervent desire for self. The will to struggle entails the threat of violence, or rather, in Gilroy's terms, counterviolence. But this will to struggle does not, at least for Douglass, imply the compulsion to kill or the sadism of power. There is in these narratives a spirit that impels Douglass. This spirit, however, does not transform him from the sensuous animal (or mythic negro) to a transcendent and peculiarly human realm but to a "power on earth." Accordingly, the narratives locate the status of the slave not alongside the realm of animals but in a position of subordination to the animals (e.g., in the critical scene between Douglass and Covey, to the horses) that the slave tends. The implication of the narrative is that the artifice of slavery reduces the human being (no less than the animal) to the unnatural status of the thing. The struggle with the slavebreaker is staged specifically in the barn—even in the animal muck of the cow yard—where slavebreaker along with slave is stripped bare of the deceptive pretensions and unnatural perversions that protect slavery and, Douglass is telling us, destroy the spirit of both black and white in America.

The European dichotomy between man and animal never eludes the speeches and writings of Douglass. Indeed, in order to counter slave ideology, Douglass cannot avoid engaging its terms. So he argues that the "lines which separate him [i.e., the colored man] from brute creation are as broad, distinct and palpable, as those which define and establish the very best specimens of the Indo-Caucasian race" (*LWFD* 3, 352–53). The slaves, he adds, "are not wolves nor tigers, but men" (*LWFD* 3, 223). However, this demarcation between rational man and brute animal does not exhaust the revolutionary potential of Douglass's writings. More significantly, these writings express a general sympathy that links the hardship of the broken spirits of the beaten-down ox or horse on the plantation with the condition of the slave, and the free spirit of the uncaged animal with manhood.

For example, in "The Heroic Slave," a fictionalized account of a slave rebellion, Douglass portrays the hero (Madison Washington) as a fearsome warrior and then compares the courage of the rebel slave not only to the spirit of a lion but also to the readiness of the snake to give battle. Douglass's earlier 1845 *Narrative* had reserved the image of the snake for the demonic Covey.[33]

Moreover, Douglass places Madison's soliloquy on freedom in nature in the woods, where Madison contrasts his life as a slave to the freedom of birds: "Though liable to the sportsman's fowling piece, [the birds] are still my superiors. They *live free*" (*HS*, 26–27). As an escaped slave, Madison's first free dwelling is among the bears and wolves (*HS*, 38). It is the realm of nature, wolves included, and not the perverse artifices of American institutions that exemplifies for Douglass the conditions for freedom (cf. *BF*, 85, 96). Douglass not only comes to question the hypocrisy of Northern Christian abolitionists along with Southern Christian enslavers, both of whom lustily dominate the black body at the same time that they proclaim their own transcendence of nature and things natural. More radically, Douglass projects an image of the free self that traverses the dichotomies between nature and spirit, animal and human, and desire and reason, which propel the pathologies of European and Euro-American culture. The slave who resists his oppressor, as Douglass writes of the rebel Bill Denby, is "full of animal spirits" (*BF*, 78).

Traditionally, the series of dichotomies that define European-based cultures have been used not only to legitimate the domination over non-European peoples but to legitimate the domination of men over women. As feminists have observed, rites of passage into manhood may enact a ritualistic separation from the mother and the sphere of female power. For example, Gilmore's statement, "Real men are made, not born," reinforces the notion that boys become real men only when they break away from a childish dependency upon their mothers and are reborn into a more powerful world of men (*M*, 14). Those boys who avoid or otherwise fail the rites of passage established by patriarchal communities are depicted by Gilmore as both weak and effeminate (e.g., *M*, 62).

Douglass's speeches and writings, however, break from this pattern. Although Douglass has very little to say about black women, and certainly focuses his narratives on his own quest for "manhood," these writings do not associate the broken-spirited slave with female imagery. Douglass does not interpret slavery as the feminization of man.[34]

On the contrary, *My Bondage* is careful to include examples of female slaves who resist some of the worst abuses of the enslavers. Especially interesting is a slave named Nelly who proved to be "a vigorous and spirited woman." When her overseer set out to whip her, Nelly "nobly resisted, and unlike most of the slaves, seemed determined to make her whipping cost Mr. Sevier [the overseer] as much as possible" (*BF*, 62). While it is true that she was whipped, Douglass notes, "she was not subdued, for she continued to denounce the overseer" (*BF*, 63). "Such floggings," Douglass observes, "are seldom repeated by the same overseer" (*BF*, 63). In fact, it is specifically from the example of this woman that Douglass draws what may be his most critical insight, namely that "the old doctrine that submission is the best cure for outrage and wrong, does not hold good on the slave plantation; . . . and that the slave who has the courage to stand up for himself against the overseer, although he may have many hard stripes at the first, becomes, in the end, a freeman, even though he sustain the formal relation of a slave" (*BF*, 63).[35] Douglass's examples of slaves who find freedom even in the mist of slavery are certainly not stoics. But they are also not necessarily male. On the contrary, the struggle for what Jean Hyppolite in his commentary on Hegel characterizes as "virile recognition" (*GS*, 169) appears not only in the shape of a woman, but paradigmatically so.

Not only does the naturalized expression of the self in the fully embodied will diverge from the dominant white conceptions of manhood; more significantly, it may pose a measure for the pathology of an antiblack, antiwoman culture. This pathology stems from a fantasy of transcendence that severs the antiblack self from its flesh-and-blood contact with the real. Its philosophical origin is in stoicism.

In order to interpret the dichotomy between the natural and the transcendental self that Hegel appropriates in his analysis of self-consciousness, Jean Hyppolite explains what he takes to be an important distinction between wolves and men. Hyppolite argues that "unlike animals, men desire not only to persevere. . . . That men are wolves, in Hobbes's phrase, does not mean that, like animal species, they fight to survive or to extend their power. The fight of each against all is a fight not only for life but also recognition" (*GS*, 169).

In fact, Hyppolite is quite mistaken. Many male and at least some female wolves engage one another in a life-and-death struggle that is primarily social in character. These struggles for honor establish one dimension of a wide range of possibilities for animal sociality.

At the same time, while struggles for recognition in various human (or more broadly, animal) societies may risk economic or physical well-being for the sake of social status, these rituals do affect power and prestige in an economic and material context (*FP*, 115). The social and psychological forces that drive the self may supersede material considerations without appropriating what Hegel terms the "absolute negation" (and understands as the alienation) of material existence. Crucially, Douglass describes his struggle for "honor" as one that at the same time renders him "a power on earth." While the concern for recognition does not, as vulgar materialists claim, reduce to a question of power, one does not achieve recognition without also achieving material power, and vice versa. Human beings, like many other animals, engage in struggles for power that aim to establish a social self. Without power, one is nothing. But so too, with power and without recognition, one is nothing.

Agency in the Slave

One of the controversial questions concerning oppressed peoples is to what degree they interiorize images of themselves that are projected from the dominant culture. For example, Orlando Patterson argues that African American ex-slaves often enough appear (at least when interviewed by whites) to be convinced of their depravity and therefore of the morality of acts of sadism that are veiled as "discipline" or "punishment": "One finds this view repeated constantly by American exslaves in their interviews. 'De massa and Missus was good to me but sometime I was so bad they had to whip me.'"[36] Many scholars also cite ways in which slaves or ex-slaves were able to define a sense of identity outside of antiblack ideology. According to these scholars, some aspects of slave culture developed apart from the dominant culture altogether. Other aspects developed as subtle forms of subversion that went right past the white gaze.[37]

Douglass constructs his narratives around the difference between slaves who submit passively to the demands of their owners and slaves who resist in open struggle. For Douglass the oppressed establishes an identity as a person through the act of rebellion. No other act has this force. The most obvious intent of the narratives is to overcome "the cowardly spirit" and incite the dialectic for a second revolution (see, e.g., *LWFD* 3, 308). In so doing, Douglass also provides an explanation for how it is that some slaves were able to resist the fantasies of their masters and in the process transform the normative terms of the dominant ideology.[38]

In each of Douglass's slave narratives, including the fictionalized narrative of Madison Washington, the emergence of a self that is independent from the projections of the dominant culture takes shape under significantly similar circumstances. Douglass recounts that his will to assert himself before his enslaver occurs during an episode in which Douglass is the object of what the dominant ideology calls "punishment." The violence of the slaveholder against the slave is legitimated in the discourse of subjugation as punishment (for insolence, laziness, etc.). In the events leading up to the critical scene with Covey, Douglass had fallen ill. It is significant that while Douglass signals his intent to obey the slavebreaker, Douglass could not make himself stand and work. Covey refuses to accept incapacitating illness as an excuse. Douglass escapes from the slavebreaker and appeals to the paternalism of the slaveowner but finds no redress. Douglass is now fully conscious of the fact that the life of the slave is not only miserable; this misery is also unjust. It is the realization that the suffering of the slave is arbitrary and, at the same time, that individuals and institutions misrepresent that suffering as due punishment which brings him to question the images and constructs of the dominant white culture. It is this questioning on the part of the slave that breaks him free not yet from slavery but, crucially, from the self-alienation of the slave mentality.

The explanation provided by Douglass in his autobiographies for the reconstruction of subjectivity of the slave extends to a number of similar narratives. For example, Madison Washington in "The Heroic Slave" frees himself from slave ideology after having been punished without proper cause by his master (*HS*, 35). So too the character of Janie in Zora Neale Hurston's *Their Eyes Were Watching God* learns to question the sacrifices that are defined by a patriarchal culture as marital duty. In particular, Janie is able to break free from the crippling self-images projected by her second husband only after he has beaten her for a dinner that was burned quite "by accident."[39] It is the gratuitous and self-refuting exercise of her husband's power—a one-sided assertion of male power over female self-effacement—that sparks the central dialectic of the novel. As Hurston explains: "She had an inside and an outside now and suddenly she knew not how to mix them."[40] The dialectic of "inside" and "outside" in the climactic scene of the Hurston narrative parallels the dialectic that structures the climactic scenes in the Douglass autobiographies. According to these autobiographies, after the critical struggle with Covey, Douglass emerges a man "in fact" if not "in form." It is the crystallization of this difference between inside and outside views of the self that animates the struggle for freedom.

Still the awareness of an inner self that differs from external projections does not suffice to build self-respect. The Self may not be free until it has attained the "gratification" of triumphant struggle before the Other. Social pain is overcome through social change. For Hurston as for Douglass, this struggle occurs when the victim of oppression challenges the authority of the oppressor and in such a way that the victim lets it be known that she or he will no longer act in deference to this dominant force.

Resistance to domination, and therefore the expression of a self, is effective when it occurs before witnesses, or on a "public stage." Therefore, Douglass not only adds witnesses to his struggle with Covey in the second revision of the autobiography; contra the stoics, writing also becomes for Douglass a way in which to cast the struggles of the self on a very large, and therefore very powerful, "public stage." Similarly, Hurston points out that Janie chooses to challenge her husband not in the privacy of their home, but before other men. Hurston writes, "Janie had robbed [her husband] of his illusion of irresistible maleness that all men cherish, which was terrible.... But Janie had done worse, she had cast down his empty armor before men and they had laughed" (*IE*, 75). Just as the enslaver reinvigorates and reasserts his self by turning the plantation into a mock battleground where he ascertains his virility before a captive audience, so too Janie's husband used his store as a whipping ground where he would establish himself by controlling his wife. The oppressed overcomes self-alienation only as he or she transforms the consciousness of the oppressive Other. This is at least one possible dialectic of freedom.

In a very different kind of narrative of self, *The Alchemy of Race and Rights*, Patricia Williams tells a similar story. She argues that "what links child abuse, the mistreatment of women, and racism is the massive external intrusion into the psyche that dominating powers impose to keep the self from ever fully seeing itself."[41] The problem is that "the self becomes subservient to the other, with no reciprocity; and the other becomes a whimsical master" (*ARR*, 64). For Williams, as for Douglass, the highest aim of freedom cannot rest in a principle of self-ownership but must instead address the dialectic of recognition. As she argues, "A fundamental part of ourselves is beyond the control of pure physical will and resides in the sanctuary of those around us" (*ARR*, 73). Williams proceeds to give a number of examples of how the dominant white culture projects images of the black self that are, from the point of view of the black, arbitrary. For example, Williams notes that in some respects, "blacks as a group are poor, powerless and a minority.... It is in the minds of whites that blacks become large, threatening, [etc.]" (*ARR*, 72). The power of Williams's work owes in part to the fact that it precipitates a dialectical tension between inner and outer perceptions of the self that is oppressed. It is this double consciousness that serves to instigate struggles for social and cultural change.

By tracing the origin of the double consciousness of the slave to the realization of the arbitrary basis for what is called punishment, Douglass accounts for the construction of agency in the oppressed. This divided consciousness is not Hegel's Christianized consciousness, or what the *Phenomenology* terms "unhappy consciousness." Douglass rejects what Marx will call the opium of the masses, the stoic and Christian dualisms of thought that, at least according to Patterson, effectively accommodated many a slave to slavery both in ancient Rome and in the American South (*SSD*, 72–73, 76). By introducing a strong concept of individual agency into a dialectical narrative of social freedom, Douglass transforms the meaning of freedom in the West.

Nietzschean and Psychoanalytic Explanations of Punishment

Oppression can be rationalized by those who have power as discipline and punishment. But if the punishment of slave by slaveholder is not motivated by the actions of the slave, what does motivate the slaveholder? After listing in *Genealogy of Morals* some of the countless rationalizations that have been used to legitimate punishment, Nietzsche locates an underlying cause in the pleasure of power.[42] Punishment hardly reforms its victim, he notes, although it may break the will. He also notes that once the victim realizes the arbitrary nature of punishment, he becomes an enemy of the system. For Nietzsche, this means that the "criminal" becomes "hardened" and thus ever more ready to commit willful acts of violence against those who hold power (*GM*, Second Essay, sec. 14).

In his slave narratives, Douglass provides examples of how the institution of slavery grants to the slaveholder the pleasures of domination. Contrary to Nietzsche, however, Douglass also points out an undercurrent of pathology in these peculiar pleasures. Douglass's most striking example of the eroticization of punishment on the plantation focuses on the relation between an aunt of his and his master. Douglass writes: "I have often been awakened at the dawn of day by the most heart-rending shrieks of an own aunt of mine [Hester], whom [the slaveowner] ... used to tie up to a joist, and whip upon her naked back till she was literally covered with blood.... Before he commenced ... , he ... stripped her from neck to waist.... He then told her to cross her hands, calling her at the same time a d – – – d b – – – h.... She now stood fair for his infernal purpose" (*N*, 51–52).

The punishment of Hester is an obvious case where the black slave stands for, mirrors, and serves antisocial desires that belong not to the slave but to the master. Historian Winthrop Jordan develops exactly this point by drawing upon the psychoanalytic notion of projection. He explains that the "common assumption [in European and Euro-American culture] that Negro women were especially passionate" served as a justification for the illegitimate passions of the white man; "It is apparent that white men projected their own desires onto Negroes: their own passion for Negro women was not fully acceptable to society or the self and hence not readily admissible. Sexual desires could be effectively denied and the accompanying anxiety and guilt in some measure assuaged, however, by imputing them to others" (*WB*, 150, 151–52). As I have argued in chapter 5, what Jordan observes as the common association on the part of the white slaveholder of the black slave with his own repressed desire (*WB*, 151) receives its most complete philosophical rationalization in Hegel's phenomenology of self-consciousness. The slave represents for the master desires that are repressed from the European psyche.

One of the major effects of the slave narratives is to demonstrate that the suffering of the slave cannot be justified and to thereby instigate a struggle for change. According to these narratives, the always more or less erotic scenes of violence against the slave may be rationalized by the enslavers as forms of punishments. In fact, however, these scenes act out the unmastered desires and repressed fantasies of the slaveholders. Without the capacity to discipline and punish, the selfhood of the dominant consciousness would crumble. It is through these means that the dominant consciousness obtains the deference of the slave. The slave holder requires the deference of the slave in order to convince himself that he has control over the monstrous desires that he "sees" in the slave and that he must distinguish from himself. In the divergence between the practices and ideology of slavery, we read the unconscious desires of the Southern oppressor writ large. It is only to the extent that the slave breaks out of the mirror of the master that he or she finds the inner resources to struggle for a self that is free.

The Pathology of the Oppressor

Hegel and other apologists for racist oppression perpetuate the myth that dependency upon the Other is the result of a weak will. According to this view, the black body prefers material pleasures over the uncertainties of freedom and therefore lacks the will to count as a full human being (see, e.g., *SSD*, 71, 78). In his slave narratives, Douglass illustrates not only that the black body does indeed possess a will but also that the will of the slave-holder is a fraud. While the slaveholder in America demanded the show of deference from the slave, this slaveholder did not typically tolerate what Hegel understands as the dialectical contradiction, i.e., resistance or chal-lenge, that establishes the test of virility for the will. The plantation was not "in fact" but only "in form" (to use Douglass's distinction) a stage set for a battle of the wills where deference could be earned by the slavemaster. Thus, the dominant consciousness in the American South perverted the struggle that he nonetheless thought necessary for the establishment of a socially recognized self. The slaveholder preempted the intersubjective rituals of battle that defined a model for the nineteenth-century self and instead used the slaves as props to act out the private illusions of his own imaginary.

Nietzschean and psychoanalytic theories fail to find the self-destructive and destabilizing dialectic that inheres in oppression precisely because they lack what Hegel had set out to develop: a conception of the self through its vulnerability before the gaze of the Other. Joel Kovel's *White Racism* exem-plifies the limited explanatory power of a psychoanalytic theory of subju-gation. Kovel distinguishes between the dominative form of racism in the Old South and the aversive form of racism in the North. According to the theory, Northern white culture suffers from the psychological fixations of the anal personality. One of the symptoms of the anal personality is the need to deny that part of the self that is associated with filth. Because of the association of filth with blackness in white racist culture, the anal white per-sonality projects an aversion for his or her own bodily filth onto the black race. In contrast, the more intimate contact that accompanies the domina-tive form of racism in the South results from symptoms of the phallic per-sonality. The white slaveholder acts out illicit sexual desires onto the black "mammy" and displaces his fears of castration onto the black man.

Kovel's account of racism would appear fairly convincing except for what, in a Freudian vein, one might call a telling slip. Kovel supposes that "being satisfied on so many counts, the culture of dominative racism in the antebellum South retained that spontaneous and graceful quality that has endeared it to American mythology."[43] According to Kovel, it is the unhin-dered freedom of the master to act out Oedipal fantasies that brings to life this mythic grace and spontaneity.

Douglass's narratives of slavery hardly support the mythology of the "spontaneous and graceful" South. According to Douglass, the behavior of the master toward the slave reduces the master to an especially miserable brute. The master is, Douglass no less than Hegel insists, socially and psychologically dependent upon the slave for his core sense of self. The problem with psychoanalytic theory is that it projects asocial narcissism and even sexual savagery onto basic human instincts. Because psychoanalytic theory reduces the sociality of the self to sublimations of savage drives, this theory cannot explain the social pathology of oppression. Without a stronger concept of sociality, psychoanalytic theory misses the dialectical ironies that destabilize what colonial mythology might present as a "spontaneous and graceful" domination. As long as the slaveowner seeks unresisting victims for domination, he preempts the agonistic sociality (or "spirit") that, for both master and slave, provides at least one model of selfhood.

The slaveowners of the Douglass narratives could not exemplify the sovereign moment for the dialectical subject of history because these would-be masters are enslaved in cycles of savage desire. It is civilized repression, not free libidinal expression, that produces the self as savage. As such the masters are not in form but are in fact deprived of both selfhood and sociality. It is no accident that slaveholders are exactly what they project onto their slaves. They are slaves to themselves.[44]

If the cruel pleasures of slavery (or what is otherwise known as "punishment") deflect guilt onto the victim, then Nietzsche's account of the origin of punishment is also incorrect, even backward.[45] According to Nietzsche, the natural and healthy expression of the instincts occurs in the polymorphous pleasures not of libido per se—Nietzsche is not a Freudian—but of a conception of power that does not exclude domination. That is, for Nietzsche (and post-Nietzscheans such as Foucault) pleasure originates in the differentials of power; pleasure is not, as for the Freudians, originally opposed to power. But while Nietzsche argues that guilt turns inward a natural instinct to break the will of the Other, the slave narratives tell a different story. The need to destroy the Other may in fact be a perverse expression of a Self that is by nature not savage but social.

The Healing Power of Music

Douglass's 1845 *Narrative* is also a story of literacy. European philosophers, including Hegel, argue that it is the capacity to use "language" that distinguishes human beings from "animals." However, while Douglass does use his acquisition of the written language of the dominant culture in order to demonstrate that he is not in its terms a "brute," his narratives also work to transform the European logos in such a way as to deconstruct the opposition between mute animal and rational man. That opposition, as it is constructed in modernist ideology, projects a disembodied and hyper-rationalist subject alienated from the full range of expressive powers that summon the social existence of human and nonhuman animals alike. As a consequence, logos is opposed to eros, and rational self-expression is opposed to nonconceptual forms of self-expression. The latter are then deemed of aesthetic and not epistemological significance, constituting for philosophers the sophistry of rhetoric and not disciplined thinking. Even the dialectical philosopher Hegel, who does address nonconceptual dimensions of language, nonetheless subordinates those modes as primitive in comparison with the systematic reason of the stoic European.

While Douglass's autobiographies engage standard European notions of education and reason, his use of personal narrative subverts the opposition between impersonal and visceral forms of self-expression. An often-cited reviewer of slave narratives wrote: "Argument provides argument, reason is met by sophistry. But narratives of slaves go right to the heart of men" (see, e.g., *FS*, 5). In an account of the pathological dimensions of antiblack racism that draws parallels between "colorphobia" and the monstrous visions of delirium tremens, Douglass makes it clear that prejudice cannot be countered by rational argument (*LWFD* 1, 385–87). The will of the opponent is met not in bare and bloodless argument but in the "aesthetic" modalities of social exchange.[46]

Iris Young explains in more contemporary terms the limits of rational argument in combatting contemporary forms of racism. She points out that while nineteenth-century ideology sanctioned explicit statements of racial inferiority, the current liberal ideology forbids such statements.[47] But if liberal social theory forbids such statements it also has difficulty accounting for the continuation of more subliminal and less discursive forms of oppression. As Young argues, much of contemporary racism is expressed in nondiscursive behaviors such as avoidance and aversion and unconscious associations of blackness with intellectual and moral inferiority.[48] Frederick Douglass's use of narrative force along with his impatience with enlightened argument suggest that even in the nineteenth century the roots of oppression lie not at the level of discursive awareness but deeper in the cultural imaginary.

But so too, the Douglass narratives intimate, the force of the imaginary lies not only in visual imagery but also in rhythm and tone. The 1845 *Narrative* resituates the problem of the will of the slave in a brief but crucial discussion of the songs of slaves. Of these songs Douglass remarks that much is expressed not in the thought but in the sound alone. "The mere hearing of these songs would do more to impress some minds with the horrible character of slavery . . . than the reading of whole volumes of philosophy on the subject could do" (*N*, 57). In fact, as William Andrews notes, it was not in a book but through a slave song that Douglass himself claims to have first grasped the injustice of slavery and the meaning of freedom (*BF*, 170). Therefore, it is not surprising that the force of Douglass's intellect expressed itself not exclusively and abstractly in stoic argument but in the full force of embodied speech.[49]

The Rhythms and Tones of Freedom

Freedom is not, as the stoics had thought, a concept. Freedom is more originally a music. So too an education for freedom must develop not the alienated superstructure of the abstract mind; on the contrary, it is the alienation of the abstract mind that secretes the image of the savage black body. In order to heal the antiblack pathology of civil-war America, Douglass subverts the mind/body dialectic that informs it and so transposes the existential basis for the self in Western culture.[50] Meanwhile the pathological symptoms of white Reason have not gone unnoticed in Europe. At about the same point in history, Nietzsche was summoning Apollonian man to return to the musical rites of Dionysian culture. But if for Douglass the will to be a man manifests itself in a reason that is also music, for Nietzsche it is music that manifests itself in the will of man. In the final chapter I interrogate the meaning of this reversal.[51]

· 7 ·
Spirit

Friedrich Nietzsche versus Frederick Douglass

*Now the slave emerges as a freeman; . . . Now man expresses
himself through song and dance. . . . Through him sounds a supernatural power, the same power which makes the animals speak. . . .*
Friedrich Nietzsche
The Birth of Tragedy Through the Spirit of Music

*This is scarcely a day for prose. It is a day for poetry and song, a
new song.*
Frederick Douglass, December 28, 1862

*Black groups digging on white philosophies ought to consider the
source. Know who's playing the music before you dance.*
Nikki Giovanni, Gemini

W. E. B. Du Bois offers one progressive image of manhood in racist
America when he holds up Frederick Douglass as "the greatest of the
American Negro leaders."[1] In order to portray a dynamic of black
manhood, however, Du Bois borrows from a white philosophy. In particular, Du Bois invokes a Hegelian dialectic of assimilation and difference in
his description of the ideals that Douglass represents.[2] What Douglass
stands for is "ultimate assimilation *through* self-assertion, and on no other
terms" (*SB*, 35).[3] But if Douglass sought recognition from the white
masters through a dialectic of identity *and difference*, then his autobiography cannot be entirely assimilated into the master narrative of white
culture, at least not as this narrative is represented in the works of Hegel.

In *Phenomenology of Spirit*, Hegel interprets historical progress from slavery to universal freedom through the dichotomies that define Euro-
Christian culture. Hegel demonstrates how the alienating conditions of
labor motivated the European bondsman to construct a rational self that
was free from the body and its affects. Like most modern philosophers,
Hegel did not believe that those of African descent were capable of

controlling the irrational impulses of the body and thus of developing the capacity to reason. Without the abstract skills of reason, the black would lack the moral criterion of the free self.

Clearly, in one respect Hegel was wrong. No doubt individuals across all cultures are equal in their capacities to learn the skills of abstraction. In another respect, however, Hegel's prejudice may distort a fact of cultural difference. At least some philosophers agree that Afrocentric cultures do not produce the kind of dichotomies that sustain Western rationality.[4] My interest here lies not in demonstrating that the African might as well as any European sever himself or herself from his or her material roots and develop some version of what the European tradition valorizes as the rational self. On the contrary, my argument is that specific African American cultures cannot be entirely assimilated into Euro-Christian culture, and that in particular the autobiographies of Frederick Douglass demonstrate that from black culture emerges a progressive conception of the free self. While the white bondsman in Western history acquired freedom only after internalizing the dichotomies of Christian culture, Douglass exemplifies the slave whose "hands were [not] tied by any religion—black or white."[5] Douglass, who rejects movements to return to Africa, also rejects the asceticism of Euro-Christian culture and instead demands from American culture the recognition of his difference.

But then if Douglass rejects white asceticism, his will to be "*a power on earth*" (*BF*, 152) would seem to anticipate the more explosive force that emerges in Nietzsche's anti-Christian concept of the sovereign master. Nietzsche's *Genealogy of Morals*, subtitled *A Polemic,* reads as a direct attack on Hegel's interpretation of the master-slave relation. While Hegel demonstrates that ascetic self-denial and other cathartic practices of the self define a dominant pole of white culture,[6] Nietzsche, like Douglass, calls for practices of the self that intensify desire, and in this sense are ecstatic. However, while Nietzsche aims to subvert the dichotomies of European culture, white asceticism recurs, I shall argue, in Nietzsche's phobia of black cultures.

On the other hand, Douglass poses an image of manhood that subverts Euro-Christian dichotomies and yet embraces what Nietzsche rejects—a concept of freedom as universal recognition. By constructing the autobiography on the principle of "assimilation *through* self-assertion, and on no other terms," the slave narratives of Frederick Douglass challenge the master narratives of both Western tradition and Nietzschean countertradition in order to project a uniquely African American conception of selfhood and freedom. This stance, I argue, emerges from neither the repressive abstraction of European asceticism nor the all-too-brute impulses of a Nietzschean will to power. Beyond this opposition lies a notion of the free self that Douglass on occasion termed "animal spirits" and that yields an original and more progressive vision of what Hegel termed "Spirit."

Warrior versus Worker: DuBois on Freedom

Hegel represents the slave (white or black) as having lacked the courage to risk her (or, for Hegel, paradigmatically his) life for freedom. Because the slave is motivated by the more limited concern for self-preservation, Hegel argues, the slave does not count as a person. This account of slavery has proven persuasive enough that even sociologist Orlando Patterson claims to find historical evidence for the moral failure of the slave. Patterson writes: "The slave was someone who by choosing physical life had given up his freedom. Although he could, of course, have kept his freedom and died, [he] . . . lacked the courage to make such a choice."[7] Because the slave fears death more than slavery, his or her lot will be to serve the master, and, at least according to Hegel, deservedly so. His cowardly nature proves that the slave is not a "person" (or again, paradigmatically, the slave is not a "man") but an "animal." On the other hand, once the master establishes that he can overcome his desires, including, most fundamentally, his animal instinct for self-preservation, he acquires the moral authority to exercise his will over the slave.

But Western history, or at least Hegel's rendition of it, does not favor the master. On the contrary, Hegel explains, the slave finds himself transformed by an overwhelming fear of death. This overwhelming fear finally serves to detach the slave from his physical and emotional existence. The slave becomes a stoic. Because the stoic is able to renounce the fears and pleasures that define animal life and serve instead a principle of reason that Hegel eventually reinterprets as Spirit, he acquires a sense of self. Hegel is thereby able to demonstrate that it is the rational will of the disciplined worker and not, for example, the warrior spirit of the rebellious slave that defines the concept of freedom and the meaning of existence in the West.

Booker T. Washington, or at least the representation of Booker T. Washington that Du Bois juxtaposes to a certain Frederick Douglass, imitates the path of the slave to freedom as this path is envisioned by Hegel. Booker T. Washington urges for the ex-slave in America the slow apprenticeship to freedom through what for both Hegel and Du Bois must be the "double consciousness" of the alienated, or "disciplined," laborer. As Du Bois explains, "Mr. Washington represents in Negro thought the old attitude of adjustment and submission" (*SB*, 36). This servile attitude takes "an economic cast, becoming a gospel of Work and Money to such an extent as apparently almost completely to overshadow the higher aims of life" (*SB*, 36). For the black American, unlike the white American, wage labor signifies dependence, not independence, and therefore a new form of slavery.[8] Washington therefore cannot provide, according to Du Bois, a progressive model for black manhood in racist America. On the contrary, Du Bois argues, Washington's program threatens to "sap the manhood" of the black race, and, Du Bois adds, "manly self-respect is worth more than lands and houses, and ... a people who voluntarily surrender such respect, or cease striving for it, are not worth civilizing" (*SB*, 36).

On the other hand, as Du Bois suggests, Frederick Douglass rejects the path of the slave entailed by the moral rules of white culture and generates an alternative dialectic of freedom. While, as Hegel explains, the white slave acquired the properties of selfhood through the discipline of work, and in particular through a stoic and then Christian philosophy of dutiful service, Douglass reconstructs a self out of slavery in terms that recall the Hegelian concept of the sovereign master.[9] Unlike Du Bois's Washington, Douglass, in his *Narrative* and its 1855 revision, *My Bondage and My Freedom*, portrays himself as choosing to stake his life (as well as his support from the paternal Christian abolitionists) in order to assert his own "manhood." As Douglass explains in a climactic scene of *My Bondage*, he becomes a "man" at that moment when he "resolves to fight" against his oppressor, here the slavebreaker Mr. Covey, "heedless of consequences" (*BF*, 149).

Similarly, in "The Heroic Slave," Douglass challenges the ideology that the black slave lacks the moral virtue of courage, and thus a primary criterion of what is called "will," via an exchange between two of the story's characters, the second of whom has witnessed the slave rebellion led by Madison Washington. To the charge that "all that is needed in dealing with a set of rebellious darkies, is to show that yer not afraid of 'em," is found the reply: "It is quite easy to talk of flogging niggers here ... , where you have the ... physical force of the government, State and national, at your command ... but ... I deny that the negro is, naturally, a coward."[10]

Frederick Douglass's narratives also demonstrate that the black slave can learn as well as any white the powers of Eurpean reason, including the ability to read and write in a European language. A primary task of the narratives, however, is to invoke the intellectual and erotic "force" of black spirit.[11] It is this spirit, and not the acquisition of the European ideology of stoic rationality, that moves the black out of slavery.[12]

Free Spirits

Because Douglass eschews the disciplinary practices of stoic reason and embraces instead the dignity of struggle, it would seem that he has exchanged the role of the Hegelian slave only in order to be assimilated into the role of the Hegelian master. Clearly, Douglass aims to establish black manhood through struggles for recognition that are, as Hegel requires of the lordly sovereign master, heedless of consequences. Hegel, however, locates the sovereignty of the master in the subjugation of the "animal self" and all that the latter represents in the European imaginary. Douglass, on the other hand, invokes the spiritedness of a fully embodied and fully social self and thereby recasts the concept of freedom in terms that are alien to Western European culture and counterculture.

The recovery of the embodied dimensions of selfhood coalesces with the accusation that slavery and its techniques of breaking the resolve, or will, of the slave constitute a perversion, i.e., a crime against nature. The Douglass narratives are not preoccupied by the task of demonstrating that the black man equals the white man in his difference from the animal. The narratives do not work only to establish that the black man is not the mythic animal that white culture makes him out to be. On the contrary, in a move that is much more daring and much more dangerous, Douglass explains the brutality of human slavery by way of an analogy to the cruelties of animal domestication. In *My Bondage*, for example, Douglass does not separate but dares to equate the breaking of the spirit of the slave with the breaking of the spirit of the ox (*BF*, 132). The ox will resist, Douglass relates, until its spirit is broken: "Tame and docile to a proverb, when *well* trained, the ox is the most sullen and intractable of animals when but half broken to the yoke" (*BF*, 132). Likewise, Douglass characterizes those slaves who resist their masters by invoking animal imagery. For example, Douglass praises the rebellious slave Bill Denby "as a powerful young man, full of *animal spirits*" (*BF*, 78; emphasis mine). By their nature, both ox and African, or rather, animals in general possess the spirited will that defines what the Douglass narratives locate as a primary ethical dimension of the person.

But if Douglass reconstructs the black self by staking risky analogies between human beings and other animals, Douglass not only subverts the traditional Western definition of the human through speciesization but transforms the European concept of the person—as transcendent, disembodied, metaphysical—into a concept imbued with the colors and shapes of a fully embodied existence. Morever, as we shall see, this transformed person, fully embodied, is also fully social.[13]

Ecstatic "Manhood"

Like Douglass, Nietzsche uses parables, extended arguments, and various narrative elements in order to beget an intellectual practice of the self that is not cathartic but ecstatic. In one form or another, the cathartic self continually reemerges in a dominant position throughout Western history and so too informs Hegel's conceptualization of freedom. As Hegel explains, the slave must "sublate" sensuous existence in order to develop the capacity to reason and thereby qualify as a person. It is the "sublation" of "natural consciousness," read as the subordination and overcoming, at times even the total purging, of embodied dimensions of human experience, that the narratives of Nietzsche and Douglass call into question.

In *Genealogy of Morals*, Nietzsche directly challenges the equation of the self with a rational will. According to the *Genealogy*, the will originates not in reason but in the murky zone of the body and its drives. Nietzsche does not deny the effects of the intellect on the self but merely recontextualizes these effects in terms of a more subterranean dialectic of the will. For, as Nietzsche writes: "To eliminate the will, to suspend the emotions altogether, provided it could be done—surely this would be to castrate the intellect, would it not?"[14] In order to support his suspicion, Nietzsche demonstrates how it is that the rationalist project of severing the self from the body breeds not a creature of virtue but the malice and misery of the wounded animal. Nietzsche's transvaluation of values would not suppress but would even intensify the instinctual force of will to power of the human animal.

Nietzsche opens the *Genealogy* with an autobiographical reflection on the underlying motivations of his own ideas. The pattern of images that express these motivations bare the core of the Nietzschean project. As Nietzsche writes, the ideals that guide the *Genealogy* "sprang from a common root, from a primary desire [or will, *Grundwillen*] for knowledge," to which he adds: "Our thoughts should grow out of [us] ... with the same necessity as the fruit out of the tree" (*GM*, Preface, sec. 2, 150). By way of images from the Biblical Genesis, the *Genealogy* reinvokes a prelapsarian garden of human origins in order to trace moral ideas not from transcendent reason or ethereal sentiment but from the hubris of carnal knowledge.

What is surprising is that while Nietzsche appropriates his premise—that moral knowledge originates in transgressive desire—from Genesis, he interprets carnality not in terms of the erotic desire of an Adam and Eve but in terms of the sovereign will of the lone warrior. Nietzsche begins his polemic against Euro-Christian culture in self-reflection and proceeds to recast the story of the "fall of man" without an Eve. In other words, the Nietzschean genealogy retraces the origins of the self to the warring spirits of a will that is not erotic and yet, or so Nietzsche claims, is not Christian, not ascetic, and not unnatural.

In his autobiographies, Douglass also recounts the development within himself of what we might call, after Nietzsche, a certain will to power. Like Nietzsche, Douglass is impatient with the excessive use of unspirited reason in the culture of the Enlightenment: "The time for . . . argument is past. For it is not light that is needed, but fire" (*BF*, xiv). Douglass, like the hubristic Prometheus celebrated in Byronic poetry, will dare to take from the gods, and, like Prometheus, what he appropriates is not the light of reason but fire. Douglass thereby incites the Euro-Christian phobia of people of color and all that color stands for—the body, violent desire, animality—not only to cleanse the black person of his dark associations with the European irrational but more centrally to transvaluate the meaning of color in white America. Like Nietzsche, Douglass seems to have very little to say about women or sexuality. And like Nietzsche, the definition, or rather practices, of an evidently masculinized self resides in the hubris of a will to power.

For it is the heat of struggle, Douglass explains, that "rekindled [within him] the few expiring embers of freedom."[15] In the pivotal confrontation with the slavebreaker Mr. Covey, Douglass invokes a practice of African American manhood in which the threat or counterthreat of violence is not gratuitous. As Douglass writes: "After resisting [the slavebreaker] . . . , I was no longer a servile coward, trembling under the frown of a brother worm of the dust, but, my long-cowed spirit was roused to an attitude of manly independence. I had reached the point, at which I was *not afraid to die*. This spirit made me a free man in *fact*, while I remained a slave in *form*. When a slave cannot be flogged he is more than half free. He . . . is really '*a power on earth*'" (*BF*, 152). Douglass ends his account of the struggle with lines from Byron's poetry: "Hereditary bondmen, know ye not/Who would be free, themselves strike the blow" (*BF*, 153).

But if, for Douglass, "A man, without force, is without the essential dignity of humanity" (*BF*, 151), what is the nature of this force? Nietzsche defines the will as an increment of power: "A quantum of strength is equivalent to a quantum of urge, will, activity" (*GM*, first essay, sec. 13, 178). The central location of will in terms of quantity rather than quality of affect corresponds to a distinction drawn in contemporary psychology between vitality affects and categorical affects. Categorical affects include happiness and sadness and tonal variations on these emotions. Vitality affects include the intensity, rhythm, and duration of self-expression. In effect, by defining the will in terms of vitality and not categorical affects, Nietzsche breaks the bounds of the utilitarian formula for the good life in favor of a terrain that is, he imagines, "wild and dangerous" (*GM*, preface, sec. 2, 150). For Nietzsche, the prudential calculus renders the human being content like the "pied cow" or other chattel. Aversive to grand risks, the utilitarian calculus drains the self of its vital force. For Douglass, too, the force of manhood exceeds the construction of the self in terms of utilitarian self-interest or conventional prudence. The slave becomes a man when he resolves to act "heedless of consequences," or at that moment when he overcomes the fear that has paralyzed him before his oppressor.

Moreover, like Nietzsche, Douglass endorses a conception of the self that by conventional and, for the nineteenth century, explicitly Christian standards must be evil. As Douglass explains, the terrain of manhood constitutes "a fallen state" in which the spirit appears as "the devil in me" (*BF*, 148, 154). Douglass portrays the slave who refuses to allow himself to be reduced to the status of chattel as a "bad sheep," or wolf (*BF*, 154), and elsewhere as a predatory "cat, ... ready for the snakish" slavebreaker (*BF*, 149). Compare Nietzsche, who also celebrates a kind of predatory violence in those of strong will. As Nietzsche writes in one of his parables, "There is nothing very odd about lambs disliking birds of prey, but this is no reason for holding it against large birds of prey that they carry off lambs.... To expect that strength of will not manifest itself as strength, as the desire to overcome, to appropriate, to have enemies ... is every bit as absurd as to expect that weakness will manifest itself as strength" (*GM*, first essay, sec. 13, 178).

Douglass presses further and openly endorses an element of criminality. As Douglass explains: "The morality of *free* society can have no application to *slave* society. Slaveholders have made it almost impossible for the slave to commit any crime, known either to the laws of God or to the laws of man. If he steals, he takes his own; if he kills his master, he imitates only the heroes of the revolution" (*BF*, 119). Here too, Douglass *seems* to anticipate Nietzsche, who also applauds the criminality of the "noble races":

> Once abroad in the wilderness, they [i.e., those of strong will] revel in the freedom from social constraint and compensate for their confinement in the quietude of their own community. They revert to the innocence of wild animals: we can imagine them returning from an orgy of murder, arson, rape and torture, jubilant and at peace with themselves ... —convinced, moreover, that the poets for a long time to come will have something to sing about and to praise. Deep within all these noble races there lurks the beast of prey, bent on spoil and conquest. (*GM*, first essay, sec. 11, 174)

At first glance, then, it appears that Douglass and Nietzsche have much in common. Nietzsche's hero revels in the freedom from social constraint. Douglass's rebel slave refuses to recognize the moral constraints of a society that he deems oppressive. Both Nietzsche and Douglass reinvoke the animality of the human self and then interpret animal potency in terms of the threat or counterthreat of violence. And for both writers, the restitution of manhood in an oppressive society can entail acts of transgressive appropriation that are experienced as a gratification, even perhaps, as ecstasy.

However, there is also a striking contrast between the two thinkers. The Nietzschean will expresses itself in the polymorphous dynamics of power. This will to power lacks qualitative definition. It is, as Gilles Deleuze argues, a quantity.[16] Joy is not a goal. It is an effect of active will. Therefore, this will does not aim toward utilitarian happiness or dialectical recognition. On the contrary, under some readings, the Nietzschean will exhausts itself in the thrill of the discharge. Even if Nietzsche's mythos of a sovereign individual constitutes an advance beyond the primitive savage, this advanced will owes its genealogy to savagery. As a consequence, the elemental will may express itself fully in the pleasures of predation. It may also express itself in the savagery of what Nietzsche traces back to the "noble races" and which he defines as a race of conquerors. Of course, as Nietzsche himself points out, the victim of conquest experiences the celebrations of the conquering will from a different perspective. The victim experiences the festivity of violations (e.g., rape) not as innocent becoming but as domination.[17] Therefore, while the weak would seek protection in the restraints of social legislation, the phallic overfullness of the free spirit, in the Nietzschean genealogy, could only be "domesticated" by social forces. For Nietzsche, the will expresses itself fully in its freedom from social constraints, or from sustained erotic attachments in general.[18] In this sense, Nietzsche, like his modernist forebears, defines freedom in terms that are negative.

Douglass, on the other hand, finds in the concept of freedom a positive goal. The rebel slave aims not only to escape from a society that is oppressive but also to establish a society whose spirit is free. The expression of a will to power apart from a positive social goal, and therefore apart from the perspective of the slave, degenerates into what for Douglass truly is "savage barbarity." According to Douglass, savage barbarity characterizes the actions of transgressive masters but not those of the transgressive rebel (*BF*, 78, 119). For example, while Douglass writes of the rebel slave leader Madison Washington, "LIBERTY, not *malice* is the motive for this night's work" (*HS*, 66; emphasis his), he charges that the aggressive actions of his slavebreaker "evinced ... meanness and not ... spirit" (*BF*, 119). One would suspect that there may be some element of revenge in the motivations of the slave rebel. Nonetheless, for Douglass, the heroic rebel does not satisfy him- or herself in either the vindictive release of pent-up emotion or in the "innocent becoming" of power. The rebel has an aim, and this aim is the establishment of a social spirit that is free from moral pathology and, in particular, from colorphobia. When Douglass incites the slave to acts of transgressive violence, he, no less than Nietzsche, reengages the element of danger in many manhood rituals. However, for Douglass, the will of the rebel does not reduce to a display of power. On the contrary, the will has a goal, and this goal is prosocial. Douglass offers a progressive redefinition of phallic manhood in terms of a "heroic resistance to oppression."[19] This is strength.

But then what would be the motive for the orgy of violence that Nietzsche glorifies in primitve man? Could it be another, perhaps even a stronger spirit—a spirit of a conquering race rather than that of a slave race? Or, to repeat the words of Douglass, might malice be the motive for this night's work?

Demythologizing Power

In order to gain a better grasp of what might motivate the peculiar ecstasies of display that Nietzsche applauds, we need to move from the mythic creature of Nietzschean lore to a flesh-and-blood exemplar of the blond conqueror that is, as Nietzsche hypothesizes, set loose in the wilderness. I would propose that such an exemplar might be found in the history of the American South. But then we might refer to the texts of Douglass for an alternative perspective on the race of conquerors.

In Nietzsche's view, the race of conquerors possesses a "typical character trait.... They speak of themselves as 'the truthful'" (*GM*, first essay, sec. 5, 163). It is curious that Nietzsche, master of dark irony, sees through hypocrisies of European morality and yet takes as transparent the claims of the race of conquerors. If the slaveholder of the American South claimed the authority for all demarcations of truth, Douglass intimates that this claim was hardly without its darker motives. One might consider what Douglass treats as a typical response of the slavemaster to one of his slaves who inadvertently revealed the unhappy conditions of his slavery: "The poor man was then informed by his overseer, that, for having found fault with his master, he was now to be sold to a Georgia trader. He was immediately chained and handcuffed; and thus, without a moment's warning he was snatched away, and forever sundered from his family and friends, by a hand more unrelenting than that of death. *This* is the penalty of telling the simple truth" (*BF*, 75). Clearly, as Douglass points out, at least in the historical example of America, much of the power of the conquering race resides in keeping the slave ignorant: "Ignorance is a high virtue in a human chattel; and as the master studies to keep the slave ignorant, the slave is cunning enough to make the master think he succeeds" (*BF*, 55).

Nietzsche not only portrays the mythic blond conqueror as truth-affirming. He also supposes that the conqueror is jubilant, at peace with himself, and thus as self-affirming. However, according to Douglass, the fragile ego of the blond conqueror in historical America relies upon the flattery of slaves. One of the greatest crimes of the slaves, Douglass notes, is impudence, or the crime of self-assertion (*BF*, 160). If a slave fails to pull off his hat before a white person or otherwise fails to affect a posture of Sambo-like dependence before the white master, he or she is punished. Drawing upon similar accounts, historian Joel Williamson concludes that "Sambo was a creature purely of the white mind, a device by which white slaveholders day by day masked a terror that might otherwise have driven them over the edge of sanity. In time, however, the Sambo role functioned to build white egos. The role was, after all, beautifully fitted to flatter the white man's image of himself. He was the superior, the Spartan warrior and the winner." Williamson adds, "Black people probably did not much internalize the Sambo role because it was ultimately unflattering. It seems clear enough that they had the strength to resist that role, to wear it as a mask when necessary and to set it aside at will."[20] In other words, there is historical evidence that much of the regard shown by the slave to the master was a farce. Clearly, the ego of the American master drew its strength not from self-affirmation, as Nietzsche would mythologize, but in "reaction" to the images projected by the slave.

There may very well be better historical analogues for the mythological conqueror celebrated by Nietzsche than the Southern aristocrats of the more isolated plantations, surrounded by their displays of power and, in their dealings with their slaves, severed from the constraints of European morality. Maybe it is the continual operation of European morality in the guilt complexes of the slaveowner that accounts for his pathology. But, maybe too it is the repressive mechanism of European morality that produces the fantasies of what Nietzsche mythologizes as will to power. Certainly the history of the conquerors in America suggests that the will to power that aims to be free from social constraint does not manifest either the virtue of truth-telling or the innocence of becoming. When the sovereign master of the Nietzschean mythology takes on the flesh and blood of history, he hardly looks so grand.

The Fear of Color

Nietzsche's mythology of the noble blond conqueror, judged from the historical experience of conquest in America, exhibits the symptoms of an escapist fantasy. Such fantasies are not unknown among philosophers, whose ideal values often enough exhibit the symptoms of a flight from the real. But then what might motivate such a retreat from the real?

For the white slaveholders, the answer is as clear as the image of the mulatto slave. The slave represents and is part product of the mixed desires of the slaveholder. As Douglass explains, "Men do not love those who remind them of their sins ... and the mulatto child's face is a standing accusation against him who is master and father to the child" (*BF*, 42). The slaveholder projects onto the slave as the very meaning of color the mythic animality that he lusts for but also must abhor as a threat to the European ideology of selfhood that he has not yet overcome. His fear of color is his fear of the desires that he might express in his relation to his slaves but that he must disavow in Christian America.

In Nietzsche, the fear of color reads only somewhat differently. Nietzsche indicates what is for him the meaning of color in his discussion of the etymology of moral terms. He writes:

> The words *kakos* and *deilos* (the plebeian, in contrast to the *agathos*) emphasize cowardice and provide a hint as to the direction in which we should look for the etymology of *agathos*.... The Latin *malus* (besides which I place *melas*) might designate the common man as dark, especially black-haired ("*hic neger est*"), as the pre-Aryan settler of the Italian soil, notably distinguished from the new blond conqueror race by his color.... Who knows whether modern democracy, ... especially that preference for the *commune* ... does not represent a throwback.... *Bonus* would then spell the man of strife, of discord, the warrior. (*GM*, first essay, sec. 5, 164)

Nietzsche's mythology of the blond warrior serves as a shield against the complications and vulnerabilities of sociality. Most mammals, excluding Nietzsche's mythic blond beast, exhibit a preference for the "commune" or some form of sociality, and this preference does not evidence regression. Even in aggressive shows of force, the wolf seeks the acknowledgment of other wolves. Nietzsche, on the other hand, hypothesizes that the whole of human misery lies in the constraints of socialization (*GM*, second essay, sec. 16, 217).[21] Clearly, Nietzsche denies what Douglass and Hegel develop, a telos of the self in recognition. Nietzsche's fear of color—what we might as well call his asceticism—signals a denial of animal sociality. No doubt, the denial of a fundamental need for recognition, or what Nietzsche dismisses as a "herd mentality," protects the self from the perspectives of others. What Douglass, in his narratives, suggests is that social perspectivalism not only supplements self-esteem but weaves the inner fabric of the self. The denial of the social eroticism of the will severs the self at its very roots. It is because Douglass understands the force of the Other in the construction of the Self that he could urge the black slave to stake his or her very life for the sake of a society whose spirit is free.

The heroic rebel of the Douglass narratives is more credible than that projected by Nietzsche in his *Genealogy*. The agonizing separations of the black slave from his or her family testify to the very natural pain of social deprivation. Meanwhile, it is not to nature but to an institution of domination, the institution of slavery, that Douglass traces the bestiality of the sovereign master celebrated in Nietzschean mythology. Douglass concludes that the "slaveholder, as well as the slave, is the victim of the slave system. A man's character greatly takes its hue and shape from the form and color of things about him" (*BF*, 54). The Other and his institutions, Douglass is telling both black slave and blond slave owner, necessarily enter into the inner life of the self (cf. *BF*, 247). Douglass knows that he cannot afford not to struggle with the alien will of the antiblack oppressor.

The double focus of the dialectic on Self and Other informs not only the life of Frederick Douglass but also, as Du Bois suggests, an ideal of African American manhood, "assimilation through self-assertion, and on no other terms." Only this double focus can address what Du Bois terms the "double consciousness" of the black in America: that "peculiar sensation; ... this sense of always looking at oneself through the eyes of others" (*SB*, 3). Taken together, our readings of Douglass and Nietzsche deconstruct the mythologies (either black or white) of phallic sovereignty. The black American is as dependent upon the white American as the white American is dependent upon the black American. There can be no freedom unless it is, not abstractly but through concrete mediation, made universal.

Tactile Recognition

For if freedom is a universal value, it is not from every perspective lived as the same. In the *Phenomenology*, Hegel works out the dynamics of intersubjectivity predominantly within the visual and conceptual registers of experience.[22] The self-conscious person emerges from the narcissistic isolation of an animal-like existence by way of the gaze of the Other. And, as Hegel makes clear, in order to be fully free and rational, European man endeavors to bring the totality of experience into conceptual articulation. Some contemporary philosophers, most prominently Luce Irigaray, have argued that the priority given to the visual, technical, and conceptual registers of experience supports the most oppressive dimensions of Western culture (see chapter 2). Irigaray also argues that a less phallic culture might give a greater place to alternative and specifically to more sensuous registers of human experience.

I have argued that the Douglass narratives present a variation on at least one of the major Hegelian themes: The emergence of a self, certainly under conditions of oppression, requires a struggle for recognition. Douglass's portrayal of the struggle differs from Hegel's in that the former locates the basis of the self not in the rational will, which is the hallmark of Western asceticism, but in the spirited will and specifically in the will to struggle against oppression. My question is whether this will responds to any of the concerns of feminists, especially as these concerns are expressed in the more thoroughgoing critique that one finds in the works of Irigaray.

In this regard, it is significant that while the *Phenomenology* locates the emergence of the self in the kind of contest that often characterizes adolescent rituals of manhood, Douglass's autobiographies point toward what may be a more originary happening of the self. In the opening chapters of *My Bondage*, Douglass writes that it is his early childhood experience, not the struggle with the slavebreaker, that provided for him "the veriest freedom" (*BF*, 32). And while Douglass writes little about his early childhood, what he does write is quite telling. Especially interesting is his focus on "the strong and spirited hands" of the grandmother who raises him (*BF*, 32). Douglass describes these hands in terms that are almost magical: "Superstition had it, that if Grandmamma Betty but touches them [seedling potatoes, but also the children that she reared?] at planting, they will be sure to grow and flourish" (*BF*, 29). The nurturing caresses that he must have received from his grandmother are acknowledged explicitly from his mistress, Sophia (*BF*, 91). Moreover, while Douglass never knew much about his mother, claiming never to have seen his mother in the daylight, warm impressions remain from her nighttime visits. Douglass writes her memory as more of a tactile than a visual or verbal image, and specifically in terms of a feeling which is strong even as it resists verbalization: "I take few steps in life, without feeling her presence; but the image is mute, and I have no striking words of her's treasured up" (*BF*, 42). While the earliest childhood experiences may be remembered as gestures and feelings inaccessible to discursive thought,[23] Douglass's mention of these memories suggests the central role of tactile recognition to the spirit that would be free.

Thus, even though Douglass, like Hegel and like Nietzsche, has little to say about women, his acknowledgment of the nurturing sources of both his self and his sense of freedom alludes to what Hegel, Nietzsche, and the Western tradition would exclude from the phenomenology of the spirit. This exclusion is not accidental. On the contrary, these patriarchal genealogies define manhood as the negation of the sphere of the mother and understand the rebirth of the self into manhood through rituals of separation. The self reemerges from alienation as a hardened will. Douglass envisions a route to manhood that invokes not separation but reconnection. The self that is reborn in a struggle against oppression is guided by images of freedom that are rooted in the social eroticism of early childhood. Douglass does not celebrate but mourns the nomadic separation of the family in American culture, suggesting that freedom must have as its goal the recognition and not the negation of the sociality that began for him in the grandmother- and mother-child relation.

Moreover, it is because recognition happens not only in a realm of concept and image but already in response to touch that the self is vulnerable to the deprivations and abuses of touch. The whip of the slaveholder breaks the spirit of the slave by hardening the skin and thereby numbing the self to the resources of touch. This numbing of the flesh does not, for Douglass, define the emergence of manhood but its undoing.

So too Douglass reclaims an essential element of the self—the tactile self as it was once tendered by the hands of the grandmother—by resisting the social humiliations of slavery in physical combat. The triumphant physicality of struggle regenerates the broken flesh and revitalizes the self. This revitalization of the lived self is experienced as a "gratification."

It is also significant that what, according to Joel Kovel, are two forms of white racism in America both work through aberrations of touch. Drawing upon psychoanalytic theory, Kovel argues that the dominative racism that historically characterizes the Old South arises from a phallic eroticism. He argues further that the aversive racism that characterizes the traditional North and still much of contemporary America owes to an anal construction of the self. In the process of developing these differences, Kovel suggests that the punishment of the whip and the violation of rape typify the more intimate contact between master and slave on the Southern plantation. The aversive racist, on the other hand, "keeps his distance, both physically and morally."[24] Kovel accounts for the distance of the aversive racist by examining the needs of the anal personality. The anal personality draws clear and distinct boundaries between the rational self and the loose fluids or unsightly excrement that recall childhood dependency upon the mother. Similarly, the aversive white racist associates the white race with purity, cleanliness, and order and the black race with filth and other impurities (*WR*, 34). The behavior of the aversive racist is especially telling with regard to touch. The aversive racist maintains an attitude of "nonspecific coldness" toward the outcast, or "untouchable" (*WR*, 34). "He does not concretely touch those black bodies so coveted by dominative racists . . . ; he is the true descendent of the Puritan" (*WR*, 60).

Douglass's narratives point to inadequacies in both Southern and Northern concepts of intersubjectivity. Most clearly, Douglass uncovers the Southern style of power as a pathological expression of the will. Douglass does not, however, expose the mythologies of Southern patriarchal power in order to embrace the ethical practices of the North. Following Kovel, the stoic concept of the free self generated by a Puritan culture rests on an anal construction of autonomy. The rational Self is detached from both the body and the Other. When Douglass tells us that the breaking up of slave families reduces the slave to a brute, he gives emphasis to a dimension of selfhood that exceeds anality. For Douglass, as for Hegel, freedom signifies not only the self-reliance valued in Enlightenment and post-Enlightenment America but also, and more critically, social recognition.[25] However, absent entirely from European dialectical philosophy is the tactile recognition that precedes but emcompasses adolescent, or even adult, struggles for recognition and that for Douglass defines "the veriest freedom."[26]

"The veriest freedom" rests on a dialectical concept of freedom as recognition, and yet it does not entail the Hegelian nightmare of the total community. Hegel's dialectical logic enlists a mirror-like series of reversals in order to reconcile differences in abstract sameness. Because Douglass finds his strength in the felt presence of those who raised him, he does not require in the Other a mirror-like image of the self. The spirited hands of the grandmother do not present a visual image of the self for the slaveboy to imitate. These maternal hands do not provide a specifically male role model for the boy to follow. Perhaps because these early resources of selfhood do not engage a psychology of narcissism, the adult Douglass can seek in freedom not a colorless mirror of abstract sameness but the concrete recognition of his specific difference.

Hegel's dialectic follows the development of the free self from immersion in an unarticulated whole and subsequent alienation to a community based on common concepts. The Hegelian community can aspire to the sameness of a universal humanity, however, only because it subscribes to a construct of sociality that is a disembodied and unerotic abstraction. Douglass's "veriest freedom" does not submerge him in a mute whole with blurred boundaries between Self and Other from which he must then separate. He and his grandmother were always two distinct individuals, each one strong and spirited. The rhythm of Douglass's narratives, like the contrapuntal cadences of African dance, does not celebrate the disconnected individual. Nor does it submerge individuals in sameness. The Douglass narratives intone the togetherness of difference.

The Birth of Freedom from the Spirit of Music

As Douglass finds the veriest freedom in the hands of his grandmother, his first "idea" of the injustice of slavery appears long before his acquisition of what is called literacy across European and Euro-American cultures. Douglass had already developed an understanding of injustice through the medium of slave music (see editor's note, *BF*, 170). The slave songs, Douglass writes, "told a tale which was then [as a child] altogether beyond my feeble comprehension.... To those songs I trace my first glimmering conceptions of the dehumanizing character of slavery" (*BF*, 65). The force of white culture on Douglass's autobiography marginalizes the influence of this music and demands that Douglass's arguments repeat the European philosophy of freedom as rational, restrained, and self-reliant. The will that defines the locus of white autonomy is rational. Douglass, however, takes up the white concept of freedom in a rhythm and tonality that is black. The will of the ex-slave expresses itself in speech that is not alienated from its sources in African music and dance.[27]

The partial reconstruction of what is called "political philosophy" in the medium of music rather than in the detached principle of stoic reason is not surprising if we consider the history of the American black. Patricia Hill Collins explains that music "assumed a similar function in African-American oral culture as that played by print media for white, visually based culture."[28] Sterling Stuckey explains the constitutive role of rhythm in black styles of self-expression. According to Stuckey, the typical "sermon [of the black preacher] ... was as Christian in message as its modes of delivery and the response it evoked were African." [29] The crucial elements of the black mode of delivery include bodily sympathy communicated through rhythms of song and, unlike Western music, an "organic tie to dance" (*SC*, 41). This is not the dance of the Nietzschean Dionysiac, the unconscious swooning in sublime rhythms before a terror that is too dark for a history. For the black in America, terror has a distinct face and a distinct history, and it is white. Nor does the black call for justice merge into mythic rhythms which, as Nietzsche describes in *The Birth of Tragedy*, annihilate individuality in the "Dionysiac stirrings of ... which all primitive races speak in their hymns" (*BI*, sec. 1, 22). What Sterling identifies as the call-and-response pattern in African rhythms sustains the hyphenated duality, or the correspondence, of Self and Other (*SC*, 40). Compare again Patricia Hill Collins, who notes that black songs "were originally sung in small communities, where boundaries distinguishing singer from audience, call from response, and thought from action were fluid and permeable" (*BFT*, 100). In these communities of song individuality was not submerged in group dynamics. Nor was individuality conceived in tension with community. "In music one effect of this oral mode of discourse is that individuality ... actually flourishes" (*BFT*, 99).

If the education of the slave signifies both a comprehension of African American sounds, rhythms, and intonations and a comprehension of the more abstract language and stoic morality of Eurocentric logocentrism, then African American freedom must carry a double meaning, one black and one white. Elementary among the differences in style between black and white freedom is what Nietzsche diagnoses as European asceticism, or what I am redescribing as the "fear of color." While the ascetic culture of the Puritan attempts to rid the self of the vulnerabilities and social resources of the body, the music culture that emerges from the black slave in America gives full measure to the whip that enslaves as well as to the hope for freedom that survives. "'Sprung from the African forests where its counterpart can still be heard, it was adapted, changed, and intensified by the tragic soul-life of the slave, until, under stress of law and whip it became the one expression of a people's sorrow, despair and hope'" (*SC*, 255; here Stuckey quotes Du Bois). The roots of the African American self emerge not from cathartic rituals of moral, intellectual, and social detachment but from the expressive sociality of song and dance.[30]

Conclusion

It has been argued that, "in a typically American gesture," Douglass portrays himself as the self-made man.[31] My claim is that the Nietzschean will to power, not the self-reliant individual of Enlightenment philosophy, better approximates the transgressive spirit of the Douglass narratives. But against both Enlightenment and Nietzschean philosophies, philosophies that celebrate the sovereign Self in freedom from social constraints, the Douglass narratives express a fundamental need for the Other. The slave-breaker's reluctance to whip Douglass after their struggle signals the respect that Douglass must have. So too, if the concept of freedom in white America ultimately signifies fathering oneself, Douglass acknowledges the roots of his self in more "maternal" sources.[32] From the spirited hands of his grandmother to the shared beds and shared dinners of his life in freedom, Douglass seeks self-empowerment in the intimate context of recognized sociality (*BF*, 245–46).[33]

It is not an accident that European conceptions of the self sustain a politics of oppression in the name of freedom. Not understanding the intellectual and erotic energy of spirit, white culture severs the rational Self from nature and sociality and then alternately projects the mythologies of the savage or the Sambo upon the unknown Other. The purge of the total outcast and the torment of the liminal Other will continue until white culture learns to cultivate the social resources of the lived body and acknowledges its desire for the desire of the Other; until, that is, white culture discovers what Douglass knew, "the veriest freedom."[34]

Notes

Introduction

1   See, e.g., Eleanor H. Kuykendall, "Toward an Ethic of Nurturance: Luce Irigaray on Mothering and Power," in *Mothering: Essays in Feminist Theory*, ed. Joyce Trebilcot, (Totowa: Rowman and Allanheld, 1983). Kuykendall's essay explains why, as she writes, "recent feminist arguments emphasize recognition rather than equality as a mark of mutuality" (264). Kuykendall develops a dimension of recognition by examining the narcissistic identity between mother and daughter. In contrast, I shall reject the theory of narcissism as an explanatory basis of this relation. However, my project, like Kuykendall's, emerges from a reading of some of Irigaray's writings. Other significant feminist reinterpretations of Hegel's concept of recognition include: Jessica Benjamin, *The Bonds of Love: Psychoanalysis, Feminism, and the Problem of Domination* (New York: Pantheon, 1988); Simone de Beauvoir, *The Second Sex* (New York: Vintage, 1989); Nancy C. M. Hartsock, *Money, Sex, and Power: Toward a Feminist Historical Materialism* (New York: Longman, 1983); Patricia Jagentowicz Mills, *Woman, Nature, and Psyche* (New Haven: Yale University Press, 1987); and Mary O'Brien, *The Politics of Reproduction* (Boston: Routledge, 1981).

On the central importance of Hegel's concept of recognition with regard to racial self-consciousness in African American cultures, see "Chapter 2: Master, Mistresses, Slaves, and the Antinomies of Modernity," in Paul Gilroy, *The Black Atlantic: Modernity and Double Consciousness* (Cambridge: Harvard University Press, 1993), 41–71, henceforth cited as *BA*; Orlando Patterson, *Slavery and Social Death* (Cambridge: Harvard University Press, 1982), henceforth cited as *SSD*; David Brion Davis, *The Problem of Slavery in the Age of Revolution, 1770–1823* (Ithaca: Cornell University Press, 1975), esp. 557–64; George Rawick, *From Sundown to Sunup: The Making of the Black Community* (Westport: Greenwood, 1972); Eugene D. Genovese, *Roll, Jordan, Roll: The World the Slaves Made* (New York: Random House, 1974), henceforth cited as *RJR*; Frantz Fanon, *Black Skin, White Masks* (New York: Grove Press, 1967); and Lewis R. Gordon, *Bad Faith and Antiblack Racism* (Atlantic Highlands: Humanities Press, 1995). See also Kenneth Liberman's unpublished manuscript, "The Dialectics of Oppression: Looking, and Being Seen."

2   Patricia J. Williams, *The Alchemy of Race and Rights: Diary of a Law Professor* (Cambridge: Harvard University Press, 1991), 73. Henceforth cited as *ARR*.

3   Williams's discussion of spirit murder speaks to what Orlando Patterson describes as the social death of the slave in his *SSD* (esp. 71) and to what Howard McGary describes as the cultural alienation of the African American in his article "Alienation and the African-American Experience," *The Philosophical Forum* 24, nos. 1–3 (Fall–Spring 1992–93), henceforth cited as *AA*. Spirit murder can also be described in terms of the political phenomenology of shame; for a development of the latter concept, see Sandra Lee Bartky, *Femininity and Domination: Studies in the Phenomenology of Oppression* (New York: Routledge, 1990), 83–98; and Drucilla Cornell, *The Imaginary Domain* (New York: Routledge, 1995).

4   Jean-François Lyotard, *The Postmodern Condition: A Report on Knowledge*, trans. Geoff Bennington and Brian Massumi (Minneapolis: University of Minnesota Press, 1985), xxiv.

5   For Emmanuel Levinas's critique of the narcissistic force of dialogue and his attempt to locate the source of ethical obligation prior to the "said" of communication, see his *Otherwise Than Being or Beyond Essence*, trans. Alphonso Lingis (Dordrecht: Kluwer Academic Publishers, 1991), 118–21. In this book, I shall appropriate various deconstructive techniques. For a full discussion of deconstruction, see Irene E. Harvey, *Derrida and the Economy of Difference* (Bloomington: Indiana University Press, 1986).

6   See, e.g., Drucilla Cornell, *Transformations: Recollective Imagination and Sexual Difference* (New York: Routledge, 1993), 2; Judith Butler, *Bodies That Matter: On the Discursive Limits of "Sex"* (New York: Routledge, 1993), 2. Butler's work is henceforth cited as *BM*.

7   Compare similar claims found in Nancy Fraser's "False Antitheses," *Feminist Contentions: A Philosophical Exchange* with Seyla Benhabib, Judith Butler, Drucilla Cornell, and Nancy Fraser (New York: Routledge 1995), 67–68; and Cynthia

Willett, "Tropics of Desire: Freud and Derrida," *Research in Phenomenology* 22 (1992), 138–51.

8   See, e.g., Kelly Oliver, *Reading Kristeva: Unraveling the Double Bind* (Bloomington: Indiana University Press, 1993), 5. Oliver explains the role of alterity in the work of Julia Kristeva: "Kristeva ... argues that the subject can relate to an other because the other is within the subject." See also the use of the personal abject to gain access to alterity in Butler, *BM*, 3; Iris Marion Young, "Abjection and Oppression: Dynamics of Unconscious Racism, Sexism, and Homophobia," in *Crises in Continental Philosophy*, ed. Arleen B. Dallery and Charles E. Scott with Holley Roberts (Albany: SUNY, 1990), 201–214; Homi K. Bhabha, *The Location of Culture* (New York: Routledge, 1994), 1–18; and Cyntha Willett, "Partial Attachments: A Deconstruction of Responsibility," *Ethics and Danger,* ed. Arleen B. Dallery and Charles E. Scott (Albany: SUNY, 1992), 273–82. These theories allow for but do not develop the possibility that colonized subjects may express a sense of self apart from the projections of alterity that originate in the dominant consciousness. For a turn toward the latter project, see Iris Marion Young, *Justice and the Politics of Difference* (Princeton: Princeton University Press, 1990), 159, hereafter cited as *JP*. It is this latter project that forms the basis of my own study as well as my critique of postmodernism.

9   Laurence Thomas, "Moral Deference," *The Philosophical Forum* 24, nos. 1–3, (Fall–Spring 1992–93), 233.

10   Ibid., 24b.

11   Like the current study, Paul Gilroy finds in hybrid currents of black culture a basis for critiquing the opposition between the rationalism of European modernism and the aestheticism of postmodernism. And, like the current study, he aims to avoid both the racism that is implicit in modern universalism and the relativism of post-modernism by seeking within the mediations of black counterculture a more global narrative that would be an "inversion of the relationship between margin and centre as it has appeared within the master discourses of the master race." See *BA*, esp. 39–40, 45.

12   Nancy Fraser and Linda Nicholson, "Social Criticism Without Philosophy: An Encounter between Feminism and Postmodernism," *Theory, Culture and Society* 5 (l988), 378.

13   For especially incisive discussions of the detrimental effects of cultural images on oppressed groups, see Susan Bordo's essay "Reading the Slender Body," in *Body/Politics: Women and the Discourses of the Sciences*, ed. Mary Jacobus, Evelyn Fox Keller, and Sally Shuttleworth (New York: Routledge, 1990), 83–112; essays by Judith Butler and Robert Gooding-Williams in *Reading Rodney King, Reading Urban Uprising*, ed. Robert Gooding-Williams (New York: Routledge, 1993); Patricia Williams's discussion of "spirit murder" (*ARR*, 73); Kaja Silverman, *Male Subjectivity at the Margins* (New York: Routledge, 1992), 2; Drucilla Cornell on the fictions and metaphors that constitute the feminine, in *Beyond Accommodation: Ethical Feminism, Deconstruction, and the Law* (New York: Routledge, 1991), 3; Iris

Young, *JP*, 123–24; and Ann E. Cudd, "Enforced Pregnancy, Rape, and the Image of Woman," *Philosophical Studies* 60 (1990), 47–59.

14   Laurence Mordekhai Thomas, *Vessels of Evil: American Slavery and the Holocaust* (Philadelphia: Temple University Press, 1993), 156. Henceforth cited as *VE*.

15   See his introduction to *The Classic Slave Narratives*, ed. Henry Louis Gates, Jr. (New York: Mentor, 1987), ix.

16   See Friedrich Nietzsche, *The Genealogy of Morals,* in *The Birth of Tragedy and The Genealogy of Morals*, trans. Francis Golffing (Garden City: Doubleday Anchor Books, 1956), esp. "What Do Ascetic Ideals Mean?" 231–99.

17   Michel Foucault, *The Use of Pleasure*, trans. Robert Hurley (New York: Vintage Books, 1990), 11. Henceforth cited as *UP*.

18   On differences between black and white cultures in the United States, see David R. Roediger, *The Wages of Whiteness: Race and the Making of the American Working Class* (New York: Verso, 1993). Roediger explains how the white working class internalized the discipline of "industrial morality" and projected fantasized images of "preindustrial" life onto blacks. While African Americans were excluded from the white work ethic, they developed alternative conceptions of ethical subjectivity, including, for example, what Eugene Genovese describes in terms of "the black work ethic" (*RJR*, 309–24).

19   Audre Lorde, *Sister Outsider* (Freedom, CA: The Crossing Press, 1984), 55.

20   These terms are borrowed from Patricia Hill Collins, *Black Feminist Thought* (New York: Routledge, 1991), 122.

Part I: Introduction

1   Thomas Hobbes, *Leviathan,* ed. Michael Oakeshott (New York: Collier, 1975), 101.

2   G. W. F. Hegel, *Phenomenology of Spirit*, trans. A. V. Miller (Oxford: Oxford University Press, 1977), sec. 171; *Phaenomenologie Des Geistes* (Hamburg: Felix Meiner, 1952), 137. Trans. altered.

3   My opening remarks owe much to Seyla Benhabib, "The Generalized and the Concrete Other," in *Feminism as Critique*, ed. Seyla Benhabib and Drucilla Cornell (Minneapolis: University of Minnesota Press, 1987): "The state of nature is the looking glass of these early bourgeois thinkers.... The state of nature is both nightmare (Hobbes) and utopia (Rousseau).... The varying content of this metaphor is less significant than its simple and profound message: in the beginning man was alone. Again it is Hobbes who gives this thought its clearest formulation" (84). See also Luce Irigaray's throughgoing critique of narcissistic projection, e.g., in "Body Against Body: In Relation to the Mother," in *Sexes and Genealogies*, trans. Gillian C. Gill (New York: Columbia University Press, 1993), esp. 13.

4   See, e.g., Susan Moller Okin, *Justice, Gender, and the Family* (New York: Basic Books, 1989), esp. 17–24. Okin argues that a condition for the just society is

parenting a moral person and that therefore justice must be brought into the family.

5 For a critique of the role that this dichotomy plays in the differences between communitarian and liberal political theory, see Iris Marion Young, *Justice and the Politics of Difference* (Princeton: Princeton University Press, 1990), 228ff. For the psychological basis for this difference, see Nancy Chodorow, *The Reproduction of Mothering* (Berkeley: University of California Press, 1978). For a discussion of the appropriation of this dichotomy in care ethics, see Owen Flanagan and Kathryn Jackson, "Justice, Care, and Gender: The Kohlberg-Gilligan Debate Revisited," in *An Ethic of Care*, ed. Mary Jeanne Larrabee (New York: Routledge, 1993), 76.

6 For a comparison of the Lacanian triad "need-demand-desire" and the Hegelian "negation of negation," see Slavoj Zizek, *Tarrying with the Negative: Kant, Hegel, and the Critique of Ideology* (Durham: Duke University Press, 1993), 120.

Chapter 1: The Origin of Ethics in Music and Dance

1 Daniel N. Stern, *The Interpersonal World of the Infant: A View from Psychoanalysis and Developmental Psychology* (New York: Basic Books, 1985). Henceforth cited as *I*. With the notion of affect attunement, Stern begins to explore the developmental impact of the tremendous amount of parental work involved in singing and dancing with the child.

2 Jessica Benjamin, *The Bonds of Love: Psychoanalysis, Feminism, and the Problem of Domination* (New York: Pantheon, 1988), 11–12. Henceforth cited as *B*.

3 "Natural desire" should be read not through the positivistic dualism between nature and culture but through the dialectical paradoxes of a nature that is always already cultural. A contemporary Anglo-American exponent of the dialectical view of nature can be found in Clifford Geertz, *The Interpretation of Cultures* (New York: Basic Books, 1973).

4 I am following a European practice of distinguishing ethics as a social practice from morality as a private code of rules. Hence, my concern for the origins of social practices is a concern for the origins of ethics. This distinction traces back to Hegel. For further explanation, see Charles Taylor, *Hegel* (Cambridge: Cambridge University Press, 1989), 368–78. My concern here is to develop what Kristeva terms "herethics," which traces the origin of the social in the bridge between nature and culture that occurs in the maternal space. For Kristeva's discussion of a herethics, or what we can also understand as a maternal ethics, see her "Stabat Mater," in *The Kristeva Reader*, ed. Toril Moi (New York: Columbia University Press, 1986), 160–86. Kristeva writes: "For an heretical ethics separated from morality, an *herethics*, is perhaps no more than that which in life makes bonds, thoughts, and therefore the thought of death, bearable: herethics is undeath [*a-mort*], love" (185). This chapter focuses on the possibilities for a maternal ethics from her earlier work, and in particular *Revolution in Poetic Language*, because of its clearer explanation of musical and kinetic dimensions of early infant experience.

5   "Revolution in Poetic Language," in *The Kristeva Reader*, 90–136. Henceforth cited as *R*.

6   For a much more comprehensive reading of Kristeva's relation of the semiotic and the symbolic, see Kelly Oliver, *Reading Kristeva: Unraveling the Double-Bind* (Bloomington: Indiana University Press, 1993). While my argument focuses on Kristeva's earlier work, Kristeva continues to portray the maternal as a site of violence that is heterogeneous to the social, or what Oliver aptly terms an "outlaw *jouissance*" (see 50ff. for Oliver's account of the role of "outlaw *jouissance*" in Kristeva's later essay "Stabat Mater"). Oliver concludes her study by arguing that the semiotic body provides a site of resistance for social change, or what Oliver calls an "outlaw ethics." My concern is that an outlaw ethics premised on the expression of asocial drives contributes to a regressive politics, at least in cowboy America, which tends to discount the social resources as well as social deprivations of oppressed people. My question to Kristeva would be, do we not need to move from an outlaw ethics to an outcast ethics, and thus to an ethics centered around the vital need for social exchange?

7   Gayatri Chakravorty Spivak, "French Feminism in an International Frame," in *In Other Worlds: Essays in Cultural Politics* (New York: Routledge, 1987), 134–53; Susan Rubin Suleiman, *Subversive Intent: Gender, Politics, and the Avant-Garde* (Cambridge: Harvard University Press, 1990), 40; Benoite Groult, "Night Porters," in *New French Feminisms*, ed. Elaine Marks and Isabelle de Courtivron (New York: Schocken, 1980), 68–75. Henceforth, *Subversive Intent* will be cited as *S*.

8   A few years later, in "Women's Time," Kristeva again examines the violence that inheres in a "jouissance which is always already a transgression" (*The Kristeva Reader*, 203). She concludes that there is no social contract and, by dialectical reversal, no countersociety that does not originate in sacrificial logic. My first and more immediate question concerns the inequality in the distribution of the sacrifice and the pleasure of jouissance. A more difficult question concerns whether or not sociality itself might not be a natural pleasure and not a sacrificial negation. Kristeva shares Hobbesian assumptions of savage desire that I am questioning. Kristeva calls for the "de-dramatization of the 'fight to the death'" (*The Kristeva Reader*, 209) as social foundation. But the glorified transgressions of the avant-garde as well as the "interiorization of the founding separation of the socio-symbolic contract" transgress or interiorize but do not overcome the dialectics of sacrifice (*The Kristeva Reader*, 210). The "de-dramatization of the fight to the death" suggests a society that is not based on the thematics of castration, sacrifice, and separation.

9   See Domna C. Stanton, "Difference on Trial: A Critique of the Maternal Metaphor in Cixous, Irigaray, and Kristeva," in *The Poetics of Gender*, ed. Nancy K. Miller (New York: Columbia University Press, 1986), 173.

10   Friedrich Nietzsche, *Beyond Good and Evil*, trans. Walter Kaufmann (New York: Vintage, 1966) secs. 13, 21; references to original German text from Friedrich

Nietzsche, *Werke*, vol. 3, ed. Karl Schlechta (Ullstein Materialien). Henceforth cited as *BGE*.

11   Friedrich Nietzsche, *The Birth of Tragedy and The Genealogy of Morals*, trans. Francis Golffing (New York: Doubleday Anchor, 1956), second essay, sec. 5, 196. References to *The Genealogy of Morals* henceforth cited as *GM*.

12   Laura E. Berk, *Child Development* (Boston: Allyn and Bacon, 1991), 125. We parents also know the tremendous range of squeaks and grunts that babies already at birth use to signal their various desires. The cry of discomfort or pain lets us know that these desires are not polymorphous but already oriented even if not object-specific. There are limits to how the parent can shape the baby.

13   The association of the womb with a tomb is pervasive in our traditional culture. See, e.g., Madelon Sprengnether, "(M)other Eve: Some Revisions of the Fall in Fiction by Contemporary Women Writers," in *Feminism and Psychoanalysis*, ed. Richard Feldstein and Judith Roof (Ithaca: Cornell University Press, 1989), 298–322; Sprengnether argues for an elegiac notion of self by noting associations in literature between womb and tomb, garden and cemetery. Gayatri Spivak like-wise locates the procreative processes of the womb within the "larger economy of death"; thus, the self is always in exile; see her "French Feminism Revisited," in *Feminists Theorize the Political*, ed. Judith Butler and Joan W. Scott (New York: Routledge, 1992), 63. Similarly, according to Drucilla Cornell, "for Derrida, the subject only becomes a self in … mourning"; thus, the figure of mother is associated with the work of mourning; see Cornell, *The Philosophy of the Limit* (New York: Routledge, 1992), 76.

Irigaray comments that as far as Freud is concerned, women represent both "havens of refuge and safety" and "the total reduction … of death." See her *Speculum of the Other Woman*, trans. Gillian C. Gill (Ithaca: Cornell University Press, 1985), 34. She believes that the womb functions as a reminder of death only because men too often conceptualize feminine sexuality in terms of the castrated man, which is itself, Irigaray charges, a symptom of womb envy (*Speculum*, 23, 27). Nonetheless, Irigaray posits a death wish as fundamental to not only the male but also the female psyche.

14   See also Alice A. Jardine, *Gynesis* (Ithaca: Cornell University Press, 1985), 32.

15   Adrienne Rich, *Of Woman Born: Motherhood as Experience and Institution* (New York: W. W. Norton, 1986), 68. Henceforth cited as *OW*.

16   Cf. Benjamin, *B*, 11–12. The first-time mother of Benjamin's narrative takes her very own response to her very own question as a sign from her mute and passive child. Thus, she reduces the child to a topic in a sentimental and monologic narrative.

17   Angela Davis discusses the history and problems with the use of the metaphor of slavery to describe the experience of motherhood in white patriarchal society in "The Anti-Slavery Movement and the Birth of Women's Rights," in *Women, Race, and Class* (New York: Vintage, 1983), 30–45. Along with many nineteenth-century

feminists, I use this term in order to establish not a commonality but a dialectical mediation (a correspondence) between the causes of feminism and Black Liberation (cf. Davis, 44).

18   The view that the boundaries between mother and child are indeterminate appears in Nancy Hartsock, "The Feminist Standpoint," in *Discovering Reality*, ed. S. Harding and M. Hintikka (Dordrecht: Reidel, 1981). This view is also found in feminist works that draw upon Kristeva's theory of the abject in order to locate a basis for racism and other social pathologies. See, e.g., Iris Marion Young, *Justice and the Politics of Difference* (Princeton: Princeton University Press, 1990), 141–48; and Kelly Oliver, *Reading Kristeva*, 5.

Chapter 2: Tactile Sociality

1   "Nature" here functions as a complex term, clearly not reducible to a positivistic conception of a domain untouched by ethical and cultural elaborations. The paradoxical formulation, that the human being is by nature a social being, indicates the cultural complicity of any theory about "nature."

2   See Andrew Cutrofello, *Kant and the Problem of Discipline* (Albany: SUNY, 1994).

3   Adrienne Rich, *Of Woman Born: Motherhood as Experience and Institution* (New York: W. W. Norton, 1986), 217.

4   Cf. Jessica Benjamin, *The Bonds of Love: Psychoanalysis, Feminism, and the Problem of Domination* (New York: Pantheon, 1988), 11–12. Henceforth cited as *B*. My essay works within the dialogic model of self as developed by Benjamin, but with one modification. I am arguing that because the infant initially lacks any awareness of a self, the comportment between caregiver and child does not begin as dialogue but as attunement. I draw the notion of attunement from Daniel Stern as reinterpreted through the work of Luce Irigaray. See Daniel Stern, *The Interpersonal World of the Infant: A View from Psychoanalysis and Developmental Psychology* (New York: Basic Books, 1985). Henceforth cited as *I*.

5   For a Freudian-inspired analysis of the erotic pleasures of infancy, see John O'Neill, *Critical Conventions: Interpretation in the Literary Arts and Sciences* (Norman: University of Oklahoma Press, 1992), 249–63.

6   Kristeva is an example of a theorist who postulates the inevitability of sacrifice and then throws the burden of that sacrifice on the mother. Kristeva's essay "Stabat Mater" neglects the social pleasures of the maternal. On the contrary, the mother is temporarily shelter against death and finally makes death acceptable. Kristeva's vision of maternal ethics participates in the tradition that reduces women to mothers, mothers to wombs, and wombs to tombs. Mother is great receptacle. In this chapter, I borrow much from Kristeva's attempt to define a maternal ethics; however, I differ from Kristeva in my attempt to understand the mother-infant relation as a primary source of pleasure. A translation of Kristeva's essay can be

found in *The Kristeva Reader*, ed. Toril Moi (New York: Columbia University Press, 1986), 160–86.

For a critique of the ways in which black women in particular have suffered through the glorification of maternal sacrifice, see Patricia Hill Collins, "Black Women and Motherhood," in *Black Feminist Thought: Knowledge, Consciousness, and the Politics of Empowerment* (New York: Routledge, 1990), 115–37.

7   For exceptionally clear explanations of Lacanian analytic theory, see Elizabeth Grosz, *Jacques Lacan: A Feminist Introduction* (New York: Routledge, 1990); and Tamsin E. Lorraine, *Gender, Identity, and the Production of Meaning* (Boulder: Westview, 1990).

8   This generalization applies across several animal species. For example, according to Elizabeth Marshall Thomas, human beings "share something with the cat tribe: the stimulus to our hunting instinct is visual." As Thomas also points out, the sense of smell and touch function differently: "A cat's sense of smell, ... seems to have relatively little importance as a hunting tool, but is more than useful as a way of learning about other cats," and in fact, she adds, different species. When cats rub on us, they mix their odors with ours in a gesture of bonding and unity. See "Strong and Sensitive," *The Atlantic Monthly* 274, no. 1 (July 1994), esp. 68–69.

9   "Feminist" is not used in opposition to expressions of masculine subjectivity but specifically to those masculinist values that require the subordination or exclusion of women and that are complicit in patriarchy. While this chapter does not address differences between nonpatriarchal expressions of masculinity and masculinist styles of domination, it does aim to avoid what Lewis Gordon terms a "Manichaean" opposition between "bad guys" and "good women." I am grateful to Lewis Gordon for comments on an earlier version of this chapter.

10 Luce Irigaray, "The Fecundity of the Caress: A Reading of Levinas, *Totality and Infinity*, section IV, B, 'The Phenomenology of Eros,'" trans. in *Face to Face with Levinas*, ed. Richard Cohen (Albany: SUNY, 1986), 231. Henceforth cited as *F*. The essay originally appears as "Fécondité de la caresse," in *Ethique de la différence sexuelle* (Paris: Minuit, 1984), 173–99.

11 For a discussion of how Irigaray uses the work of Merleau-Ponty in order to interpret the experiences of early childhood, see "Chapter 4: Lived Bodies: Phenomenology and the Flesh," in Elizabeth Grosz, *Volatile Bodies: Toward a Corporeal Feminism* (Bloomington: Indiana University Press, 1994), 86–114. For a discussion of Merleau-Ponty's account of the intersubjective aspects of early infancy, see "Chapter 7: Childhood and Embodiment," in John O'Neill, *The Communicative Body* (Evanston: Northwestern University Press, 1989), 46–57. For a related discussion, see Robert Switzer, "Together in the Flesh," in *The Deniscence of Responsibility*, ed. D. Davis (forthcoming).

12 Jean-Jacques Rousseau and Johann Gottfried Herder, "An Essay on the Origin of Languages," *On the Origin of Language*, trans. John H. Moran and Alexander Gode (Chicago: University of Chicago Press, 1966), 39. Irene Harvey notes that Michelangelo's god uses his index finger.

13 Peggy Reeves Sanday argues that patriarchal cultures develop cosmologies (Heidegger's fundamental ontology) that emphasize creation *ex nihilo*, as if by magic. She characterizes these patriarchal cosmologies as outer-oriented. More balanced cultures include more feminized cosmologies, or stories that present inner-oriented tales of creation. These stories draw upon the fact that women create children within themselves and not outside themselves. See her *Female Power and Male Dominance: On the Origins of Sexual Inequality* (Cambridge: Cambridge University Press, 1991).

14 See Luce Irigaray, "The Invisible of the Flesh: A Reading of Merleau-Ponty, *The Visible and the Invisible*, 'The Intertwining—The Chiasm,'" in *An Ethics of Sexual Difference*, trans. Carolyn Burke and Gillian C. Gill (Ithaca: Cornell University Press, 1993), 162.

15 Luce Irigaray, *The Irigaray Reader*, ed. Margaret Whitford, (Cambridge: Basil Blackwell, 1991), 80. Henceforth cited as *R*.

16 Here I am reinterpreting what Iris Young describes as the sexual eroticism of motherhood. See her essay "Breasted Experience," in *Throwing Like a Girl and Other Essays in Feminist Philosophy and Social Theory* (Bloomington: Indiana University Press, 1990), esp. 196–200. She finds in the mother infant relation an erotic pleasure akin to intercourse. It is interesting that the work of socialization is assumed to be a burden demanding self-sacrifice rather than a potential source of pleasure akin to (although, as I am arguing, distinct from) that of sexuality. No doubt this assumption is due in part to the lack of regard on the part of the American capitalist system and its rationalization in liberal ideology for the social dimension of the person and, consequently, the lack of regard for the caregiver.

17 W. Golbfarb, "Effects of Psychological Deprivation in Infancy and Subsequent Stimulation," *American Journal of Psychiatry* 103 (l945), 18–33; R. A. Spitz, "Hospitalism: An Inquiry into the Genesis of Psychiatric Conditions in Early Childhood," *Psychoanalytic Study of the Child* 1 (l945), 113–17.

18 Diane Ackerman, *A Natural History of the Senses* (New York: Vintage, 1991), 73. Henceforth cited as *NH*.

19 Alessandra Piontelli, *From Fetus to Child: An Observational and Psychoanalytic Study* (New York: Routledge, 1992), 42. Henceforth cited as *FC*. Unfortunately, Piontelli's fascinating findings with regard to the social activities of the fetus are marred by her projection of social roles such as "whore" onto the observed fetus. Piontelli overlooks the possibility that women become whores because of a history of abuse or poverty and instead attributes to the whore an indelicacy of taste that develops already in the womb (see, e.g., her full remarks concerning the case of Giulia, 40–68).

20 See title essay in Luce Irigaray, *Ce sexe qui n'en est pas un* (Paris: Minuit, 1977), 23–32. Translation by Catherine Porter, *This Sex Which Is Not One* (Ithaca: Cornell University Press, 1985), 24–29. References to translation henceforth cited as *NO*.

21 Enrique Dussel, *Philosophy of Liberation*, trans. Aquilina Martinez and Christine

Morkovsky (Maryknoll: Orbis Books, 1980), 21. Dussel wrote his book in "the sorrow of exile."

22 These remarks owe much to discussions with Dianne Rothleder.

23 Ann Ferguson raises this question in her essay "On Conceiving Motherhood and Sexuality: A Feminist Materialist Approach," in *Mothering: Essays in Feminist Theory*, ed. Joyce Trebilcot (Totowa: Rowman and Allanheld, 1983), 159.

24 The asceticism of a care ethic dominates the tone of such standard guides to pregnancy as Arlene Eisenberg, Heidi Eisenberg Murkoff, and Sandee Eisenberg Hathaway, *What to Expect When You're Expecting* (New York: Workman Publishing, 1988). This guide depicts maternity as a chore full of risks for infant and sacrifices for the mother by focusing on the hazards of pregnancy and neglecting the social pleasures between mother and fetus. Niel H. Lauersen, *Childbirth with Love: A Complete Guide to Fertility, Pregnancy, and Childbirth for Caring Couples* (New York: Berkeley Books, 1985) addresses the paucity of research on the emotional life of the unborn child in the United States in comparison with Europe by mentioning some of the findings on prenatal psychology (see chapter 14). Nonetheless Lauersen's guidebook also focuses on what I would characterize as the ascetic practices that seem to be required for a successful pregnancy.

25 H. F. Harlow and R. Zimmerman, "Affectional Responses in the Infant Monkey," *Science* 130 (1959), 421–32.

26 B. Seay, B. K. Alexander, and H. F. Harlow, "Maternal Behavior of Socially Deprived Rhesus Monkeys," *Journal of Abnormal and Social Psychology* 69 (1964), 345–54.

27 The same mechanistic language continues in the best of contemporary work on infancy. See, e.g., T. Berry Brazelton et al., "The Origins of Reciprocity: The Early Mother-Infant Interaction," in *The Effect of the Infant on Its Caregiver*, ed. Michael Lewis and Leonard A. Rosenblum (New York: John Wiley and Sons, 1974), 49–76. The article makes the important observation that it is "the interdependency of rhythms ... [that] seemed to be at the root of [parent-child] 'attachment' as well as communication.... [And that] the interdependency of the dyad seemed to be more powerful in shaping each member's behavior than did any other force—such as the individual member's style or wish of the moment" (74). However, the article also uses computer imagery in order to explain the interaction despite the fact that computers cannot experience touch. While the article uses the computer model as though this model expresses what "literally" appears to the observer, the article distances itself from more humanistic and participatory language through the use of quotation. I will return to this problem later in this chapter.

28 For Irigaray, the lover's caress touches off reminiscences of the oceanic fluids of the maternal womb; see *F*, 233.

29 See "The 'Mechanics' of Fluids" in *NO*, 106.

30 Luce Irigaray, *Je, Tu, Nous: Toward a Culture of Difference*, trans. Alison Martin (New York: Routledge, 1993), 39.

31 Jacques Derrida and Christie V. McDonald, "Choreographies," *Diacritics* (Summer 1982), 66.

32 Here I am thinking of the women of Chile, whose protest of the Pinochet government took the form of dancing with their arms stretched open to absent partners on the square of Chile's capital.

33 This chapter was supported by a University of Kansas General Research Grant.

Part II: Introduction

1 Seyla Benhabib, *Situating the Self: Gender, Community and Postmodernism in Contemporary Ethics* (New York: Routledge, 1992), 148–77. Henceforth cited as SS.

2 Here I am sliding over an equivocation between the expressive individual of the existential tradition and the possessive individual of the modernist tradition. These differences will be explored in chapters 4 and 5.

3 My project emerges from various attempts to develop an account of a heterogeneous sociality, including Iris Young, "Impartiality and the Civic Public: Some Implications of Feminist Critiques of Moral and Political Theory," in *Throwing Like a Girl and Other Essays in Feminist Philosophical and Social Theory* (Bloomington: Indiana University Press, 1990), 92–113. Henceforth cited as TG.

4 Emmanuel Levinas, *Ethics and Infinity*, trans. Richard A. Cohen (Pittsburgh: Duquesne University Press, 1985), 86.

Chapter 3: The Greeting

1 Or, as Kojève writes, the human person emerges in "le Desir qui transforme l'Etre." See Alexandre Kojève, *Introduction a la lecture de Hegel* (Paris: Gallimard, 1947), 11. For English translation, see *Introduction to the Reading of Hegel*, trans. James H. Nichols, Jr. (New York: Basic Books, 1961), 3. Henceforth cited as IH.

2 Cf. Judith Butler, *Subjects of Desire: Hegelian Reflections in Twentieth-Century France* (New York: Columbia University Press, 1987), 61ff. Henceforth cited as SD.

3 Martin Heidegger, *Basic Writings*, trans. David Farrell Krell (New York: Harper and Row, 1977), 108. Henceforth cited as BW. For German text, see *"Was ist Metaphysik?"* in *Wegmarken* (Frankfurt am Main: Vittorio Klostermann Verlag, 1967), 1–19.

4 See translator's "Analysis," Martin Heidegger, *Nietzsche*, vol. 4: *Nihilism*, trans. David Krell (New York: Harper and Row, 1982), esp. 273ff.

5 Friedrich Nietzsche, *Ecce Homo: How One Becomes What One Is*, trans. R. J. Hollingdale (New York: Penguin, 1979), sec. 9. For commentary on this image in Nietzsche, see Gary Shapiro, *Alcyone: Nietzsche on Gifts, Noise, and Women* (Albany: SUNY, 1991), 134ff; and Kelly Oliver, *Womanizing Nietzsche* (New York: Routledge, 1985), 150

6 Hans-Georg Gadamer, *Hegel's Dialectic: Five Hermeneutical Studies*, trans. P.

Christopher Smith (New Haven: Yale University Press, 1976), 60. Henceforth cited as *HD*.

7   Butler makes this point in a slightly different way and with very different results. See *SD*, 74ff.

8   My criticism here is not meant to displace a more complete postcolonial critique of those theorists who argue that we Europeans have provided the civilizing principles for the en-light-enment of the colonized world and that it is up to them (e.g., those dark Latinos) to provide the raw courage. See, e.g., Homi Bhabha's critique of Richard Rorty, "Postcolonial Authority and Postmodern Guilt," in *Cultural Studies*, ed. Lawrence Grossberg et al. (New York: Routledge, 1992), 62. Why is it that we Europeans are allowed to characterize our principles of justice as "universals" that in some obscure way transcend "the walls of the city" (e.g., Seyla Benhabib, *Situating the Self*, 228), while Latinos are to contribute nothing more than courage?

9   Cf. Butler, who argues that Kojève successfully constructs a notion of community that respects individuals; *SD*, 78.

10 I will examine more carefully Hegel's own account of the dialectic of Self and Other in part 3. There I will argue that Hegel is not exempt from these two related problems. In this respect, my interpretation of Hegel, and of the difference between Hegel and Kojève, differs somewhat from Judith Butler's.

11 Cf. the later Hegel, who in fact denies that the duel exemplifies the struggle for recognition, *Philosophy of Mind*, trans. William Wallace (Oxford: Clarendon, 1978), sec. 432.

12 Jacques Lacan, *Écrits: A Selection* (New York: W. W. Norton Co., 1977), 2. Henceforth cited as *E*.

13 See Nancy Hartsock, *Money, Sex, and Power* (New York: Longman, 1983), 172.

14 For an account of Freud's location of the first self in narcissism, and an interpretation of narcissism through autoeroticism, where the individual's own body is taken as his first love-object, see, Bice Benvenuto and Roger Kennedy, *The Works of Jacques Lacan* (New York: St. Martin's, 1986), 50. Irigaray attempts to feminize the Freudian-Lacanian account of autoeroticism in tactile sociality rather than the objectifying dynamics of the visual gaze.

15 See Tamsin E. Lorraine, *Gender, Identity, and the Production of Meaning* (Boulder: Westview, 1990), 49. Here I think Kelly Oliver is right to argue that Lacan takes the mirror as the model of the social rather than vice versa. Oliver writes, "For Lacan, the subject can see itself only as the image reflected in the mirror. This becomes the model for subsequent relations and self-definition.... Following the mirror stage, the mother takes the place of the mirror image as Other." See her *Reading Kristeva: Unraveling the Double-Bind* (Bloomington: Indiana University Press, 1993), 37.

16 I am grateful to Barry Shank for helping me to strengthen my argument here.

17   Jonathan Bennett, "Thoughtful Brutes," in *American Philosophical Association Proceedings* (December 1987), 197–209. Henceforth cited as *TB*.

18   See Susan Bordo, *The Flight to Objectivity* (Albany: SUNY, 1987), esp. 54, for a critique of the representational model of the self, or the division of an inner self from the body; see 65, for a critique of the perspective model of experience, which interprets objects primarily in the visual register, and thus excludes nonvisual, including affective, knowledge of an object. Bordo points out that medieval European and African cultures do not apprehend the objects in the world as objects in a mirror but in multiple dimensions of sensory experience and hermeneutic significance.

19   It is significant that Bennett assumes that his project, which is to conceptualize the difference between "man and beast," can be performed simply by examining our representations or mental pictures of "man" and "beast." His concept of the self cannot be based on anything more real than our (whose?) representations, or the myths and fantasies that Lacan characterizes as the "imaginary." Lacan more carefully distinguishes the fictive representations that comprise our "specular self" from the discourse that comprises our "social self." Ironically, Bennett concludes by arguing that there is no specular self, i.e., no image of the self that, for example, might appear in the mirror, but only a concept of the self (or the subject that is referred to in propositional speech). Nondiscursive representations of the human self and the animal, the representations that were supposedly the beginning points of Bennett's analysis, are themselves delegitimated as sources of self-knowledge by Bennett's conclusion. Meanwhile, neither Lacan nor Bennett deals with the historicity of the imaginary. See Michele Wallace "The Search for the 'Good Enough' Mammy," *Multi-Culturalism*, ed. David Goldberg (Cambridge, MA: Basil Blackwell, 1994), 26.

The American imaginary is no doubt largely swayed by the American media. The antisocial outlaw is a popular image in American culture. And if originally this liberating image was reserved for the male subject, the film *Thelma and Louise* "emancipates" the female imaginary by reconstructing femininity in the same old terms. Only as antisocial outlaws can American protagonists assert their freedom. And, as Lacan argues, the liberal unweaving of the individual from the social fabric marks a step toward pathological derealization.

Chapter 4: The Figure of the Face

1   For a discussion of the role of the face in ethics and the motif of the stranger in the later writings of Levinas, see Robert Bernasconi, "Levinas Face to Face—With Hegel," *Journal of the British Society for Phenomenology* 13, no. 3 (October 1982), 267–75; and Ewa Ziarek, "Kristeva and Levinas: Mourning, Ethics, and the Feminine," in *Ethics, Politics, and Difference in Julia Kristeva's Writing: A Collection of Essays,* ed. Kelly Oliver (New York: Routledge, 1993), 62–78. For the remarks concerning infant babbling, see Emmanuel Levinas, *Otherwise Than Being or Beyond Essence*, trans. Alphonso Lingis (Dordrecht: Kluwer Academic Publishers,

1991), 147; for original French text, see *Autrement qu'etre ou au-dela de l'essence* (The Hague: Martinus Nijhoff, 1974), 188. References to *Otherwise Than Being* are hereafter cited as *O* with pagination in English translation preceding that of the original French text. For an alternative but related critique of Levinas, see John D. Caputo, *Against Ethics* (Bloomington: Indiana University Press, 1993).

2 But on the specific Jewish origins of ethics as a response to the stranger in distinction to the classical Greek and Christian location of ethics and justice in freedom, see Orlando Patterson, *Freedom,* vol. 1 (New York: Basic Books, 1991). Patterson explains how "what the Egyptian sojourn taught the Israelites was a ... passion for justice, including justice for the stranger" (34).

　　For an alternative but related reading of the influence of Rousseau on Levinas, see Robert Bernasconi, "Levinas and Derrida: The Question of the Closure of Metaphysics," in *Face-to-face with Levinas,* ed. Richard A. Cohen (Albany: SUNY, 1986), 181–204.

3 Jean-Jacques Rousseau and Johann Gottfried Herder, *On the Origin of Language: Two Essays,* trans. John H. Moran and Alexander Gode (Chicago: University of Chicago Press, 1966), 13. Henceforth cited as *OL.*

4 This remark follows Levinas's use of the metaphor of the maternal to describe a particular dimension of the ethical experience. I will return to his use of the maternal in a later section. It is important to note that even in his references to the maternal nature of the ethical relation, he quickly returns to a discussion of ethics as fraternity.

5 For a discussion of this problem with respect to Hegel, see Heidi M. Ravven, "Has Hegel Anything to Say to Feminists?" *Owl of Minerva* 19, no. 2 (Spring 1988), 149–68.

6 But it is also true that Levinas's account of the metamorphosis is not always the same. Importantly, his later work, *Otherwise Than Being,* emphasizes the dependence of existence upon the ethics and justice. For example, he writes, "the absurdity of the *there is* [is] a modality of the-one-for-the-other" (*O,* 164/208–09).

7 Emmanuel Levinas, *Time and the Other,* trans. Richard A. Cohen (Pittsburgh: Duquesne University Press, 1987), 46–47. Henceforth cited as *TO.*

8 Emmanuel Levinas, *Totality and Infinity,* trans. Alphonso Lingis (Pittsburgh: Duquesne University Press, 1969), 63; *Totalité et Infini* (The Netherlands: Martinus Nijhoff, 1971), 58. Henceforth cited as *TI,* with English pagination followed by pagination from the original French.

9 For the argument that Levinas presupposes war as natural, see Adrian Peperzak, "Some Remarks on Hegel, Kant, and Levinas," in *Face to Face with Levinas,* 214.

10 Emmanuel Levinas, *Ethics and Infinity,* trans. Richard A. Cohen (Pittsburgh: Duquesne University Press, 1985), 88.

11 Lacan observes that charity often invokes an aggressive reaction from its recipient. This is because altruism may be motivated by an intention to humiliate. In any

case, altruism has that effect. Lacan quotes La Rochefoucauld: "I can't bear the thought of being freed by anyone other than myself." See "Aggressivity in Psychoanalysis," in *Écrits: A Selection* (New York: W. W. Norton Co., 1977), 13. If so, then altruism once again reverses into its opposite, the will to violate. See chapter 1, where I interpret the gift-giving virtue in Nietzsche as violation.

12 Sandra Lee Bartky makes this point in "Feeding Egos and Tending Wounds," in *Femininity and Domination: Studies in the Phenomenology of Oppression* (New York: Routledge, 1990), 99–119.

13 Adrienne Rich, *Of Woman Born: Motherhood as Experience and Institution* (New York: W. W. Norton, 1986), 36, henceforth cited as *OW*.

14 Theodore de Boer argues that Levinas understands pleasure to be fundamentally asocial in "An Ethical Transcendental Philosophy," in *Face to Face with Levinas*, 98, 110. In some respects, I am attempting to find what Fabio Ciaramelli calls a "more positive evaluation of reciprocity and symmetry" within the ethical dyad. See his "Levinas's Ethical Discourse between Individuation and Universality," in *Re-Reading Levinas*, ed. Robert Bernasconi and Simon Critchley (Bloomington: Indiana University Press, 1991), 100–101.

15 I take this to be the main point of her essay, "The Fecundity of the Caress," in *Face to Face with Levinas*, 231–56.

16 For a less poetic and more scientific study that comes to the same conclusion, see T. Berry Brazelton et al., "The Origins of Reciprocity: The Early Mother-Infant Interaction," in *The Effect of the Infant on Its Caregiver*, ed. Michael Lewis and Leonard A. Rosenblum (New York: John Wiley and Sons, 1974), 49–75. The article concludes: "The strength of the interdependency of the [parent-infant] dyad seemed to be more powerful in shaping each member's behavior than did any force—such as the individual member's style or wish of the moment"; and specifically the "interdependency of rhythms seemed to be at the root of their 'attachment' as well as communication," 74.

17 Daniel Stern, *The First Relationship: Infant and Mother* (Cambridge: Harvard University Press, 1977), 72.

18 Daniel Stern, *The Interpersonal World of the Infant: A View from Psychoanalysis and Developmental Psychology* (New York: Basic Books, 1985), 139, emphasis mine; hereafter cited as *I*.

19 Not always do caregiver and infant respond in a way that resonates. But these misattunements are useful in shaping or changing the affective state of the Other (*I*, 148).

20 In effect, Jessica Benjamin draws upon this possibility in *The Bonds of Love: Psychoanalysis, Feminism, and the Problem of Domination* (New York: Pantheon, 1988), 11–12.

21 Laurence Thomas, "Moral Deference," *The Philosophical Forum* 24, nos. 1–3 (Fall–Spring 1992–93), 235. Henceforth cited as *MD*.

22 Along these lines, see Aldo Leopold's transfiguration before the face of a dying wolf in *A Sand County Almanac* (New York: Oxford University Press, 1966), 130. I thank James Woelfel for this reference.

For an account of the role of the fully expressive face in the social life of cats, see Elizabeth Marshall Thomas, "Strong and Sensitive," *The Atlantic Monthly* 274, no. 1 (July 1994), 66–71. Moreover, Thomas finds that cats have developed a vast repertoire of vocalizations and facial expressions in order to communicate across species.

23 Thomas, "Strong and Sensitive," 69.

Part III: Introduction

1 Luther H. Martin, Huck Gutman, and Patrick H. Hutton, eds., *Technologies of the Self: A Seminar with Michel Foucault* (Amherst: University of Massachusetts Press, 1988), 146. Henceforth cited as *TS*.

2 Michel Foucault, *The Use of Pleasure* in *The History of Sexuality* 2, trans. Robert Hurley (New York: Vintage Books, 1990), 242. For an alternative, and more distinctly stoic, ritual for testing manhood independence, see Michel Foucault, *The Care of the Self,* in *The History of Sexuality* 3, trans. Robert Hurley (New York: Vintage Books, 1988), 58–59.

3 See, e.g., Sterling Stuckey, *Slave Culture: Nationalist Theory and the Foundations of Black America* (New York: Oxford University Press, 1987).

4 Henry Louis Gates, Jr., ed. *The Classic Slave Narratives* (New York: Mentor, 1987), ix. Henceforth cited as *CSN*.

5 Broadus N. Butler locates as essential moments of African American philosophy what I am arguing to be two dimensions of postcolonial philosophy in his "Frederick Douglass: The Black Philosopher in the United States: A Commentary," in *Philosophy Born of Struggle*, ed. Leonard Harris (Dubuque: Kendall/Hunt, 1983), 1–10. First, Butler interprets what (as I shall argue) dialectical philosophy understands as the social dimension of the free self in terms of the specifically African value of belonging. Secondly, he argues that any authentic philosophy of freedom must emerge from the standpoint of the oppressed. His example, as will be mine, is Frederick Douglass.

6 Frederick Douglass, *Narrative of the Life of Frederick Douglass, An American Slave*, ed. Houston A Baker, Jr. (New York: Penguin, 1986). Frederick Douglass, *My Bondage and My Freedom*, ed. William Andrews (Chicago: University of Illinois Press, 1987). Henceforth cited as *BF*.

7 William L. Andrews, *To Tell a Free Story* (Urbana: University of Illinois Press, 1988), 217 and 124–29. Henceforth cited as *FS*. While Andrews argues that the 1845 *Narrative* adopts Euro-American individualism, he also argues that the Douglass narrative challenges conventional literary expectations with surprising rhetorical devices.

8   Georg Wilhelm Friedrich Hegel, *The Philosophy of History*, trans. J. Sibree (New York: Dover, 1956), 40–41.

9   Cf. Thad Ziolkowski, "Antitheses: The Dialectic of Violence and Literacy in Frederick Douglass's *Narrative* of 1845," in *Critical Essays on Frederick Douglass,* ed. William L. Andrews (Boston: G. K. Hall, 1991), 148–65. Thad Ziolkowski argues that the Douglass *Narrative* appropriates the European dialectic of freedom exactly as it is conceptualized by Hegel in his *Phenomenology of Spirit.* I shall be developing the ways in which Douglass eschewed the worker-self encouraged of the slave by the slaveholder and justified philosophically by Hegel. Note however that Sterling Stuckey criticizes Douglass on exactly this point. Stuckey argues that Douglass fails to acknowledge the African origins for agriculture and handicraft skills, which defined an African American slave culture. See his "'Ironic Tenacity': Frederick Douglass's Seizure of the Dialectic," in *Frederick Douglass: New Literary and Historical Essays*, ed. Eric J. Sundquist (Cambridge: Cambridge University Press, 1990), 23–46.

10 Orlando Patterson makes a very powerful case for the dialectical dependency of freedom on slavery as "thesis upon antithesis." See his *Slavery and Social Death* (Cambridge: Harvard University Press, 1982). For another appropriation of the master/slave dialectic in Hegel, see David Brion Davis, *The Problem of Slavery in the Age of Revolution: 1770–1823* (Ithaca: Cornell University Press, 1975), epilogue: "Toussaint L'Ouverture and the Phenomenology of Mind," 557–64.

11 For a historical account of the association of Africans and African Americans with brute animality, see Winthrop D. Jordan, *White Over Black: American Attitudes Toward the Negro, 1550–1812* (Chapel Hill: University of North Carolina Press, 1968). For example, according to Jordan, such products of the Enlightenment as the Linnaean classification of the various species or the philosophical classification of the various faculties were used to justify slavery. The Linnaean classification of the species was used to place the African in a species between man and orangoutangs (236). One exemplary philosopher of the Enlightenment, Thomas Jefferson, drew upon philosophical argument in order to conclude that the African lacks the reflective and rational capacities of the European (436–37).

12 Hegel terms this moment of individual difference "moral spirit." See *Phenomenology of Spirit*, trans. A. V. Miller (New York: Oxford University Press, 1977), sec. 796.

Chapter 5: Hegel's Master Narrative of Freedom

1   G. W. F. Hegel, *Phenomenology of Spirit*, trans. A. V. Miller (Oxford: Oxford University Press, 1977); *Phaenomenologie des Geistes* (Hamburg: Felix Meiner, 1952). Henceforth cited as *PS*.

2   For a brief discussion of the central role of Hegel's concept of recognition in African American philosophy, see Robert C. Williams, "W. E. B. Du Bois: Afro-American Philosopher of Social Reality," in *Philosophy Born of Struggle: Anthology of Afro-American Philosophy from 1917*, ed. Leonard Harris (Dubuque: Kendall/Hunt, 1983), 17. There are several excellent philosophical studies that examine the effects of slavery

on African American identity. However, each of these works—including Laurence Mordekhai Thomas, *Vessels of Evil* (Philadelphia: Temple University Press, 1993); Howard McGary and Bill Lawson, *Between Slavery and Freedom* (Bloomington: Indiana University Press, 1992); and many of the essays in the Harris anthology— borrow their methodology from neo-Kantian or modernist philosophies rather than nineteenth century dialectical philosophy. There are essays in the Harris anthology (e.g., Angela Davis, "Unfinished Lecture on Liberation–II," and Cornel West, "Philosophy, Politics, and Power") that are in the dialectical tradition. See also Frantz Fanon's critique of the Hegelian model from the point of view of his own cultural history in *Black Skin, White Masks* (New York: Grove Press, 1967). As far as I am aware, however, there are no extended philosophical discussions of the relation between Hegel's master/slave dialectic and the African American experience of slavery. This is despite the fact that a reference to Hegel is almost obligatory in social histories of slavery, and that W. E. B. Du Bois, a major African American thinker, appropriated Hegelian themes and a dialectical methodology throughout his writings on racism.

3   One of the deeper problems in Hegel's discussion of the master/slave relation is the presupposition that both master and slave are warriors and, as the tradition requires, are therefore most likely male. While I will touch upon the gender issue, I have chosen to focus on the issue of race. Nonetheless, it should be remembered that most slaves in Western history were female; see Orlando Patterson, *Freedom*, vol. 1: *Freedom in the Making of Western Culture* (New York: Basic Books, 1991), 9–10. Henceforth cited as *F*. It is disappointing that even while Patterson provides evidence for the fact that most slaves have in fact been female, he nonetheless perpetuates one of the major myths of the Western philosophical tradition, namely, that the slave was defeated in battle and therefore fails to exhibit manly courage.

4   As Andrew Cutrofello reminds me, this asceticism is sublated and finally resolved when evil and judging consciousnesses come to recognize that we are all "evil"— i.e., determined in part by primitive desires rather than duty. The *Phenomenology* concludes that we finite creatures must forgive one another and live happily thereafter in community. I am arguing that the dialectic of duty and desire does not occur in African American culture as it does in northern European cultures. As will become clearer in chapters 6 and 7, desire for such exemplary African American thinkers as Frederick Douglass does not define an evil and liminal dimension of the self that must then be overcome even if this overcoming finally amounts to nothing more than mutual forgiveness. Desire is not for Douglass a sin.

5   In German, Hegel's discussion of what scholars typically refer to as the master/slave relation occurs in terms of *Herrschaft und Knechtschaft*, which, as Lewis Gordon has remarked, may allude more directly to the German history of indentured servitude than to European slavery. David R. Roediger has written that in pre-Revolutionary America, "indentured servitude, impressment, apprenticeship, convict labor, farm tenancy, wage labor ... made for a continuum of oppression" and that after the Revolution, whites came to set up a sharp opposition between the freeman and the black slave. See his *The Wages of Whiteness: Race and the*

Making of the American Working Class (New York: Verso, 1993), 25, henceforth cited as *WW*. Rather than attempt to locate the single correct interpretation of the Hegelian model of self-consciousness, I aim to develop one version of the Hegelian problematic that might give some insight into the dynamics of American slavery. I translate Hegel's passages on self-consciousness with this aim in mind.

6   Cf. Robert R. Williams, *Recognition: Fichte and Hegel on the Other* (Albany: SUNY, 1992), 141–68. Williams argues for the pure and a priori status of Hegel's introductory discussion of self-consciousness.

7   On the concept of experience as a historical presentation, see, e.g., Werner Marx, *Hegel's Phenomenology of Spirit: A Commentary Based on the Preface and Introduction*, trans. Peter Heath (New York: Harper and Row, 1975), 12–15. For Hegel's critique of the use of intuition in philosophy, see *PS*, sec. 17. For his critique of mathematical thinking, see *PS*, secs. 42–48.

8   Frank M. Kirkland, in his commentary on the version of this chapter read at the Central Division of the American Philosophical Association (May 1994), argues that the historical considerations that I am incorporating into Hegel's dialectic of self-consciousness are premature. No doubt, he is on good scholarly grounds to argue that these historical considerations should only come into play in chapters 6 and 7 of the *Phenomenology*. However, while I am defending my interpretation of chapter 4 as a transformative reading of Hegel's text, I could also use my interpretation as a critique of the latent Cartesianism of Hegel's first few chapters in the *Phenomenology*. In particular, I would ask, on what basis can the Hegel scholar justify what Hegel reifies as *the* experience of self-consciousness? What guarantees that this experience does not vary in accordance with such factors as race, culture, and gender as well as the specific historical and material grounds from which the self emerges?

On this same issue, John McCumber argues that the master/slave dialectic of the *Phenomenology* "appears to be based on a halcyon view of slavery in the ancient world" and adds that "the historical source of what is described is less important than the way Hegel appropriates it in his narrative as a stage in the development of Spirit." See his *Poetic Interaction: Language, Freedom, Reason* (Chicago: University of Chicago Press, 1989), 40–41. My aim is not to return to a positivistic notion of history but to transform the historical and political-ethical sources of a Hegelian-style narrative of Spirit from those masterpieces of the Western tradition in which slavery is depicted in terms that are halcyon to texts that view the master/slave dialectic from the more troubled perspective of the slave. In the process, I aim to show that Hegel's definition of the self (or moral person) is not the only one.

9   Clark Butler develops this thesis in his psychoanalytic reading of Hegel. See "Hegel and Freud," *Philosophy and Phenomenological Research* 36 (June 1976), 506–22. Here I develop the same thesis, but draw more upon Hegel's own writings than those of Freud.

10 I borrow the term "psychohistory" from Joel Kovel, *White Racism: A Psychohistory* (New York: Pantheon, 1970), for reasons that will become clearer in chapters 6 and 7.

11   On the association of women with the passive receptivity of the plant world and of men as the primordial hunters, see Hegel, *Philosophy of Nature*, trans. A. V. Miller (Oxford: Clarendon Press, 1970), 413.

12   The standard reading of Hegel argues that hedonism fails as an end of history due to the endless cycle of dependence of self on other. The hedonistic self depends on the external object that it consumes. For example, see Judith Butler, *Subjects of Desire: Hegelian Reflections in Twentieth-Century France* (New York: Columbia University Press, 1987), 36. Ivan Soll, however, points out that the hedonist cherishes the endless cycle of desire and satiation. See his "On Desire and Its Discontents," in *Ratio* 2, (1989), 169–84. Indeed, if the Hegelian absolute demands not a static and eternal unity of subject and object but only a cyclical equation of subject and object, then such an absolute could be exemplified in the eternal return of hedonistic pleasure. It seems to me that Kojève implies some such vision of pleasure in his depiction of "posthistorical" America or even the more refined Japanese tea ceremony. See Alexandre Kojève, *Introduction to the Reading of Hegel*, ed. Allan Bloom (New York: Basic Books, 1969), 160–62. Therefore, I have modified the standard interpretation in order to locate what I take to be a more central motivation of the passage from hedonism and desire to willful battles for recognition.

13   Cornel West explains the same idea in more contemporary terms: "The quest for identity is fundamental. The quest for community is basic. For what? Protection, meaning, value, the means by which human beings are willing to face their extinction, with a sense of significance." See his "Beyond Eurocentrism and Multiculturalism," in *Prophetic Reflections: Notes on Race and Power in America* (Monroe: Common Courage Press, 1993), 122.

14   I am relocating the context of Hegel's writing from the modern French focus on desire to the more Germanic focus on will. The interpretation of self-consciousness, indeed of the entire Hegelian project, in terms of desire occurs in Kojève's *Introduction to the Reading of Hegel* as well as in numerous American interpretations of Hegel, including, e.g., Butler's *Subjects of Desire*, 35ff. and Stanley Rosen, *G. W. F. Hegel: An Introduction to the Science of Wisdom* (New Haven: Yale University Press, 1974), 30. Rosen writes that Hegel "recognizes desire as the 'engine' of world-history (thereby uniting the Platonic Eros with the directedness of historical development)." Hegel explicitly uses the language of will in the account of the battle for recognition that appears in the *Philosophy of Mind*, trans. William Wallace (Oxford: Clarendon Press, 1971), sec. 432, *Zusatz*; this text is henceforth cited as *PM*. For references to the German edition of *PM*, see *Werke, bande 10: Enzyklopaedie der philosophishen Wissenshaften im Grundrisse, Dritter Teil, Die Philosophie des Geistes mit den muendlichen Zusaetzen* (Frankfurt: Suhrkamp Verlag, 1979). There Hegel writes that Spirit presupposes that "der Einzelne seinerseits macht sich dieser Anerkennung dadurch wuerdig, dass er, mit Ueberwindung der Natuerlichkeit seines Selbstbewusstseins, einem *Allgemeinen*, dem *an and fuer sich seienden Willen*, dem *Gesetze gehorct*" (sec. 432, *Zusatz*).

15   In other terms, "moral authorship requires a break in the natural causal chain (in

Kantian parlance: an act of will)." I borrow these terms from John McCumber, "Is a Post-Hegelian Ethics Possible?" in *Research in Phenomenology* 18 (1988), 129.

16   Here it might help to recall Doctor Johnson's refutation of Bishop Berkeley's idealism. Doctor Johnson's proof of the existence of the world was to kick a stone outside the door of his home in London. On the masculinist presuppositions of this style of argument, see chapter 2.

17   Cf. Robert C. Solomon, *In the Spirit of Hegel* (New York: Oxford University Press, 1983), 450. Solomon points out that "one can risk one's life *and* win approval of others without trying to kill anyone (for instance, in some death-defying feat of courage), and it is not at all clear that 'risking one's life' had to be taken literally." I agree with the latter point. One must risk one's natural self, which, for Hegel, includes the instrumental self. Therefore, a test of courage might involve risking one's career or status. For example, in various interviews after her testimony before Congress on the Clarence Thomas nomination, Anita Hill indicated that she has indeed been tested. I am less clear about Solomon's first point. If freedom emerges only in sociality, a test of self against nature cannot display the supreme test of self. This test must involve—directly or indirectly—a contest of wills. A contest of wills might involve putting various contestants through trials (e.g., elephant hunting) that pose each contestant directly against nature and only indirectly against one another.

18   Luce Irigaray, *Je, Tu, Nous: Toward a Culture of Difference*, trans. Alison Martin (New York: Routledge), 39; Daniel N. Stern, *The Interpersonal World of the Infant: A View from Psychoanalysis and Developmental Psychology* (New York: Basic Books, 1985), 11.

19   The role of the gaze in the scene of recognition is developed in Jean-Paul Sartre's dialectic of "Being-for-Others" in *Being and Nothingness*, trans. Hazel E. Barnes (New York: Washington Square Press, 1956), part 3, chapter 3. For the discussion of feminist psychoanalysis, see chapter 2 above.

20   Note that while the first active engagement of the will of another occurs in struggle, the first encounter with the other person is passive and harmonious. As Quentin Lauer explains, "Before facing the challenge of another consciousness, self-consciousness finds all the recognition it wants in itself." See his *A Reading of Hegel's Phenomenology of Spirit* (New York: Fordham University Press, 1982), 104. Therefore, self-consciousness develops in a Rousseauian state of peaceful coexistence before it asserts itself in a quasi-Hobbesian struggle.

21   Hans-Georg Gadamer mentions the example of the duel in his "Hegel's Dialectic of Self-Consciousness," in *Hegel's Dialectic: Five Hermeneutical Studies*, trans. Christopher Smith (New Haven: Yale University Press, 1976), 65. Cf. Hegel: "Duelling must definitely not be confused with the fight for recognition.... Duelling does not belong to the natural state of men, but to a more or less developed form of civil society and the State" (*PM*, sec. 432, *Zusatz*).

22   I am grateful to Greg Conrad for helping me to clarify my argument.

23 Georg Wilhelm Friedrich Hegel, *The Philosophy of History*, trans. J. Sibree (New York: Dover, 1956), 95–96. Henceforth cited as *PH*.

24 Stephen Houlgate comments on these passages in *Freedom, Truth and History: An Introduction to Hegel's Philosophy* (London: Routledge, 1991), 86–88.

25 Cf. Bill Lawson's argument in "Oppression and Slavery," in *Between Slavery and Freedom*, ed. Howard McGary and Bill Lawson (Bloomington: Indiana University Press, 1992), 1–15. Lawson is right to argue that the reduction of the person to property differentiates slavery from other forms of oppression. My interest is in expanding his argument in order to account for the social and psychological dynamics common to slavery and other forms of oppression.

26 Clearly, the argument that Western culture is the product of the slave-worker cannot extend to those societies in which the slave contributes to the economic or cultural wealth of the slaveholder. Patterson argues that while the assumption that hunter and gatherer societies do not take slaves is a myth, the slaves of these societies contribute only to the honor and not the economic well-being of their masters; see Patterson, *F*, 12–16.

27 Hegel's analysis here supports in part the analysis of American slavery in Stanley Elkins, *Slavery* (Chicago: University of Chicago Press, 1959), chapter 3.

28 As Lewis Gordon reminds me, the inability of the individual to acquire a sense of self without looking into the eyes of the other person not only accounts for the fact that African Americans have often been punished for looking into the eyes of whites; Gordon also suggests that this unwillingness to admit the selfhood of the black accounts for the artistic rendering of African Americans during the period of slavery as dark bodies without faces. On the importance not only of the eyes but of the full expressive features of the face-to-face interaction for acquiring a sense of self, see part 2.

29 Orlando Patterson, *Slavery and Social Death* (Cambridge: Harvard University Press, 1982), 80. Henceforth cited as *SSD*.

30 Patterson argues against what Kojève in his reading of Hegel terms the "existential impasse" for the master. According to Patterson, it is a matter of historical fact that "the master could and usually did achieve the recognition he needed from other free persons, including other masters" (*SSD*, 99). Allen W. Wood focuses on logical grounds in order to criticize Hegel on the same point. Wood argues that masters would not logically be dependent upon their slaves for recognition but instead could seek recognition among other masters. For Wood's argument, see *Hegel's Ethical Thought* (Cambridge: Cambridge University Press, 1990), 93.

31 Frederick Douglass, *My Bondage and My Freedom*, ed. William L. Andrews (Chicago: University of Illinois Press, 1987), 61. Cf. Harriet Jacobs, writing as Linda Brent, *Incidents in the Life of a Slave Girl*, collected in *The Classic Slave Narratives*, ed. Henry Louis Gates, Jr. (New York: Mentor, 1987), 393; see also her observation that even poor whites sought to gain some recognition of their power by torturing or raping blacks (408).

32   Philip S. Froner, ed., *The Life and Writings of Frederick Douglass: The Civil War* 3 (New York: International Publishers, 1975), editor's introduction, 25.

33   John W. Blassingame, *The Slave Community: Plantation Life in the Antebellum South* (New York: Oxford University Press, 1974), 148–51. Henceforth cited as *SC*.

34   Lewis Gordon mentions here the importance of understanding that slaves risked their lives perhaps even more to save their families than to display their own courage and thereby reclaim their selfhood.

35   Eric J. Sundquist, *To Wake the Nations: Race in the Making of American Literature* (Cambridge: Harvard University Press, 1993), 51ff. Henceforth cited as *WN*.

36   Along these lines, it is interesting that in his analysis of another African American culture, specifically the "street families" of the contemporary poor inner-city black community, Elijah Anderson notes that the respect sought in violent rituals of manhood is often referred to in the street lingo as "juice." See his "The Code of the Streets," in *The Atlantic Monthly* (May 1994), 81–94, and especially the section entitled "Self-Image Based on 'Juice.'" My hypothesis is that this notion of respect based on "juice" repeats but also alters significantly themes developed in the Hegelian battle of self-consciousness.

37   Paul Gilroy, *The Black Atlantic: Modernity and Double Consciousness* (Cambridge: Harvard University Press, 1993). Henceforth cited as *BA*.

38   Eugene D. Genovese, *Roll, Jordan, Roll: The World the Slaves Made* (New York: Random House, 1976), 288–324.

39   Ibid., 285–324.

40   See Andrew Cutrofello, "Speculative Logic, Deconstruction, and Discourse Ethics," *The Philosophical Forum* 24, no. 4 (Summer 1993), 319–30; and Cynthia Willett, "The Shadow of Hegel's *Science of Logic*," *Essays on Hegel's Logic*, ed. George di Giovanni (Albany: SUNY Press, 1990), 85–92.

41   Note that because Patterson develops his analysis of the several concepts of freedom from the point of view of eighteenth-century Enlightenment rationalism, he overlooks the nineteenth-century dialectical concept of freedom as recognition; see Patterson, *F*, 3–4. Yet only the latter concept of freedom can account for the primary deprivation of the slave, which Patterson describes as a "social death." The slave lacks not only what Patterson defines as personal or civic freedoms but the social support required to develop a sense of dignity. Hegel's point is that one cannot attain a sense of dignity without social recognition. Therefore, the struggle against oppression must occur at the level of the social imaginary, or what Hegel identifies as the realm of Spirit.

      Note also that Patterson's uncritical allegiance to the philosophy of the Enlightenment accounts for his perception of non-European cultures as "pre-civilized" and "primitive"; see his discussion of the Tupinamba, 11–17.

42   I am especially grateful to Robert Bernasconi, Richard Cole, Andrew Cutrofello,

Lewis Gordon, Frank M. Kirkland, Julie Maybee, and John McCumber for very helpful comments on an earlier version of this chapter.

Chapter 6: A Slave Narrative of Freedom

1   G. W. F. Hegel, *Phenomenology of Spirit*, trans. A. V. Miller (Oxford: Oxford University Press, 1977). Henceforth cited as *PS*.

2   Robert Bernasconi makes an analogous argument with regard to a distinction between "White reason" and "Black reason" that he finds in one of the essays of Frederick Douglass. Black reason finally includes white reason inasmuch as it appeals to a more inclusive concept of liberty. See "The Constitution of the People: Frederick Douglass and the *Dred Scott* Decision," *The Cardoza Law Review* 13, no. 4 (December 1991), 1291ff. See also Leonard Harris, "Introduction," in *Philosophy Born of Struggle* (Dubuque: Kendall/Hunt, 1983). As Harris writes, "What we all have in common may be well explicated through the conceptual contours that form Afro-American culture" (x–xi).

3   For what little we know about Douglass's acquaintance with German idealism, see William S. McFeely, *Frederick Douglass* (New York: Simon and Schuster, 1991), 263. Henceforth cited as *FD*. McFeely has traced Douglass's exposure to texts of Goethe and Feuerbach to his friendship with Otillia Assing. My understanding is that he met her only after having written his 1855 *My Bondage and My Freedom*. Assing translated the second autobiography into German.

4   Douglass puts to an existential test what Bernard R. Boxill argues for in his clarification of the difference between Booker T. Washington and W. E. B. Du Bois: "Washington's position was that if a person felt wronged, he should do something about it; if he could do nothing he should hold his tongue and wait his opportunity; protest in such cases is only a servile appeal for sympathy; stoicism, by implication, is better. Du Bois strongly contested these views. Not only did he deny that protest is an appeal for sympathy, he maintained that if a person failed to express openly his outrage at injustice ... , he would in the long run lose his self-respect." See his "Self-Respect and Protest," *Philosophy and Public Affairs* 6, no. 1 (1967), 58. In effect, I am recasting Boxill's point by way of a Hegelian dialectic for recognition rather than a Kantian notion of self-respect. I return to problems with adopting an Enlightenment concept of self later in the chapter.

Secondly, I am attempting to avoid reading the character of Frederick Douglass as yet another example of a black man who invokes the patriarchal model of phallic manhood. See bell hooks's critique of the absence of sensuality in the construction of the masculine self in "Reconstructing Black Masculinity" in *Black Looks: Race and Representation* (Boston: South End Press, 1992), esp. 94.

5   On the ways in which racism and sexism enter into the very construction of Western concepts of rationality, see Nancy Leys Stepan, "Race and Gender: The Role of Analogy in Science," and Christian Delacampagne, "Racism and the West: From Praxis to Logos," both in *Anatomy of Racism*, ed. David Theo Goldberg

(Minneapolis: University of Minnesota Press, 1992); and David Theo Goldberg, *Racist Culture: Philosophy and the Politics of Meaning* (Cambridge: Blackwell, 1993), esp. chapter 2, 14–40. Henceforth cited as *RC*. The classic statement of the problem is found in Jacques Derrida, "Racism's Last Word," *Critical Inquiry* 12, no. 1 (Autumn 1985), 290–99. For the effect of culture on the construction of rationality, see Mario Sáenz, "Memory, Enchantment and Salvation: Latin American Philosophers of Liberation and the Religions of the Oppressed," *Philosophy and Social Criticism* 17, no. 2 (November 1991), 149–72; and John Russon, "Heidegger, Hegel, and Ethnicity: The Ritual Basis of Self-Identity," *Southern Journal of Philosophy* (forthcoming).

6   I am also suggesting an alternative reading to that of Henry Louis Gates, Jr., who argues that Douglass plays the trickster who deconstructs oppositions in order to show that these "oppositions, all along, were only arbitrary, not fixed." See "Binary Oppositions in Chapter One of *Narrative of the Life of Frederick Douglass, an American Slave Written By Himself*" in *Figures in Black: Works, Signs, and the "Racial" Self* (New York: Oxford University Press, 1987), 93. While Douglass deconstructs the oppositions that inform the plantation, his deconstruction yields a dialectic of social and historical progress. The evils of the plantation are not arbitrary; they are, for Douglass, unnatural.

7   Douglass, like W. E. B. Du Bois, accepted the romantic German notion that each culture has its unique gift to contribute to humanity. Douglass also argued for the relative superiority of the hybrid culture produced by the mulattoes over either Eurocentric or Afrocentric cultures. As Waldo E. Martin, Jr., explains, mulatto culture represented for Douglass a more perfect revision of the white American ideal of a melting pot. See Martin, *The Mind of Frederick Douglass* (Chapel Hill: University of North Carolina Press, 1984), 222–23. Henceforth cited as *MFD*. On the "hybrid" aspects of Douglass's reinterpretation of Hegel's dialectic of master and slave, see Paul Gilroy, *The Black Atlantic: Modernity and Double Consciousness* (Cambridge: Harvard University Press, 1993), 61. Henceforth cited as *BA*.

My own aim is not to assume with Douglass the cultural superiority of the mulatto but only to argue that Douglass presents one progressive model of freedom and selfhood. As I have argued in the introduction, this book is part of a larger project that aims to pluralize the conceptions of the moral self on the basis of such factors as race, gender, and culture. Because a single conception posing as the universal excludes other viable conceptions of freedom and selfhood, any claim to establish a universal is racist, etc.

For the citation from Du Bois, see his *The Souls of Black Folk* (New York: Bantam, 1989), 35.

8   For a discussion of the use of this criterion to justify slavery in the philosophy of Locke, see Goldberg, *RC*, 27.

9   Frederick Douglass, *Narrative of the Life of Frederick Douglass, An American Slave*, ed. Houston A. Baker, Jr. (New York: Viking Penguin, 1982), 112–3. Henceforth cited as *N*.

10   The 1855 revision was written after Douglass's break with the Garrisonians and prior to his more accommodationist stance to the virtues of social Darwinism in American capitalism. On Douglass's later philosophy, see Martin, *MFD*, 256.

11   Frederick Douglass, *My Bondage and My Freedom*, ed. William L. Andrews (Urbana: University of Illinois Press, 1987), 151. Henceforth cited as *BF*.

12   Douglass uses this language among other places in an 1863 article in the *Douglass Monthly*. See *The Life and Writings of Frederick Douglass*, 4 vols., ed. Philip S. Foner (New York: International Publisher, 1972), vol. 3, 352. Henceforth cited as *LWFD*.

13   So too I am to some extent questioning Henry Louis Gates, Jr.'s, reading of the slave narrative through the influence of the sentimental novel on the European picaresque. See "Binary Oppositions in Chapter One of *Narrative of the Life of Frederick Douglass an American Slave Written By Himself*," 81; and Eric J. Sundquist's argument that "the literature of American slavery transplants the language of oppression and liberation from the romantic and gothic traditions, where it had been a particular spur to Britain's successful antislavery movement, into a new national setting where it is bound together with the language of American Revolutionary sentiment." See his introduction to *Frederick Douglass: New Literary and Historical Essays* (Cambridge: Cambridge University Press, 1990), 11.

14   Cf. Cornel West: "The point is that if you view yourself as part of a tradition of freedom fighting, . . . understanding what you're up against can become a question of life and death. . . . The real danger is that traditions of freedom fighting will slowly but surely wane in our culture of consumption. . . . In that kind of society, I'm not willing to live." See "Beyond Eurocentrism and Multiculturalism," in *Prophetic Reflections: Notes on Race and Power in America* (Maine: Common Courage Press, 1993), 124.

15   See Michel Foucault, "Technologies of the Self," in *Technologies of the Self*, ed. Luther H. Martin, Huck Gutman, Patrick H. Hutton, (Amherst: University of Massachussets Press, 1988), 27. Henceforth cited as *TS*.

16   Through my reading of the Douglass narratives, I am arguing that Douglass did in fact hold onto a dialectical view of history but not to that version of dialectic that predominates in Christian or post-Christian European thinking. Cf. Philip Foner, who points out that the "'very core and vital element'" of his "'philosophy of the strife'" presupposed that freedom for the slaves was part of "'the inexorable logic of events'" having very little to do with "'the virtue of the North.'" For Foner's argument and excerpts from Douglass's writings, see editor's introduction, *LWFD* 3, 14. Foner finds similarities between Douglass's philosophy and the scientific socialism of Marx and Engels (e.g., 3, 15). My reading of the writings and speeches of Douglass through the Civil War era finds more links between Douglass and the existential anthropology of the early Marx than the positivism of the later Marx.

17   See Winthrop D. Jordan, *White Over Black: American Attitudes Toward the Negro, 1550–1812* (Kingston, Tenn.: The University of North Carolina Press, 1968). Henceforth cited as *WB*. Jordan argues that the association of "aggressive sexual-

ity" with the black African traces back to fifteenth-century Europe. He explains that a primary tactic that white Americans used to handle their fear was to castrate their slaves: "Castration of Negroes clearly indicated a desperate, generalized need in white men to persuade themselves that they were really masters and in all ways masterful, and it illustrated dramatically the ease with which white men slipped over into treating their Negroes like their bulls and stallions whose 'spirit' could be subdued by emasculation" (156). At the same time, black male and female house slaves were scantily dressed so that they were clearly exposed for the sexual enjoyment of the white masters.

Douglass provides a phenomenological description of the pathology of white culture in his "Colorphobia in New York!" (*LWFD* 2, 384–87).

18 Gilroy's conception of death is Sartrean, not dialectial, and therefore not consistent with the philosophies of either Douglass or Hegel. Sartre proposes to locate human freedom through the capacity of man to annihilate himself, most radically, in the act of suicide. The baring of the human soul through the possibility of suicide does align the Sartrean philosophy of freedom with stoicism, albeit a different stoicism than what Hegel identifies. For the key existential text, see Jean-Paul Sartre, *Being and Nothingness*, trans. Hazel E. Barnes (New York: Washington Square Press, 1956), esp. 66–69.

19 Eric J. Sundquist, *To Wake the Nations: Race in the Making of American Literature* (Cambridge: Harvard University Press, 1993), 87–88. Henceforth cited as *WN*.

20 Cornel West, "A Matter of Life and Death," *October* (Summer 1992), 20. West explains that the "older universalist projects of the left have been shattered … because they did not speak effectively to desire and death," which he defines in terms mentioned in the text.

21 "The Colored Race in America," in *LWFD* 3, 352.

22 William McFeely, *Frederick Douglass* (New York: Simon and Schuster, 1991), 271.

23 David D. Gilmore, *Manhood in the Making* (New Haven: Yale University Press, 1990). Henceforth cited as *M*.

24 Hans-Georg Gadamer, *Hegel's Dialectic: Five Hermeneutical Studies*, trans. P. Christopher Smith (New Haven: Yale University Press, 1976), 65.

25 And this is despite the motif of the self-made man that inspired one of Douglass's most popular speeches, itself entitled "Self-Made Men." See Martin, *MFD*, 253–78.

26 For a brief discussion of the importance of dialectic in Douglass's view of history, see Foner's introduction to *LWFD* 15.

27 See Robert Gooding-Williams, "Evading Narrative Myth, Evading Prophetic Pragmatism: Cornel West's *The American Evasion of Philosophy*," *The Massachusetts Review* (Winter 1991–92), 525.

28 It is on this point that Douglass's autobiographies provide grounds for disagreement with Bernard Boxill's reflections on self-respect. While Boxill claims that "reassurance does not come from persuading others that [one] … has self-respect,"

I am arguing that Douglass's sense of self-respect cannot be separated from the evidence that he has proven himself before his oppressors (for Boxill's argument, see "Self-Respect and Protest," 69). For the same reason, I would question the claim that African Americans could retreat to self-defined communities and thereby protect themselves from the effects of racist America. However, Douglass's involvement with African American communities also supports a conclusion drawn by Howard McGary, "that supportive [ethnic] communities can, in some cases, minimize the damaging effects caused by a racist society"; see his "Alienation and the African-American Experience," *The Philosophical Forum* 24, nos. 1–3 (Fall–Spring 1992–93), 295.

29   See Alexandre Kojève, *Introduction to the Reading of Hegel*, ed. Alan Bloom (New York: Basic Books, 1969), 5; Simone de Beauvoir, *The Second Sex*, trans. H. M. Parshley (New York: Vintage Books, 1989), 63; Jean Hyppolite, *Genesis and Structure of Hegel's Phenomenology of Spirit*, trans. Samuel Cherniak and John Heckman (Evanston: Northwestern University Press, 1974), 169, henceforth cited as *GS*; and Gadamer, *Hegel's Dialectic*, 61.

30   Beauvoir, *The Second Sex*, 63.

31   Alicia Suskind Ostriker, *Stealing the Language: The Emergence of Women's Poetry in America* (Boston: Beacon Press, 1986), 11.

32   For a contemporary feminist rendition of the same thesis, see Peggy Reeves Sanday, *Female Power and Male Dominance: On the Origins of Sexual Inequality* (Cambridge: Cambridge University Press, 1981). Henceforth cited as *FP*. Sanday elaborates on the different cosmologies that emerge from cultures that recognize women and childbearing practices and those that prevail in cultures that give power exclusively to men defined by their traditions as hunters.

33   See Frederick Douglass, "The Heroic Slave," in *Three Classic African-American Novels*, ed. William L. Andrews (New York: Mentor, 1990), 28, 27. Henceforth cited as *HS*.

34   See also Angela Y. Davis, *Women, Race, and Class* (New York: Vintage, 1983), 9–11. Davis accounts for what she sees as a strong element of egalitarianism in African American cultures through the fact that women and men shared the same tasks on the slave plantation. While many slave women may have been broken by slavery, many others developed qualities of strength and spirit that were, Davis notes, considered taboo by the nineteenth-century ideology of womanhood. This white ideology severed the sphere of the mother and her morality from the political, social, and cultural spheres.

35   See also the role of Covey's slave Caroline in Douglass's struggle with Covey (*BF*, 134).

36   Orlando Patterson, *Slavery and Social Death: A Comparative Study* (Cambridge: Harvard University Press, 1982), 12.

37   See Eric J. Sundquist, "Frederick Douglass: Literacy and Paternalism," *Raritan* 6,

no. 2 (Fall 1986), 108–24; and William L. Andrews, *To Tell a Free Story* (Urbana: University of Illinois Press, 1988), 280ff. Henceforth cited as *FS*.

38 In this section, I am attempting to account for what John McCumber terms "reflective reflection," by which he means a counterpractice or act of resistance that transforms established conceptions and practices of ethics. See his "Is a Post-Hegelian Ethics Possible?" *Research in Phenomenology* 18 (1988), 125–47, esp. 142ff.

39 I cannot address here the question of whether or not burning dinner was already an unconscious form of resistance. So too Douglass's illness might have served as an unconscious form of resistance to slavery. These liminal forms of resistance might in turn serve to precipitate the battle of wills represented in dialectic.

40 Zora Neale Hurston, *Their Eyes Were Watching God* (New York: Harper and Row, 1937), 68. Henceforth cited as *TE*.

41 Patricia J. Williams, *The Alchemy of Race and Rights* (Cambridge: Harvard University Press, 1991), 63. Henceforth cited as *ARR*.

42 Friedrich Nietzsche, *The Birth of Tragedy and The Genealogy of Morals*, trans. Francis Golffing (Garden City: Doubleday Anchor Books, 1956), second essay, sec. 13, sec. 6. Henceforth cited as *GM*.

43 Joel Kovel, *White Racism: A Psychohistory* (New York: Pantheon Books, 1970), 59.

44 Jordan discusses as a cause of slavery "the Puritans' fondness for the Old Testament and their stress on the depravity of man" in his *WB*, esp. 199.

45 Given that much of Euro-American culture during the time of slavery originated in "low-church English Protestantism strongly tinged by Calvinism" (*WB*, 199), my analysis of the punishments inflicted upon the slave as a screen for the liminal moments of the self could be seen as a modification of what Santayana characterizes as the essence of Calvinism: "Calvinism, essentially, asserts three things: that sin exists, that sin is punished, and that it is beautiful that sin should exist to be punished"; cited in Cornel West, *The American Evasion of Philosophy: A Genealogy of Pragmatism* (Madison: University of Wisconsin Press, 1989), 245, no. 25. For the white American we could say "that black exists, that black is punished, and that it is beautiful that black should exist to be punished."

46 Cf. William Andrews's discussion of the use of metaphor as argument in the Romantic discourses of the nineteenth century (*FS*, 11ff.); and Leonard Harris's discussion of the African American oral tradition in the editor's introduction to *Philosophy Born of Struggle*. Harris writes that "those [oral] forms were ... argument methodologies only partially conveyed in writing. The word, as power, as force, as intonation and nuance, carried justificatory modalities" (xi).

47 Iris Marion Young, "Abjection and Oppression: Dynamics of Unconscious Racism, Sexism, and Homophobia," in *Crises in Continental Philosophy*, ed. Arleen B. Dallery, Charles E. Scott, and Holley Roberts (Albany: SUNY, 1990), 201–214.

48 Judith Butler provides an especially nice example of this problem in her "Endangered/Endangering: Schematic Racism and White Paranoia," in *Reading*

Rodney King, Reading Urban Uprising, ed. Robert Gooding-Williams (New York: Routledge, 1993), 15–22.

49   Paul Gilroy explains that "art, particularly in the form of music and dance, was offered to slaves as a substitute for the formal political freedoms" and that black expressive culture connected subjectivity with rationality only in "a contingent manner." He also points out that Douglass had been a slave and exemplifies these aspects of African American slave culture alongside aspects of rationality that he appropriates from European modernism. See *BA*, 56–59.

For descriptions of the musicality of Douglass's speeches, see *LWFD* 1, 48, 58.

50   Cf. Cornel West: "The older universalist projects of the left have been shattered … because they did not speak effectively to desire and death" ("A Matter of Life and Death," 22).

51   I would like to thank Julie Maybee for helpful comments on an earlier version of this chapter.

Chapter 7: Spirit

1   W. E. B. Du Bois, *The Souls of Black Folk* (New York: Bantam, 1989), 35. Henceforth cited as *SB*.

2   For the influence of Hegelian philosophy on Du Bois's thought, see Joel Williamson, *The Crucible of Race: Black-White Relations in the American South Since the Emancipation* (Oxford: Oxford University Press, 1984), chapter 13, 399–413. Henceforth cited as *C*.

3   Like Paul Gilroy, I interpret Du Bois through Hegel and therefore in terms that deconstruct any purist demand for cultural authenticity. Unlike Gilroy, I find in Du Bois a conception of dialectic that emphasizes individual self-assertion and that does not, as Gilroy writes, yield to a so-called "feminine … form dissolving individuality into the tides of racial identity." See *The Black Atlantic: Modernity and Double Consciousness* (Cambridge: Harvard University Press, 1993), 135. Henceforth cited as *BA*.

4   See, e.g., Albert G. Mosely, "Negritude, Magic, and the Arts: A Pragmatic Perspective," in *Philosophy Born of Struggle: Anthology of Afro-American Philosophy from 1917*, ed. Leonard Harris (Dubuque: Kendall/Hunt, 1983), esp. 276. Henceforth references to the Harris anthology are cited as *PS*.

5   Citations from Frederick Douglass, *My Bondage and My Freedom*, ed. William L. Andrews. (Urbana: University of Illinois Press, 1987), 148, 149. Henceforth cited as *BF*.

6   Frederick Jameson elucidates on a contemporary variant of the Christian dichotomy between ascetic self-denial and hedonistic consumption that drives postindustrial capitalism in his *Postmodernism, or, The Cultural Logic of Late Capitalism* (Durham: Duke University Press, 1992). For a feminist interpretation

of the effects of this dynamic on female identity, see Susan Bordo, "Reading the Slender Body," *Body/Politics: Women and the Discourses of Science*, ed. Mary Jacobus, Evelyn Fox Keller, and Sally Shuttleworth (New York: Routledge, 1990), 83–112. According to Bordo, "The axis of consumption/production is gender-overlaid ... by the hierarchical dualism which constructs a dangerous, appetitive, bodily 'female principle' in opposition to a masterful 'male will'" (105).

7   Orlando Patterson, *Slavery and Social Death* (Cambridge: Harvard University Press, 1982), 71. Henceforth cited as *SSD*.

8   Paul Gilroy argues this point in *BA*, 40. It is also interesting that, according to David R. Roediger, "work" signifies whiteness, at least in popular culture and since the nineteenth century. See his *The Wages of Whiteness* (New York: Verso, 1993), 19–20.

9   Cf. Paul Gilroy, "One Nation Under One Groove," in *Anatomy of Racism,* ed. David Theo Goldberg (Minneapolis: University of Minnesota, 1990), 274. Gilroy argues that one of the constant themes of African culture in the diaspora is the critique of productivism, which he traces back to the experience of forced labor in slavery. Africans in the diaspora, Gilroy explains, view labor as an evil and define themselves and their freedom in terms of nonwork time.

10 William L. Andrews, *Three Classic African-American Novels* (New York: Mentor, 1990), 61–62. Henceforth cited as *HS*.

11 Cf. Du Bois, who argues, according to Williamson, that "blacks in slavery had yearned after the ideal of freedom, in Reconstruction they had turned still again, to follow the ideal of 'book-learning.' But it was white books and white learning that they sought, so long, so hard, and with so little profit" (*C*, 401).

12 I am arguing that manhood (and even more generally the moral status of the person) is something that has to be exhibited in experience and in this sense "tested." My point here is not to return to an individualistic concept of manhood that dominates right-wing America. I have also argued that there can be no self-realization is hindered in socially deprived circumstances. My point here is to counter the formalism of Anglo-American philosophy. This formalism appears, for example, in two excellent essays on the moral status of the African American. See Laurence Thomas, "Self-Respect: Theory and Practice," and Bernard R. Boxill, "Self-Respect and Protest" (*PS*, 174–89, 190–99, respectively). Both articles borrow from the Kantian tradition of moral philosophy, which focuses on self-respect, in contrast to the Hegelian tradition, which defines the self in terms of recognition (see chapter 5 in this book) and thus gives more credence to the intersubjective components of the self. Moreover, this latter tradition, unlike the former, locates the self in history and culture and thus provides a basis for pluralizing the concept of moral person. The Kantian tradition tends to produce abstractly universal and ahistorical claims regarding the person. As a consequence, this tradition provides very little basis for a social transformation of the conditions of the development of the self in our culture.

13 There are African American writers who appropriate from European dialectic the opposition of human and animal. See, for example, Maulana Karenga, "Society, Culture, and the Problem of Self-Consciousness: A Kawaida Analysis," in *PS*, 213. The life of Frederick Douglass, however, traces a dialectic of self that does not simply repeat these problematic dichotomies.

14 Friedrich Nietzsche, *The Birth of Tragedy and The Genealogy of Morals*, trans. Francis Golffing (Garden City: Doubleday Anchor, 1956), third essay, sec. 12. Henceforth cited as *GM*. References to the German are from *Werke*, vol. 3, ed. Karl Schlechta (Frankfurt: Ullstein Materialien, 1981).

15 Frederick Douglass, *Narrative of the Life of Frederick Douglass, An American Slave* (New York: Penguin, 1986), 113.

16 See Gilles Deleuze, "Active and Reactive," in *The New Nietzsche*, ed. David B. Allison (New York: Dell Publishing Co., 1977), 80–106. Deleuze writes that for Nietzsche, "all reality is already a quantity of force. There are nothing but quantities of force 'in a relation of tension' between one another.... In a body, the superior or dominating forces are called *active*, and the inferior or dominated forces are called *reactive*.... The forces that enter into relation with one another have no quality *per se*" (80–81).

17 Ofelia Schutte argues that one can separate what Nietzsche celebrates as the "innocence of becoming" from those Nietzschean texts that define the will to power in terms of the pleasure of domination in her *Beyond Nihilism: Nietzsche without Masks* (Chicago: University of Chicago Press, 1984), 83ff. Henceforth cited as *NM*. My argument is that what from the point of view of the violator may be experienced as innocent self-expression might from the point of view of the victim be experienced as domination. Moreover, just as I suspect that much of the pleasure of rape is in power, so too I suspect that Nietzschean becoming is never as innocent as he might at least on occasion like to suppose.

18 As Ofelia Schutte points out, Nietzsche's Zarathustra is incapable of love. See *NM*, 212, n. 52.

19 William L. Andrews, *To Tell a Free Story* (Urbana: University of Illinois Press, 1988), 144.

20 Joel Williamson, *A Rage for Order* (New York: Oxford University Press, 1986), 16.

21 My own reading of Nietzsche emerges out of dominant themes in Nietzsche's texts. For a reading that is more sensitive to an alternative sociality, and, specifically, to what Nietzsche called a star friendship, see Alphonso Lingis, "Cargo Cult," in *Excesses: Eros and Culture* (Albany: SUNY, 1983), 135–66, esp. 138. Because, as Lingis explains, the star friendship is not based on "abiding presence" but is "an ephemeral friendship," it cannot explain the misery suffered in the breakup of the slave family.

22 The visual dimensions of the Hegelian recognition become explicit in Jean Paul Sartre's reinterpretation of the concept of recognition in *Being and Nothingness*, trans. Hazel E. Barnes, (New York: Philosophical Library, 1956), part 3, chapter 3.

23   Albert G. Mosely makes this point in his essay, "Negritude, Magic, and the Arts: A Pragmatic Perspective," where he writes: "Freud revolutionized psychology by showing that events experienced without the aid of verbal reference (as in early childhood, before speech is learned) are remembered nonetheless in nonverbal forms" (*PS*, 281).

24   Joel Kovel, *White Racism: A Psychohistory* (New York: Pantheon, 1970), 60. Henceforth cited as *WR*.

25   For the classic liberal definition of freedom, see John Stuart Mill, "Bentham," in *Utilitarianism (and Other Essays)*, ed. Mary Warnock (London: Collins, 1962), 100–01. See also Howard McGary, "Alienation and the African-American Experience," *The Philosophical Forum* 24, nos. 1–3 (Fall–Spring 1992–93), 282–96. McGary argues that liberal and Marxist concepts of freedom fail to address the alienation experienced by African Americans, who internalize the hostile images of themselves projected by white culture. For a comparison between liberal and Hegelian concepts of freedom, see Charles Taylor's essay in *Multiculturalism and "The Politics of Recognition"* (Princeton: Princeton University Press, 1992), 25, 57.

26   Not only the slaveboy learns from the rhythms and intonations of the African American slave who raises him; Douglass writes that "even 'Mas' Daniel, by his association with his father's slaves, had measurably adopted their dialect and their ideas" (*BF*, 53).

27   Cf. Paul Gilroy: "The stubborn modernity of ... black musical forms would require a reordering of Hegel's modern hierarchy of cultural achievements. This claim, for example, that music should enjoy higher status [than reason] because of its capacity to express a direct image of the slaves' will." Gilroy also demonstrates how this musical heritage functions to unite those of distinct cultural and political backgrounds in a "distinct mode of lived blackness." See *BA*, 74, 82.

28   Patricia Hill Collins, *Black Feminist Thought* (New York: Routledge, 1991), 99. Henceforth cited as *BFT*.

29   Sterling Stuckey, *Slave Culture* (New York: Oxford University Press, 1987), 40. Henceforth cited as *SC*.

30   Albert G. Mosely explains the centrality of emotion for traditional African culture by way of a citation from Senghor: "'In African society, technical activities are always linked with cultural and religious activities, with art and magic.... It is complete consciousness, because the subject moved and the moving object are united in an indissolvable synthesis, or as I have put it, in a dance of love'" (*PS*, 278).

31   Eric J. Sundquist, "Frederick Douglass: Literacy and Paternalism," *Raritan* 6, no. 2 (Fall 1986), 108–24. Henceforth cited as *LP*.

32   For the reading of the concept of freedom in terms of the trope of fathering the self, see Sundquist, *LP*, 108ff.

33   Here I refer to incidents that occurred during Douglass's travels with William A. White, Esq., in 1843.

34 On the therapeutic effects of African spirituality, see Albert G. Mosley, "Negritude, Magic, and the Arts," in *PS*, 272–82. There he cites historical evidence for the healing power of African music on the more ascetic Eurocentric peoples after World War I and otherwise during times of a "bankrupt spirituality" (278). Mosely adds, "Unfortunately, modern man is prone to think of the expression of emotion as the ejaculation of spasmodic cries and uncontrolled convulsions" (278). This modern theory of emotions is reflected in the psychoanalytic theory of libido as well as in the postmodern affirmations of alterity that borrow from the psychoanalytic tradition. My conclusion should not be read as an endorsement of modern or postmodern theories of desire, emotion, or alterity. In part I of this book, I have argued in favor of models of desire that locate the origin of the self not in narcissism or its abjection but in sociality.

Index

DATE DUE

MAY 0 5 1998			
GAYLORD			PRINTED IN U.S.A.